The *Tokunbo* Phen
and the Second-H
in Nigeria

Africa in Development

Volume 10

Series Editor: Jeggan C. Senghor
Institute of Commonwealth Studies
University of London

Ayokunle Olumuyiwa Omobowale

The *Tokunbo* Phenomenon and the Second-Hand Economy in Nigeria

PETER LANG
Oxford · Bern · Berlin · Bruxelles · Frankfurt am Main · New York · Wien

Bibliographic information published by Die Deutsche Nationalbibliothek.
Die Deutsche Nationalbibliothek lists this publication in the Deutsche Nationalbibliografie; detailed bibliographic data is available on the Internet at http://dnb.d-nb.de.

A catalogue record for this book is available from the British Library.

Library of Congress Control Number: 2012952371

ISSN 1662-1212
ISBN 978-3-0343-0785-7

Hochfeldstrasse 32, CH-3012 Bern, Switzerland
info@peterlang.com, www.peterlang.com, www.peterlang.net

Printed in Germany

This book is dedicated to all the people who bear the name 'Tokunbo' and who have experienced derision following the transfer of *tokunbo* values from humans to goods. It is also dedicated to all who, for socio-economic reasons, are constrained to consume *tokunbo* goods and who thus rationally symbolize the imported second-hand as the alternative 'standard'. Thanks are also due to all respondents who participated in this study: without their willing support, the research that appears here would have been unachievable.

Contents

Illustrations

Figures

Tables

Foreword

I feel greatly honoured to have been asked to write the Foreword to this book by Dr Ayokunle Olumuyiwa Omobowale. Indeed, it is also with a sense of pride that I am doing this task of presenting a general overview of fundamental importance to the underdevelopment process in Nigeria, representing the whole picture for most of Africa. Many efforts have been made to 'develop' the so-called 'developing' economies with little to show for it. With little or no deep thought as to the reasons for the impracticability of these policies, people from the 'developing' nations are being made to say to themselves: 'Something must be wrong with us'. It is disturbing that, after decades of independence, still nothing seems to be working. All predictions have continued to fail in spite of the immense skilled human and natural resources. 'What a waste!' people claim. Unfortunately, all these agitations and concerns have not led to solutions as very many efforts refuse to acknowledge the 'why' of the situation before proffering a 'cure' for the ailments. As medical doctors will acknowledge, without proper diagnosis, there can never be right prescriptions.

This book is a central contribution to the understanding of why policies and efforts fail. Using historico-sociological insights, combined with in-depth and concise empirical data, Dr Ayokunle Olumuyiwa Omobowale has shown how the *tokunbo* phenomenon, a concept once conveying symbolic meanings of superiority for 'imported' children (babies born overseas), has changed its meaning to 'superiority' of imported second-hand goods. The author beautifully presents the development of the underdevelopment process wherein 'waste' from the 'more developed' nations becomes the consumers' preference in the developing nations, even against new imported products from a comparative nation like China whose products they denigrate with such euphemisms as '*Chinco*'. Interestingly, the *tokunbo* idea also typifies almost all aspects of former colonized territories. For instance, nations and kingdoms that once had their own kings began, with the advent of colonialism, to go to *Ilu oba* ('the Monarch's country') outside their territories, where the sovereign reigned supreme. By implication their erstwhile kings ceased to exist. As such, even as the economic institution became subordinated to the conquering hegemony, the political terrain was not left undefiled.

Unfortunately, what is now appreciated are only products in the historical situation of the developed world, where pressures on waste disposal facilities, landfills and the challenges of e-waste have necessitated the recycling and export of used goods. Without a commensurate historical experience in the former colonies, the histories of the colonizing nations continue to dictate the pace or, indeed, what is termed development, in the 'neo-colonies'. On the contrary, however, these only apply to what is considered relevant in the 'ruling nations'. For instance, in many of the former 'home' countries, to date, the monarchical institution continues to be relevant, whereas indigenous political institutions in former colonies have been subjected to relative non-existence or, at best, have become largely irrelevant to governance. Consequently, hegemonic nations, due largely to their superiority in arms and ammunitions, continue to use their ideas to determine what happens in other parts of the world.

Clearly therefore, one is able to discern how internal challenges in one part of the world have been subordinated and have become gains for the developed nations due to their advantaged position in the world economy. More fundamental, however, is the incapacity of the developing nations to re-construct their socio-economic and political situations within the global economy, as their attitudes – perhaps more appropriately, 'cultures' – have been globalized in inferiority. Thus, as the dependency theorists once suggested, the perpetuation of historico-sociological relationships engendered during the colonial period is further producing a neo-colonial structure still tied (albeit in inferiority) to the world economy controlled by the developed nations. This control, some have argued, is enhanced by the behaviour of the indigenous peoples of these developing nations.

Nonetheless, this perspective neglects the all-important role of education in the creation of privileged elites in these nations, and ignores too their inferior position vis-à-vis 'partners' in the relationship. Of course, it was those 'educated abroad' who felt privileged to give birth to '*Tokunbo* children'. In the same vein, their education abroad was perceived to be superior to that of people who studied at home, a view that continues in the present-day perceived 'superiority' of the Diaspora. Ironically, the relevance of the environment in knowledge-generation is driven to the background. Indeed, formal education has been dissociated from the informal economy within which it subsists, and thus has a sort of lack of relevance to survival in society. This is contrary to what existed in pre-colonial Nigeria, and indeed, Africa, where the exploitation of the environment informed the social-political relations developed around it.

In fact, the criticism of dependency theory neglects – unfortunately – the textile industries that were well developed in various parts of pre-colonial Nigeria and the social relations built around them. Just as the textile industries were well developed to satisfy the needs of the people, other industries relevant to their existence were created for survival. The textile industry, for instance, did not exist without the required technology to process raw cotton to manufacture clothes.

Put simply, the underdevelopment process engendered through the incorporation of Africa into the world capitalist system, albeit in a peripheral role, created a historical situation that needs to be appreciated in our understanding of 'how we got to where we are'. Where we are, and our ability to go forward, are fundamentally dependent on our capacity and capability to restructure our former relationship in a fundamental way. Unfortunately, 'where we are' has become almost unimportant because of who we have become! We have not become ourselves but what we have been made to be by others, and they loom larger than us in all aspects of our existence.

As it is for second-hand goods, signifying 'inferiority', so it is with what is seen as knowledge, politics, religion and all aspects of the economic institution. They are of 'second-hand' status in so far as they have virtually no relevance to the environment within which they subsist, except they are perceived within the world-view of those from outside the borders. A nation that cannot determine its needs, based on an ability to control the internal and external environments, exists only as a 'second-hand' economy – an inferior nation constructed from the perspective of others, which continues to exist only as long as the others determine its existence.

— AKINPELU OLANREWAJU OLUTAYO, PhD
University of Ibadan, Nigeria
August 2011

Acknowledgements

I wish to express appreciation for funding from the American Council of Learned Societies (ACLS), provided under the 2010 African Humanities Programme (AHP) Post-Doctoral Fellowship. The ACLS also provided a Residency Fellowship for the final drafting of the manuscript: it was taken up at the West African Research Centre (WARC), Dakar, Senegal. I would like to acknowledge the support of the Director of WARC, Prof. Ousmane Sene, and other members of staff of the Centre. Appreciation is also due to the family of Madam Diallo, my host family in Dakar, for the support and welfare extended to me throughout my stay.

The research for this book has benefited from the comments and scholarly contributions of the faculty and participants at the 2011 BIARI Institutes (Development and Inequality in the Global South) of the Watson Institute for International Studies, Brown University, Providence, USA. Special thanks are due to Professor Lanre Olutayo and Professor Yinka Aderinto for their contributions to the successful completion of the ACLS Post-Doctoral Fellowship. I must also acknowledge the input of these two academics and Professor Otite to my intellectual development as a whole. Professors Otite, Aderinto and Olutayo supervised my bachelor's, master's and doctoral research, respectively. Professor Olutayo has been my mentor, from whom I have gained enormous support over the years: I deem him a teacher of teachers and a mentor of the noblest humility. In similar measure, I appreciate Professor Felicia A. D. Oyekanmi for her intellectual support and encouragement during the short span of my career at the University of Lagos. Professor Oyekanmi is a role model who takes special interest in the advancement of upcoming younger colleagues. I thank Dr Yinka Akanle, Messrs Kayode Jegede, Wale Adesina and Charles Eguaoje for all their support during the course of the research for this book. I also thank all my research assistants, and all others who have supported this research in one way or another. My employer, the University of Ibadan, granted me one year's leave under the Staff Development Programme to carry out the study, for which I am very grateful. I similarly appreciate the anonymous reviewer and Dr Jeggan C. Senghor, the General Editor of the Peter Lang *Africa in Development* series and his team for their comments and contributions, which have, without a doubt, improved the quality of this book.

Finally, I am grateful to my wife, Mofeyisara, my son, Babafemipoju and my daughter, Babafeyikemi for their love, support and understanding. They put up with my absence and encouraged me to achieve my professional goals. I also thank my parents, Pastor and Mrs E. O. Omobowale, and my siblings, Tunde, Tope, Tayo and Yimika, and their respective spouses Eyitayo, Ayo, Bukola and Folashade for their support to me and my family.

Special Words and Acronyms

aloku	local (not imported) second-hand
auto	automobile
bend-down	the way buyers bend down to pick second-hand clothes
bosikoro	'go to a hidden place'; the second-hand clothes market
Chinco	substandard electronic devices of Chinese origin
Cotonou tokunbo	smuggled (via Cotonou in the Republic of Benin)
crosser	professional smuggler
DRL	daytime running lights
FGD	focus group discussion
'glocal'	fusion between globalized values and local culture
HDI	Human Development Index
ICT	information and communications technology
IDI	in-depth interview
ikose	apprenticeship
ilu oba	'the Monarch's country' (Great Britain)
IMF	International Monetary Fund
imported ni	imported
KII	key informant interview
Lagos cleared	legitimately imported
MDAN	Motor Dealers Association of Nigeria
mitumba	'dead man's clothes'; the second-hand clothes trade (Tanzania)
Naira (N)	the Nigerian currency unit

oja oyinbo	goods produced in the West
okaraka	'torn' – and thus second-hand clothes
oke okun	'the other end of the sea'
okrika	second-hand clothes
okun	the ocean
olaju	'modern' man with Western values
omo ale	bastard child
omo oyinbo	white man's child
onibaranda	trickster, tout
oyinbo	'white men'
re-use value	the residual utility value of used goods
SAP	Structural Adjustment Programme
Taiwan	substandard products of Asian origin
tear-rubber	new car with polythene covered seats
tokunbo	'from across the seas'

Preface

This book is the outcome of a post-doctoral research project funded by the American Council of Learned Societies (ACLS) under the African Humanities Programme (AHP) (2010). It is an empirical study focused on the values attached to the *tokunbo* phenomenon and the second-hand economy in South-Western Nigeria. *Tokunbo* ('from across the seas') evolved in response to the colonial experience of the Yoruba-speaking people of South-Western Nigeria. 'Tokunbo' was a name reserved principally for children conceived and/or delivered in Europe and North America. The name indicated that a child had been born abroad and, by extension, it momentarily conveyed meanings of membership of the elite class on the name-bearer and his/her family, with the accompanying social respect and dignity that went to privileged members of society.

In like manner, goods produced by Western manufacturers were a consumers' preserve as material elements of 'modernity' and class in colonial Nigeria. South-Western Nigeria gradually came under British rule with the annexation of Lagos as a British crown colony in 1861. The remaining parts of the Yoruba nation eventually became part of the British Protectorate following a treaty that was signed in Ibadan in 1893. Between 1861 and 1960, when Nigeria gained independence, the local population was very heavily exposed to 'modern' (in this case Western) culture. Western culture thus became the dominant culture for the region. Its non-material aspects were propagated through the indirect rule system and by educational and religious institutions (especially by mission schools and missionaries). The material aspects of 'modernity' were accentuated through the importation and consumption of products manufactured by Western industries under the active control of the colonial government.

Western goods, as elements of modern material culture, symbolized the transformation into modernity for the native and, as such, they were also status symbols representing an 'induction' into modern culture and into an elitist class and psyche. In fact, it was common for consumers of products with local alternatives (for example fabrics and clothing accessories such as belts, shoes and ties) to emphasize that the item was *imported ni* ('imported'). The label *imported ni* differentiated such possessions from the local alternatives, and conferred a social notion of superior quality on the product, and social appreciation and class on the consumer. The superiority accorded to Western material and immaterial culture was, of course, carried over to the post-independence period.

By the 1980s, Nigeria was experiencing deplorable socio-economic conditions, with most Nigerians falling below the poverty line. This was primarily due to economic maladministration and to corruption by successive governments who failed to utilize the country's huge oil earnings appropriately for economic development and transformation. The quest to plug leakages and maintain an austere fiscal policy resulted in the introduction of the Structural Adjustment Programme (SAP) in 1986. SAP entailed: the withdrawal of government from the provision of social services such as education and health; an embargo on salary increments and public service employment; devaluation of the national currency, the Naira (₦); and the adoption of laissez-faire principles in the running of the national economy. The programme was a disaster. By 1996, about 70 per cent of Nigerians had fallen below the poverty line due to its debilitating consequences.

Poor, but imbued with a taste for Western material culture, Nigerians initially opted for substandard Asian alternatives. These cloned products, popularly called *Taiwan* were a consumers' nightmare: they tended to give out or disintegrate shortly after purchase. By the 1990s, astute and shrewd importers started importing second-hand goods to the delight of consumers, and these subsequently assumed the description *tokunbo*.

Qualitative data was collected to research the *tokunbo* phenomenon in the form of observational data, archival research, 27 key informant interviews (KII), 150 in-depth interviews (IDIs) and 24 focus group discussions (FGDs). The sites of enquiry were Abeokuta, Ibadan and Lagos in Nigeria as well as Cotonou in the Republic of Benin. Lagos was expressly chosen because it is Nigeria's economic nerve centre and has the principal imported second-hand markets in the country. Abeokuta and Ibadan were selected due to their proximity to Lagos and because of the location of major imported second-hand markets in the two cities.

The resultant book is divided into twelve chapters. While the first four deal with the theoretical background and present a literature review, the others mainly discuss substantive empirical material. Chapter 1 introduces the research, briefly discussing the social value attached to *tokunbo* as a reflection of the social reality of the 'transatlantic experience' for the Yoruba of present-day South-Western Nigeria. CHAPTER 2 integrates the theories of symbolism and rational choice as a theoretical guide and framework for the study. Symbolism affirms that human actions are symbolic and bear contextual meanings, while rational choice theory presents individuals as rational beings capable of choosing amongst alternatives the action that has the greater utility. Hence, Nigerian society symbolically views Western culture as 'modern' and 'superior'. Those who are able to acquire and utilize elements of Western material culture are part of the elite class in this society, capable of setting the standards for the practice of modernity locally. In the course of striving to attain 'modern' standards, economically disempowered actors opt for relatively cheap second-hand goods, with re-use value, that convey elitist modern culture and practice notwithstanding.

CHAPTER 3 reviews the relevant literature on the rational symbolism of name, showing that names are imbued with meanings across cultures. The meanings so bestowed impact on the social milieu and inform social action and interaction.

CHAPTER 4 reviews the literature on the second-hand economy and modernity diffusion. It shows that many authors attribute the growth of the second-hand economy (especially in the Third World) to pure economic reasons, without giving consideration to the rational symbolic meanings second-hand goods may hold and convey.

The discussion of empirical data generated from the field starts with CHAPTER 5, which discusses the social value of 'Tokunbo' as a human name. The chapter affirms that in colonial and immediate post-colonial Nigeria, the name Tokunbo symbolically conferred honour and prestige on the name-bearers as the privileged elite. It gave them and their families enhanced social status, evoking images of the cultured and wealthy, imbued with modern Western culture.

CHAPTER 6 illustrates the transfer of the term *tokunbo* from human to imported second-hand goods, a development which occurred from the 1990s on. The chapter explains how the goods were appreciated locally. CHAPTERS 7–10 discuss Nigerians' experience with *tokunbo* automobiles, automobile spare parts, electronic goods and clothing.

CHAPTER 11 specifically analyses the *tokunbo* economy as a harbinger of modernity practice: it allows access to modern consumer goods and thereby levels social inequality in symbolic terms, though not economically. Finally, CHAPTER 12 summarizes the study. It concludes that, although the second-hand economy affords the greater majority of Nigeria's low-income earners access to modern consumer goods that symbolically offer a semblance of participation in the globalization process, the real 'glocal' experience is increasingly making Nigeria a dump for waste. Nigeria will continue to have to deal with this waste so long as the consuming population receives imported second-hand goods as seemingly viable alternatives.

CHAPTER I

Introduction

The first thing to note about the *tokunbo* phenomenon is that it is intricately associated with the contact the Yoruba nation made with Europeans who, from about the fifteenth century, were traversing the Atlantic Ocean to conduct trade and missionary work.[1] *Tokunbo* literally means 'from across the seas'. To native Africans, the transatlantic venture of the Europeans attracted deep admiration: it conveyed symbolic notions of superiority – not only superiority of the Europeans themselves but also of the goods they had to offer for exchange. The focus of the research presented in this book, therefore, is the study of *tokunbo* dynamism in the construction and sustenance of symbolic values given to peoples and goods. The study also examines the accompanying impact of the *tokunbo* on modernity practice and on the second-hand market in South-Western Nigeria, both historically and now.

In a related study, Ogundiran (2002) rightly shows how economic and symbolic values were constructed for cowries in West Africa between the sixteenth and nineteenth centuries. Ogundiran posits that the phenomenal economic and symbolic transformation of cowries was associated with the transatlantic experience, which significantly transmuted the cultural and political structure of Africa in general and Yoruba society in particular. The social and monetary value created for cowries was not unconnected with the fact that they came from across the seas. They came from a land beyond the vast and seemingly unending waters that could not be easily crossed by natural human efforts. Thus, Ogundiran (2000: 455) concludes:

1 Due to boundaries set by the colonialists, the Yoruba are presently found in Nigeria, the Benin Republic and Togo, with the larger population of Yoruba indigenously located in Nigeria (Asiwaju 1985).

> The social valuation of cowries in Yorubaland between sixteenth and nineteenth centuries did not therefore emerge in a vacuum, nor was it imposed by European traders. It was a cultural and political economic re-interpretation of the pre-sixteenth century cultural construction of beads as political objects.[2]

Force may not have accompanied the 'transatlantic experience' during the bead years, as it did in the period of the slave trade and colonialism; but it was a recognized instrument for ensuring compliance among the native population. Consequently, though the economic and symbolic values attached to goods and people coming from beyond the seas cannot be dissociated from the 'transatlantic experience' thesis, coercive and ideological forces of the colonial state also contributed immensely to the social construction ascribing superiority to Western culture and civilization. Starting with the natives' 'transatlantic experience' through merchandise and the slave trade between the fifteenth and eighteenth centuries, local dependency was sustained through colonial force between 1861 and 1960. Even now the post-colonial peripheral state is dominated in the international political economy by Western countries in a complex world capitalist system and globalization process (McMichael 2008; Ejiogu 2007; Hall 2004; Wallerstein 1989, 1986, 1984).

The 'transatlantic experience' thus explains the symbolic value Africans attached to European goods such as umbrellas, mirrors, spirits and items of Western clothing, among other goods that were exchanged for African slaves (Sherwood 2004; Beckford 1989; Foster 1976). Similarly, as has often been pointed out, the colonization of Africa and the subsequent construction by force of dependent societies and cultures framed along Western lines had a detrimental impact on indigenous cultures. Subjection to colonial rule explains why the indigenous population attached so much economic

2 Beads are glasslike cultural artefacts worn by traditional title-holders as symbols of authority, power and respect. Thus a Yoruba proverb alludes to the credence of beads thus: *Ade l'a fin n mo Oba, Ileke l'a fi n'mo Ijoye* (The king is recognized by his crown while the chief is recognized by his beads). In reality, whereas the chief wore only beads, the king wore beads along with a crown. The use of these cultural artefacts as traditional office paraphernalia has persisted till contemporary times among traditional title-holders (see Ogundiran 2002; Drewal 1998; Thompson 1970).

and symbolic value to transatlantic goods (used ones as well) and to services originating from Western nations. This tendency persists even into contemporary times (Omobowale and Olutayo 2009, Omobowale 2008).

For the Yoruba, the 'transatlantic experience' was intricately associated with transatlantic symbolism. Transatlantic symbolism, in this sense, describes the meaningful values created by Yoruba society in its relationship with Europeans. In this context, transatlantic symbolism is intimately associated with the *tokunbo* phenomenon. As already explained, *tokunbo* is associated with the people's contact with the Europeans. It is permeated with symbolic meanings signifying the assumed or perceived origin, status, class, standard and quality of the human beings or goods to which it is attached. Use of the term began as a name for Yoruba children conceived or born in Western nations, especially in the colonial period and up to the 1990s; but the term *tokunbo* is now more generally employed for imported second-hand goods, distinguishing them from locally used goods, which are nowadays referred to as *aloku* (Omobowale 2008).

Starting with the increasing purchase of imported second-hand vehicles by all who could afford them (including public and private bureaucracies), the consumption of imported used goods now cuts across virtually all categories of the second-hand market, and embraces items both legally and illegally imported. The second-hand goods involved include electronic appliances, clothing, spare parts and books. This market is not unconnected with Nigeria's precarious socio-economic conditions caused by the oil gluts of the 1980s, official corruption, mismanagement and maladministration by successive governments, and unbalanced and exploitative exchange relations within the global capitalist system (Omobowale 2009a; Rothstein and Eek 2009; Uche 2008; Omeje 2006; Davis and Ruhe 2003; Ahunwan 2002; Kraus 2002).

The nation's precarious socio-economic state has resulted in an abysmal descent into poverty for about 70 per cent of the Nigerian population. Every aspect of socio-economic life has been affected, to the extent that (using figures for 2010) Nigeria has a Human Development Index (HDI) of only 0.423 and life expectancy at birth is as low as 48.4 years – making the nation the 142nd out of 179 countries with HDI data (United Nations Development Programme 2010). One of the ways Nigerians have responded to the economic crisis and the ensuing poverty is by opting to buy used goods imported from Europe and North America as rational alternatives with deep symbolic values. Hence, not only in West Africa but in the continent as a whole, Nigeria stands out as an important destination for used goods imported either through legal routes or smuggled in (especially through the Republic of Benin). This is due mainly to its huge population of about 160 million people and its relatively large economy compared to other neighbouring countries (Buchert, Hermann, Jenseit, Stahl Osyguß and Hageluken 2007; Beuving 2006, 2004; Niger-Thomas 2001; Flynn 1997; Allen 1992).

Quite apart from the burgeoning market for second-hand goods in Nigeria, the *tokunbo* phenomenon unarguably impacts on local trading. In fact, it conveys symbolic value which attracts patronage for its own sake. The *tokunbo* phenomenon has been dynamically transferred from human naming to a name tag for imported used goods with attendant expectations from consumers. Hence, this study aims: (1) to analyse historically the value attached to *tokunbo* as a name for a person; (2) to examine the social reconceptualization of *tokunbo* with respect to imported used goods, and (3) to find out the possible impact the *tokunbo* second-hand economy has on modernity practice in South-Western Nigeria.

Colonization, Modernity and the *Tokunbo*

The latter part of the nineteenth century witnessed crucial developments in the Yoruba nation. Prior to this period, the Yoruba had had transactions with European merchants and missionaries for more than three centuries and the introduction of the Yoruba to European civilization had begun. European merchants introduced European goods and merchandise while missionaries exposed the natives to Christianity and socialized them into European culture through mission schools that were established by evangelism. Christian missions, including the Church Missionary Society

(Anglican Communion), the Catholic Mission and the Methodists, pioneered missionary work in Yorubaland (Lindenfeld 2005; Mary 2005; Wariboko 2004; Kolapo 2000; Peel 1990; Atanda 1980).

Starting with the annexation of the coastal city of Lagos as a crown colony in 1861 (Hopkins 1980; McIntyre 1963), British colonial interest gradually penetrated the Yoruba hinterland (Crowther 1968). From the Colony of Lagos, the British government proclaimed its 'protectorate' over the rest of Yorubaland, following the signing of the Protectorate Treaties of 1893 and consequent integration of Yorubaland into the Protectorate of Southern Nigeria (Omobowale 2006; Johnson 1921). The Protectorates of Northern and Southern Nigeria were later amalgamated in January 1914, forming the uniform colonial state of Nigeria. Britain adopted a system of indirect rule for the administration of the natives. Indirect rule allowed the continued reign of local political leaders, who had their appointments approved by colonial officials. The local leaders assisted in local administration, collecting taxes and keeping the people in check under close supervision from colonial officials. With British imperial power superimposed on Yoruba society and culture, European and especially British culture became the ideal. The imperial culture became the 'modern' culture through which development could be accessed and assessed. This was a major milestone in the socio-cultural, political, economic and overall structural transformation and development of the Yoruba. The British imperial presence introduced them to new ways of life, civilization and culture, specially packaged as 'superior' and symbolically accepted by the indigenous population as being of better quality.

Among the Yoruba, the Europeans' white skin found representation within the indigenous *Oyinbo* mythology and belief system, where it depicts purity and righteousness; thus, Europeans were called *oyinbo* (Omobowale and Olutayo 2009). Hence, Europe became *Ilu Oyinbo* ('White Man's Land') while goods produced in Europe were referred to as *oja oyinbo*. The aura and beauty symbolically applied to the *oyinbo* were transferred to things associated with the *oyinbo*. This was all the more engaging because of the *tokunbo*-'transatlantic experience' and the values that conveyed European superiority. As Europe and North America became the ideals, especially from the start of the colonial period, things originating from the West also became the preferred items. Nigerian society grew increasingly dependent on Western values as a norm, and so Yoruba men and women who had the privilege to travel to Europe suddenly became part of an elite class.

Excursions of people from this privileged class to Europe and their eventual return home with pregnancies and/or children led to the social construction of *tokunbo* as a name for persons. The children could not be called *omo oyinbo* ('white man's child') because of the literal implications for paternity, which the Yoruba take as very sacrosanct; otherwise the child would be stigmatized as *omo ale* (bastard). *Tokunbo* thus became the preferred name conveying the symbolic meaning that the child had been conceived or born abroad. Right from this stage, *tokunbo* became a widespread symbolic label indicating an association with Western civilization and culture with a 'superiority' value attached.

There has, however, been a change to this social practice in recent times. Children conceived or born in Europe and North America are hardly ever named *Tokunbo*. The term is now more closely associated with imported used goods, a trade whose value currently runs into several millions of dollars annually. *Tokunbo* goods are bought not only by most households, but by public and private bureaucracies as well.[3]

The second-hand imports market in Nigeria is indeed flourishing, despite official regulation. One explanation for this is that there is an ever-increasing production of 'new' and 'better' products in the developed nations, which inevitably results in the disposal of unwanted goods by households and institutions. Also, as argued above, the increasing demand for second-hand goods in Nigeria is due to the deplorable socio-economic conditions prevalent there. Beyond this simplistic economic explanation, however, there is a symbolic one. It is imperative to uncover the symbolic construction of the *tokunbo*, and its historical impact on society, first with its use in human naming and later as a tag for imported second-hand goods within the context of the adoption of modernity among classes not as privileged as the elite. This will thus show Nigeria's position in the web of global interconnections that make up the production and consumption

3 Above all, public and private bureaucracies buy imported used vehicles.

chain creating the flourishing second-hand market in the Third World. It will also reveal how imported second-hand goods are rationally and symbolically accepted within the local culture as elements of the social reality of the adoption, consumption and practice of diffused modernity.

Rationale for the Research

The literature is replete with arguments demonstrating that African culture has been structured along Western lines from the colonial period onwards (see, for example, Kusiak 2010; Lange, Mahoney and von Hau 2006; Schuerkens 2003; Gray 1982). Many Africans not only view Western culture as 'superior' but regard it as the culture that should be emulated. This tendency is, in fact, even more evident in the present era of globalization, as Western culture becomes increasingly diffused and adopted among the global population. It should be noted, however that societies receive Western culture in varying forms. The modern culture received from outside also blends with the indigenous culture producing a unique fusion of the modern and the local – a fusion generally described as the 'glocal' (Giulianotti 2006, 2002). This study therefore examines the *tokunbo* phenomenon within the context of this assumption. *Tokunbo* symbolically reflects elements of the transatlantic interaction with Western culture. Within the local culture, it overtly reflects the geographical origin and, to an extent, a degree of social appreciation within the Yoruba cultural space. It is thus important to uncover the social context within which symbolic meaning is attached to *tokunbo* and its possible impact on social and economic relations in contemporary Yorubaland.

Furthermore, it is imperative to investigate the dynamics of the *tokunbo* phenomenon, tracing contextual changes over time, from use of the term in human naming to its becoming a socio-cultural label for imported second-hand goods. This will give insights into the developing social construction of *tokunbo*. The research reveals the symbolic meanings attached to *tokunbo* within the local culture and how these meanings structure actions and interactions taken in their context. It also shows that people's patronage of the imported second-hand goods market cannot be sufficiently explained in simple rational-economic terms (see, for example, Waldman 2003, 1996, Thomas 2003). Rather, it shows that there is a significant nexus between the symbolic meanings attached to the *tokunbo* and the increasing attraction to imported second-hand goods, which is a direct consequence of the diffusion and adoption of modernity and/or Western values. Thus, the study reveals how the *tokunbo* phenomenon impacts on the consumption of imported second-hand goods in the practice of modernity.

Methodology

The methodology adopted for the study is basically qualitative – mainly because such an approach enables an interpretive understanding of meanings attached to symbolic actions. A mass of data was collected expressly for this project in Nigeria and the Republic of Benin. (In the course of the research it was discovered that the bulk of second-hand goods imported into Nigeria enter through this neighbouring country, which is why it was covered as well.) In Nigeria, the bank of data was collected in three purposely selected locations: Lagos (the commercial nerve centre of Nigeria and the centre of the biggest second-hand market in all South-Western Nigeria); Abeokuta, and Ibadan (see Figure 1).

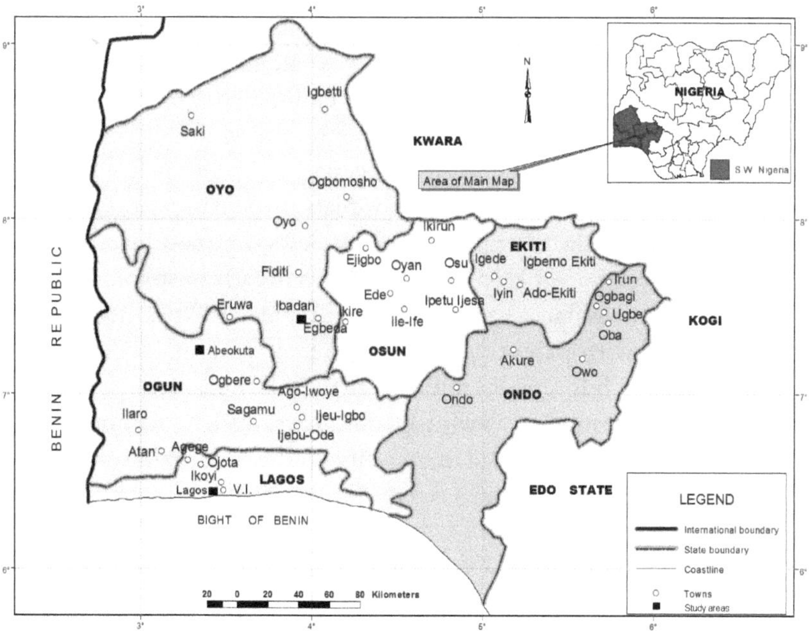

Figure 1 *Map of South-Western Nigeria, showing the study areas*

Abeokuta and Ibadan were selected because of their proximity to Lagos and because of the location of major imported second-hand markets in both cities. In the Republic of Benin the contributions to the data bank were collected at Mesebor, the main wholesale second-hand market. Some data were also collected in areas close to the Benin side of the border. Further items of qualitative data were collected through observation, consultation of archival resources, key informant interviews (KII), in-depth interviews (IDI), focus group discussions (FGD) and the gathering of material in the form of pictures and videos.

All this was collected in the following ways:

1. Observation at the major second-hand markets. The researcher observed transactions and the social and physical arrangements of the markets.

2. Archival research into Nigeria's second-hand economy from the colonial period. Historical information was gathered from the National Archive located in the premises of the University of Ibadan, Nigeria. The National Archive is a department coming under the Federal Ministry of Information, Abuja, Nigeria.
3. Key informant interviews with individuals affected by *tokunbo* naming (KIIa). In Nigeria, key informant interviews were conducted on the social value of the *tokunbo* in the colonial and early post-colonial periods with individuals (4 per city: 2 males, 2 females) bearing *tokunbo* names and with parents (4 per city; 2 males, 2 females) who have named their children 'Tokunbo' at birth (8 KII per city).
4. Key informant interviews with Yoruba experts (KIIb). Key informant interviews were conducted in each city on the social value of *tokunbo* with a Yoruba historian or an elderly Yoruba with good grasp of Yoruba culture (1 per city).
5. In-depth interviews (IDIs). IDIs were conducted with buyers and sellers of *tokunbo* goods. These goods included vehicles, vehicle spare parts, electronic devices and clothes. Two sellers and ten buyers of each category of goods were subjected to IDI in each city in Nigeria (i.e. twelve IDIs for each category of *tokunbo* goods; forty-eight IDIs per city; a mix of both male and female interviewees was ensured). In the Republic of Benin, six IDIs were conducted with wholesale sellers of *tokunbo* goods (mainly clothes) in Cotonou.
6. Focus group discussions (FGDs). Eight FGDs (two each for buyers of *tokunbo* vehicles, vehicle spare parts, electronic items and clothes) were conducted at Abeokuta, Ibadan and Lagos.
7. Case studies:
   a. One case study each with a person bearing the appellation 'Tokunbo' and with a parent who has named his or her child 'Tokunbo' in each city (2 Case studies per city)
   b. One case study each for a seller and a buyer of *tokunbo* goods under each category (8 case studies per city; for both sellers and buyers selection was on the grounds that they must have been involved with *tokunbo* goods for at least five years).

8. Pictures and videos. Pictorial documentation was collected in Ibadan, Lagos and Abeokuta (in Nigeria) and in Cotonou (in the Republic of Benin). The videos were collected from youtube.com and Aljazeera.net. They were essentially videos of clothes recycling and e-waste.

In all, 27 KIIs, 150 IDIs, 24 FGDs and 30 case studies were conducted. The items of data collected were subjected to content analysis.

CHAPTER 2

Theoretical Underpinnings: Symbolic-Rational Choice

The primary aim of this chapter is to present the theoretical framework for the study, which is based on a fusion of symbolism and rational choice theories. Symbolism reveals the context within which meaningful actions are taken while rational choice theory explains the ability of actors to choose – rationally – a particular course of action from among several alternatives.

Symbolism

Symbolism as a theoretical perspective posits that human actions are not taken in isolation of the cultural environment. Rather, the cultural environment gives meaning to actions. And meanings are relative. They differ from one cultural environment to another and from one period to another. Human beings have a capacity for deep thinking and they are capable of interpreting their social and physical environments. Through interactions, actors build meanings for the objects and elements of the social world they come in contact with within their environments. These objects and elements of the social world become symbols with varied meanings, as conceptualized by the actors. The actors then name, classify and remember the meanings of the symbols; if they did not, the social world would appear in a confused and disordered state for them (Ritzer 2008; Ritzer and Goodman 2003). Meanings are not static, however. They are subject to change, as the actors consciously or unconsciously reconstruct meanings on the basis of prevailing and present realities. According to Hatas (2002: 356, 357, 361):

> Symbols indicate social relations in which people are situated and consolidate social order ... Symbolism is not some peculiar 'autistic' reality, contained in an autonomous semiotical-linguistic system, but is socially produced. Symbol possesses a triple structure: it simultaneously means something for belief. To paraphrase ... one can say that symbol 'gives something to think about', but likewise, on even footing, presents something for belief and 'persuades one to be obedient'. This power of symbol is not intrinsic, but is of a social character ... A symbolic approach does not mean ignoring 'real issues' and structural limitations; however, the cultural and symbolic aspect is considered as most important in the forming and informing of the social world.

What Hatas has shown above is that meanings attached to symbols are not biologically created. They are, rather, socially generated through social interaction. Meanings generated through social interactions have binding impacts on the actors who are socially engaged in the interpretation of the meanings. The interpretation they give builds notions of 'the truthful' around socially accepted convictions. Socially accepted and meaningful convictions in turn impact on the construction of the social world through the imputation of meanings to symbols. This also directly impacts on the actors' construction of the 'self' (Ritzer 2008). Actors socially construct self-concepts through the meanings they make out of symbolic realities. The 'self' – an embodiment of internalized values and the meanings attached – informs the action processes of actors and the meanings such actions convey to other actors.

Using this theoretical perspective, several scholars have shown how meanings attached to symbols influence the actions of actors in all kinds of spheres. For example, Choi (2006) has revealed the symbolism of women's hairstyles in Japan and Korea and how they convey meanings of supernatural protection, beauty, marital status, social position and wealth. The attached meanings inform the hairstyles and govern reactions from the interacting public. From a mere viewing of her hair, a woman's status, social class and belief system can be understood within the context of the cultures (Japanese or Korean). In like manner, the research of Chugh and Hancorck (2009) reveals the aesthetics of hairdressing saloons, especially in terms of artefacts, tools, architecture and hairdos offered. These aspects present symbolic meanings, attracting customers whose preferences also inform the style and quality of the services offered in the saloons. Thus, the features of the hairdressing saloon are symbols conveying meanings. The aesthetic meanings attached to the features impact on customers' actions and preferences and the meanings also have the potential to attract patronage.

To take another example, Lilley (2004) reveals how the landscaping and structural organization of medieval European cities reflected the Christian symbolism that was central to European culture and identity at the time. Structural elements (such as cross shapes) were therefore not mere architectural and aesthetic designs: they expressed symbolic values representing medieval European Christianity and held a lot of meaning. Velikonja's (2003) research uncovers how, during the Balkan Wars, the various warring sides, including Orthodox Serbs, Catholic Croatians and Muslim Bosnians, resorted to religious symbols such as the cross, the crescent, and various titles and appellations to attract popular support and justify military actions. This is an attestation of the power of religious symbolism to influence social action. The same religious symbols that reflected religious piety and faith in time of peace became the symbols of conflictual faith and difference in time of war. The meanings attached to the religious symbols were re-constructed to signify conflictual separation from opposing religious groups: they conferred a separatist identity and encouraged an urge to vanquish the opposing group in war. Their war-like meanings now propelled social action against opposing ethnic and national armies.

Symbolism is important in politics. Otite (1977) has explored the relation of symbols to political behaviour, stability and instability in Nigeria. He identified political associations such as the Action Group (AG), the National Convention of Nigeria Citizens (NCNC) and the Northern People's Congress (NPC) as cultural symbols of the Yoruba, Igbo and Hausa-Fulani respectively. Otite posits that these symbols have significantly structured Nigeria's political landscape from the early post-colonial period on.

The conclusions Otite made about the symbolism of political associations remain valid up to present times. During the Second Republic, which lasted from 1979 to 1983, political associations followed an ethnic arrangement, with the Unity Party of Nigeria (UPN) succeeding the AG among the Yoruba, the National Party of Nigeria (NPN) succeeding the NPC among the Hausa-Fulani, and the Nigerian Peoples Party (NPP) succeeding the NCNC among the Igbo (Joseph 1991, Okpu 1985). Nigeria's erstwhile military president, General Babangida attempted to discourage ethnic configurations in political participation during the moribund Third Republic by granting licences to only two national parties – namely the Social Democratic Party (SDP) and the National Republican Convention (NRC). The country's political structure ended up with the NRC dominating the Hausa-Fulani north and the SDP dominating southern Nigeria, which is predominantly Yoruba and Igbo (Dinneya and Tsegaye 2004; Kieh and Agbese 1993). The political arrangement in the present Fourth Republic is not much different. Though the Peoples Democratic Party (PDP) has continually won national elections since 1999, the political terrain has not been devoid of ethnic symbolism in party politics. Hence, the Action Congress of Nigeria (ACN) is supposedly a resurrection of the defunct AG and UPN among the Yoruba while the All Progressives Grand Alliance (APGA) reincarnates the defunct NCNC and NPP among the Igbo; and the All Nigeria Peoples' Party (APP) and quite recent Congress for Progressive Change (CPC) are like resurrections of the NPC and NPN among the Hausa-Fulani in northern Nigeria.

In a further study of the power of symbolism in politics, Vandi (1979) presents the developing nations as peripheral countries subject to capitalist exploitation, but ones whose development and progress are symbolized in the adoption of Western institutions, culture and infrastructure. What this means is that, even though developing nations may not experience development in real terms, the symbolic meanings derived from westernization and 'modern' infrastructures convince the local populations that development is taking place: they continually aspire to westernization as a symbol of development.

On the plane of a people's culture, Diakparomre's (2010) study reveals that mask performances among the Urhobo are not mere ceremonial engagements but are deeply symbolic and imbued with meanings conveying norms and values. Urhobo mask performances thus assist internalization of the socialization process that preserves Urhobo culture and integrates the Urhobo people.

It is clear, therefore, that symbols convey meanings that condition social interactions and actions. The meanings they convey are imbued with acceptable norms, values and expectations, within the context of which actors choose which actions they can consider taking. The ultimate choice of actions is dependent on the actors' socially constructed rationality (Jaeger 1993). So from here we can move on to the realm of rational choice.

Rational Choice Theory

Rational choice theory has its roots in neoclassical economics (Ritzer 2008; Ritzer and Goodman 2003; McGovern 2003; Lindenberg and Frey 1993; Srubar 1993). It posits that actors are purposive and are able to choose a course of action from available alternatives (Lahno 2007; Lovett 2006; Eding and Stern 2003). The actions they can take are dependent on the surrounding constraints and their ability to circumvent such constraints. Two major constraints an actor may be faced with are scarcity of resources and the power of social institutions (Sato 2010; Best 2009; Gagne 2007; Esser 1993a, 1993b; Farmer 1992). On the one hand, due to scarcity, an actor is constrained to submit to the logic of selection: he or she has to draw up a scale of preferences and determine which resource could have a greater utility within the context of availability and affordability. The actor must also consider the implications of foregoing the most preferred action. On the other hand, it is social institutions that determine the values, norms, social expectations and contexts within which actions can acceptably be taken. Thus, as much as actors are capable of rationally making decisions for the best outcome or use, they are bound in the eventual decision by the limits inherently defined and conditioned by the prevalent social institutions.

Despite its relevance in social theorizing, rational choice theory has been variously critiqued. For example, Zafirovski (1999) dismissively describes the theory as 'dubious-wanting' to colonize and dominate older sociological theories by attempting to unify them. Likewise, Denzin (1990: 182) claims that rational choice theory does not provide an explanation of how 'society is possible' and consequently dismisses it as having 'limited utility for contemporary social theory'. (For other critiques, see Mellor 2000 and Rule 1992.)

These critiques, however, take short-sighted views of the relevance of rational choice theory. The theory in its present state explains the social world beyond the limits of *homo oeconomicus* (Esser 1993; Jaeger 1993). Rational choice theorists have revised the theory in recent years and have been able to show that human actions are imbued with meanings that must be rightly deciphered (Elster 2009; Stolz 2006) and that these meanings are constructed over time and are based on historical social experiences and contexts (Pedriana 2005; Vanberg 2002; Hill 1997). The meanings so constructed are imbued with values that, of course, guide actors in choice-making (Hechter 1994; Jaeger 1993). Hence Pedriana (2005: 356) states: 'how rational actors construct and interpret their options and why those actors choose one path instead of other available paths are conditioned by broader structural arrangements ...'

The structural arrangements Pedriana refers to here are institutionalized social and cultural expectations, the norms and values within which actions should be taken. Without these, actions would take place in a state of social dereliction. Thus, both Mehlkhop and Graeff (2010) and Becker and Mehlkhop (2006) have empirically shown that internalized norms lessen the possibility of people committing crimes. This is because internalized norms indicate the actions that are acceptable and the consequences of delinquencies. Hence, rational actors with internalized norms prefer to choose alternatives that are institutionally acceptable. Indeed, the prevalent culture, as defined by actors who operate within the contexts of generally acceptable norms, values, actions and their attached symbolic meanings, informs those same actors' selection processes. The meanings attached to rational actions are not static, however. They are subject to change in time and space on the basis of prevalent interactions and ensuing institutionalized cultural norms, values and expectations. Rambo (1999: 324–325, 326) succinctly describes it thus:

> A resource is whatever makes possible the attainment of interests. All resources, taken together, form the limit of what it is possible to attain. For any interest in meaning, cultural structure is the resource base. It is, in effect, the language within which meaning is made, but extends far beyond words to any image or sound associations with other significant objects. Cultural structure is the universe of possibilities for making meaning, a pattern of relationships among signs, the reality of which emerges

> from the intersection and combination of symbolic actions. Like price in a competitive market, it is a constraining and facilitating structure produced by human intentions, without being intended as such ... The capacity of actors to control symbolism constitutes a power to shape cultural structure, by creating texts that capture actors' interests and form new relationships among signs.

Rambo rightly notes that actors have the capability to control symbolism. Institutionalized cultures and structures do not possess the power to enforce ultimate compliance on actors, as actors are able to modify institutional expectations in line with currently existing situations. A situation of scarce resources, demand and utility could potentially generate social interaction that reconstructs meanings as regards acceptable actions. Such reconstruction of meanings, due to scarcity and demand for the same resources that are germane for survival, potentially reconstructs the utility values of alternatives. This in turn can lead to the generation of institutional and socially acceptable values for alternatives that may hitherto have been outside socially acceptable realms.

Symbolic-Rational Choice and the Second-Hand Market

To sum up: the rational actions of actors are symbols imbued with meanings, which are dependent on the prevailing social context. It is in this context that actors' preference for *tokunbo* second-hand goods becomes meaningful. The meaning springs primarily from the 'superiority' and quality value attached to the total gamut of elements of Western culture. It is further strengthened in contemporary times by the increasing cultural globalization process, which lends Western culture an aura of being the 'ideal'. The capability of a local population to absorb and reflect Western culture is, of course, dependent on its ability to utilize Western material cultural goods. Access to these goods constructs assumed 'elitist' values for the actor (that is, the consumer).

Nigerian local society and culture have thus reconfigured and modified the meanings generally and contextually attached to used goods (*aloku*). Thus, a distinction has arisen between locally used second-hand goods and those imported. Locally used second-hand ones have retained the now derisive descriptive, '*aloku*', while imported used goods are dignified by the term *tokunbo*, a term already imbued with a centuries-long freight of meaning emphasizing the Western origin and 'superiority' transferred to it. So long as the goods are from overseas, the resonances of the imported second-hand have therefore been reconstructed, achieving a promotion from 'inferior' to the 'superior'. The social interaction prevalent in post-colonial Nigeria has thus reconstructed the meanings attached to second-hand goods and as a result, the local population across classes rationally opts for second-hand goods imported from the West, believing that they facilitate the practice of the modernity they wish to adopt.

The utility value of imported second-hand goods has thus been socially reframed, with connotations of high quality, enabling such goods to offer the same satisfaction as the new Western products that are unafforda-ble. Having rationally modified the symbolic meanings attached to used goods and consequently differentiated between locally used goods (*aloku*) and imported used goods (*tokunbo*), the growing imported second-hand economy now allows ordinary people access to modern (Western) goods at affordable prices. '*Tokunbo* second-hand' is a reflection of affordable modernity attracting patronage across class boundaries and is a product of 'symbolic-rational choice' within Nigerian society.

CHAPTER 3

The Rational Symbolism of Name

One of the methods human beings have adopted to identify and remember objects and elements of the social and physical environments is through the creation of names. Name construction stands as a rational action within the social environment, which gives symbolic meanings to identified objects, social processes, interactions and phenomena. A phenomenon, whether physical or social, may not be comprehensible unless the social environment and subsisting culture are able to construct a rational meaning for it on the basis of prevalent social experiences and interactions. The meanings constructed will, in turn, inform the name given and vice versa. Name signifies the forms, nature and identity of elements within the environment. Name is context-bound, dynamic and relative. The socio-cultural environment has a primary role to play in the construction and adoption of an acceptable name. Names are therefore not given in isolation, but within the context of the experiences and meanings constructed out of the immediate environment.

Names are symbolic and meaningful. The meanings attached are dependent on social experiences within the immediate social environment and this, of course, also impacts on social interactions and culture that border on name symbolism. According to Charmaz (2006: 396):

> … names classify objects and events and convey meanings and distinctions. Names carry weight, whether light or heavy. Names provide ways of knowing and being. Names construct and reify human bonds and social divisions. We attach value to some names and dismiss others. Names are rooted in actions and give rise to specific practices.

Names depict the class and quality of human beings, goods, services and all other aspects of social life. As elementary parts of the value system, names give conditions within which actions may be taken. They solidify relationships and bring social relations within the realms of the observable and identifiable. Names bring what is ordinarily imaginary into the realm of the real, and thus concretize social experiences in the real world. It should be noted, however, that human beings are not totally subject to name symbolism. Actors are rationally capable of constructing and reconstructing meanings attached to names based on subsisting social realities. Names are therefore universal but dynamic and very congruent in interactions as symbols of identification, categorization, objectification and realization of social and physical environments.

The literature variously shows the symbolic significance of names attached to human beings, goods, places and all other aspects of human processes. For example Dandeker, Wessely, Iversen and Ross (2006) describe how the meanings attached to the tag 'veteran' condition how societies determine who should be qualified in the allocation of scarce resources to those who have served in the military. The meanings attached vary across countries. The authors identify four categories including: (1) all who have served in the military for more than a day; (2) those who have finished a basic military training; (3) those who have completed a specified period of engagement; and (4) those who have been actively involved in a tour of duty. According to Dandeker and his colleagues, Great Britain has adopted the all-inclusive definition of 'veterans' which accommodates all personnel who have served for more than a day. The British meaning of 'veteran' thus includes all who have had minimal experience in the military, whether they have seen war or not. This, they claim, is indeed is an indicator of a country desirous of taking care of the welfare of its heroes and heroines.

Hansen's (2004) study discusses how the appellation 'Europe' defines the countries accepted as European and excludes other countries on the borders of Asia, especially Turkey. Thus, Turkey may be within the continent of Europe geographically but the name symbolism of 'Europe', as presently constructed, excludes the country; and this, of course, impacts on social and international relations between Turkey and Europe and the definitions of Western heritage within Europe. While Turkish citizens view themselves as Europeans with a historical Muslim civilization and Arab links, the rest of Europe (especially Western Europe) sees Turkey as part of Asia though, as geographically delineated, projecting into Europe

(Baban and Keyman 2008; Keyder 2006; Hudson 2000). The meanings attached to 'Europe' symbolism with regard to Turkey may change if and when Turkey is admitted into the European Union.

Another example of the symbolic significance of naming can be seen in the work of Furusa (2009) and Reid-Merritt (2009), who have focused on the problem of adopting the most apposite and generally acceptable name for the field of African Studies. Various nomenclatures have been adopted by scholars, including 'Black Studies', 'Black American Studies' and 'African and Diaspora African Issues', among others. The search finds a parallel in Mysterud's (2004) study on the quest to adopt a uniform name for the field of evolutionary study, which currently is variously called 'Human Socio-Biology', 'Evolutionary Anthropology', 'Human Ethnology' and 'Evolutionary Psychology' among other names. Scholars who specialize in these disciplines are concerned about the plethora of names because they have implications for the nature and acceptability of their disciplines in the wider scholarly arena. Different names for the same disciplinary area suggest a schismatic field in which everyone is trying to create areas of influence and identity cliques, and this could affect disciplinary unity, teamwork and development adversely.

Furthermore, the literature also affirms the importance of names for goods. Dawar and Parker (1994) posit that brand names have the potential to attract the patronage of consumers, along with price, physical appearance and reputation (see also Semmann, Krambeck and Milinski 2004). A brand name gives a product a unique identity that may attract customers' attention. Hence, it is a prerequisite for producers to come up with brand names that can enhance the marketing of their products. Klink (2000: 5) states that:

> An effective brand name can enhance awareness and create a favourable image for the product ... On the other hand, not all brand names are well received by consumers. In fact, an ineffective name can spell a product's demise ...

He (2000) therefore posits that sound name symbolism impacts on brand patronage. Products should thus have names that are meaningful to consumers. The meaning the brand name conveys has the potential to attract consumers' interest and patronage. A successful name could be created by ensuring a link between the brand mark (such as target group, colour and picture) and the brand name (Klink 2009, 2003; Lee and Ang 2003).

Above all, it is for human individuals themselves that name is principally fundamental. Finch (2008) describes name as a mark of individual identity and social connection. Human beings must provide and respond to their names in everyday social interactions in order to carry out even the most basic tasks involving other parties. The state and other social institutions within which an individual operates relate to that individual first and foremost on the basis of the name he or she has provided. Names also indicate social connections, experiences, profession, ethnicity, gender and nationality among other indices. In short, names are cultural capital (Thorne 2008; Almack 2005; Silva 2005; Ward 2003; Lord 2002; Orie 2002).

Confirming again the relevance of names as cultural capital, Aceto (2002) discusses the importance of ethnic personal names among descendants of Anglophone West Indies Creole-speaking migrants in Bastimentos Island, which belongs to Panama, where the predominant language is Spanish. The residents of the island have both Spanish and Creole names. Having Creole-derived names signifies the identity and history of the residents of the island, and Aceto therefore posits that this is one way of resisting the pressure to Hispanicize. Within the community, everybody knows and calls the other person by his or her Creole name. Outside the island, and especially in official documents, the Spanish name is used. Within this context, the adoption of dual names of diverse historic-cultural traditions shows the overriding impact of names as rational symbolism in the construction and adoption of human nomenclature within a society.

The Anglophone-Creole community finds itself in a predominantly Spanish community. It has no chance of accessing its citizenry rights unless it accepts elements of the Spanish culture generally practised in Panama. So, in order to ensure its acceptance and integration into the larger Panamanian society, the island community adopts Spanish names as official names through which resources may be sourced from the state. However, it retains a consciousness of its Anglophone history and identity under Panamanian sovereignty by also adopting Anglophone-Creole names. These give the community a feel of distinctiveness from the larger Panamanian society. The names symbolize the Caribbean origin and history of the island residents.

Despite this, it can be argued that the Creole names only keep the memory of the people's cultural and/or ethnic origin within their consciousness and provide some means of practising their culture. Clinging on to the names does not make them fully immune from the process of Hispanicization. That Anglophone Creoles in Bastimentos Island are not immune from the Hispanicization process is evident in the fact that they have to identify with Spanish culture by adopting official Spanish names. It is through these Spanish names that they are recognized and exist within the Panamanian society. In this context therefore, both the Panamanian and Creole societies and cultures provide the rational symbolic context for the social construction of names of Bastimentos islanders.

Along the same lines, a study by Copeland (2010) focuses on the name 'slave' and how it bound enslaved Africans, as 'property', to their masters in America. Validated by judicial pronouncements, the term 'slave' socially and symbolically transformed enslaved Africans from human beings into 'things'. Being 'things', they became properties of their masters without rights. They were subject to uncontrolled exploitation and use, even to the point of exhaustion and death. This shows the power of a society and the interacting socio-cultural environment to impute meanings and values to names. The just-a-'thing' value attached to slaves conditioned their interactions with their masters and society as a whole. It denied them rights and subdued them under the most heinous and inhumane conditions (Afigbo 2009; Mason 2009; Fandrich 2007; Benson 2006; Ogunleye 2006; Peterson 2001).

Aside from this classificatory naming, as a means of recreating the psyche of newly arrived slaves, the slave merchants and masters gave them new personal names. Thus the forcefully abducted Africans assumed their new identities as bondmen. Berlin (1996: 251) believes that this renaming of slaves was a way of 'separating them from their African inheritance'. It was indeed a means of resocializing them into slavery and the life of being mere 'property' whose fate, services and future were at the discretion of their masters. Though they were enslaved, powerless and devoid of rights, Handler and Jacoby's (1996) research shows the persistence of African names among slaves in Barbados. Slaves adopted plantation names that differed from the names given them by their masters by which they were formally known. These alternative names bestowed on them some sort of historical consciousness and affinity to Africa. This rational symbolic adoption of African names shows the perpetuation of some continuing African consciousness even among these supposedly powerless people reduced to 'things'.

In the long run, as the slaves were emancipated, they were classified as 'Negro'. Within the last five decades, however, the social name for Africans in the United States has been reconstructed from 'Negro' to 'Black' (the term adopted in the 1960s) and lately (from the 1980s) to 'African-Americans'. According to Martin (1991: 83), the Rev. Jesse Jackson puts the rationale behind the change thus:

> To be called African-Americans has cultural integrity ... It puts us in our proper historical context. Every ethnic group in this country has a reference to some land base, some historical cultural base. African-Americans have hit that level of cultural maturity. There are Armenian-Americans and Jewish-Americans and Arab-Americans and Italian-Americans; and with a degree of accepted and reasonable pride, they connect their heritage to their mother country and where they are now. (See also Smitherman 1991.)

Today, as a way of socio-symbolically recreating and realigning their social consciousness away from the social realities of slavery and disadvantage to a sense of being proud Africans, many black people in the USA have started to adopt unique names rooted in African culture and quite distinct from Anglo-Saxon tradition. This is noted by Khabib (1995) and by Lieberson and Mikelson (1995). The trend is a reflection of rational response to the meanings attached to name symbolism. African Americans adopting African names have simply reacted to the memories of slavery and have sought to reconstruct their freedom and identity through the symbolic adoption of names that emphasize their roots and African-ness.

This takes us to the naming culture in Africa. Africa remains a continent rich in traditions, despite centuries in which its indigenous culture and social values have apparently been weakened, due to integration into the modern world system. The birth of a child and the child's subsequent naming are deeply rooted in traditional African cultural values. Children are valued as the hope and social insurance of their parents and of society, and are seen as the future facilitators of societal development. They are regarded as God-given, and so the circumstances of their birth are taken into account when they are named. Describing naming among the Ga of Ghana, Abarry (1997: 365) states that:

> The naming ceremony … [is] a multifaceted communicative system through which the people express, not only their ideas of personhood, self, and group identities, but world view, aesthetics, creativity, moral, social, and religious values as well.

Naming amongst the Ga takes place on the eighth day of a child's life. The ceremony denotes the child's presentation to the world in which he/she will live and be subjected to the social experiences that will contribute to the construction of his/her self-concept and essential being throughout life. Hence, naming appears to give the child a personality and identity and an assurance of acceptance into society.

Naming practices are similar across Africa. It is worth looking at the practices among the Yoruba-speaking people, who are of direct relevance to this study. These people number up to about 24 million and are geographically situated in Nigeria, the Republic of Benin and Togo. Nigeria has the highest concentration of the Yoruba. Here they are located in the six states of South-Western Nigeria (the Ekiti, Lagos, Ogun, Ondo, Osun and Oyo states) and in the Kogi and Kwara states in North-Central Nigeria. Yoruba society is rich in traditions that have survived through the centuries despite the foreign influences since colonialism. The Yoruba regard conception and birth as divine. The circumstances of birth are therefore taken into consideration in the naming of a child. As with the Ga people of Ghana, this usually takes place on the eighth day after birth. The naming principle is encapsulated in the socio-cultural notion '*Ile ni a n wo ki a to so omo ni oruko*', meaning that the condition of the home determines a child's name (see Akinnaso 1980: 279; Ekundayo 1977: 57).

The circumstances of birth and, by extension, the condition of the home are, of course, informed by the prevalent social reality. By merely hearing a person's name, anyone with a good knowledge of Yoruba culture can infer the social affinities of the bearer and the circumstances surrounding his or her birth. The fact that Yoruba names are meaningful emphasizes the need to 'integrate culture and second language teaching through Yoruba personal names' (Akinyemi 2005: 115).

Akinyemi has identified different types of names among the Yoruba. These include: (a) names children are born with (i.e. *oruko abiso*); (b) names describing the child-parent relationship; (c) death prevention names; (d) praise names; and (e) nicknames (Akinyemi 2005: 117; see also Oyetade 1995). The names children are born with are the ones describing the physical nature of their birth. For example, a breech birth child is called *Ajayi*. The first born of a twin birth is called *Taiwo* or *Taye*, while the second is called *Kehinde*. The Yoruba presume the *Kehinde* to be the older of the two: He/she sends *Taye* to go out first to view the earth while the *Kehinde* follows behind.

Names depict the child-parent relationship; indicate professional affiliation, religious affiliation, social status and the fortune or misfortune of the parents at the time of the named child's birth. Furthermore, Yoruba mythology presumes that some children have supernatural powers to determine their birth and death. Such children are generally called *Abiku* (see also Okonkwo 2004; McCabe 2002). Akinyemi (2005) affirms that the Yoruba believe such children can be prevented from dying by possessing names such as *Malomo* ('do not go again') and *Banjoko* ('sit down' or 'stay with me') (Akinyemi 2005: 119–120).

Names depicting social status can have prefixes such as *Ade* ('crown') and/or *Ola* ('honour/prestige'). Examples of such names include *Adeniyi* ('the crown is honourable') and *Bolanle* ('has met honour at home'). *Ade* is principally the paraphernalia of a Yoruba *Oba* or king. People with names prefixed with *Ade* are assumed to be of the royal family. *Ola*, on the other hand, depicts the wealth, honour and prestige of a family. A person with the name prefix *Ola* is assumed to be from an honourable and prestigious background. Praise names depict valour and heroism. They are given in hope of what the parents wish their children will become. Akinyemi identifies some, such as *Ajani* ('he who fights to possess'), *Akande* ('one who has been intentionally selected') and *Aduke* ('one people shall contest to pet') (Akinyemi 2005: 120). Nicknames are names that are given by friends and associates in later life, eventually becoming accepted as personal names signifying identity. The works of Akinyemi (2005), Akinnaso (1980) and Ekundayo (1977) show that Yoruba names are symbolic and are rationally selected based on prevalent circumstances within the home.

A major gap in this literature of names is that none of the authors discusses 'Tokunbo' as a name given to children conceived or delivered abroad. As already noted, the social construction of value around conception and birth abroad has its roots in Nigeria's colonial experience. This links it with the recent construction denoting imported second-hand goods. It is noteworthy that the *tokunbo* prefix for second-hand goods does not indicate any brand name. It is a social construction generated by the local marketing and consuming public to describe imported second-hand items, irrespective of the original producers. It is a reflection of a rational symbolic construction in society conveying a meaningful label to consumers. The *tokunbo* tag, just as is the case of humans, conveys the meaning of good quality, attracting admiration.

CHAPTER 4

The Second-Hand Economy and Modernity Diffusion

Within the last three decades, more than ever before, second-hand goods and markets have become a booming reality in the Third World. Aided by increasing globalization and modernization processes, the world is culturally becoming united, while Western lifestyles are gaining almost universal dominance (Eisenstadt 2010; Smith 2010; Smith 2009; Domingues 2009, 2002; McMichael 2008; van Der Bly 2005; Kaya 2004; Roche 2003). The socio-economic dimension of the ensuing modernization process is increasing people's preference for Western goods. In Nigerian local culture Western goods symbolically depict a sought-after standard, an elitist class and modernity. Those who are able to access Western goods are deemed to have acquired prestige products and they are also seen as members of an elite class who are up with modern culture (see, for example, Parkins 2010; Trentmann 2009; Money 2007; Entwistle 2006; Schulz 2006; Mills 2005; Yurchisin and Johnson 2004; Hill 2002, 2001; Jansson 2002). Since many Nigerians are unable to afford good quality new products from Western nations and also find the readily available, cheaper Chinese alternatives rather inferior (Pang 2008), the second-hand market provides their main channel for accessing the Western goods they require – items imbued with the aura of 'modern constructs'. These come at relatively cheap prices but are, of course, of a better quality than the inferior new goods. This indeed is a dimension of the local experience of the globalization process (the 'glocal') in Nigeria as it affects the value-consumption chain of Western goods. It confirms Martinelli's (2003a: 291) assertion that:

> Today globalization implies not only the emergence of a new object of study, the world as such, but requires that any specific study be framed in a global context, since each part of the world is increasingly interdependent with many others and the

> world as such is increasingly present in all parts. The contemporary world looks more and more like a laser beam hologram, where every point contains the information of the whole, since each human being increasingly tends to consume information and resources coming from everywhere. Hence there is the need to shift the level of analysis at the global level and to take a world system perspective in any study. The study of world society and its relations with national and local realities should become a central theme of research. The higher the degree of interconnectedness of social relations at the world level, the greater the need to analyse the links between global social reality and multiple local social realities. 'Glocal' is an increasing relevant neologism in our lexicon.

Hence, in Nigeria in particular, and the Third World in general, the contemporary second-hand economy is an aspect of the 'glocal', which requires in-depth study to reveal the social reality of the local second-hand economy and local consumption within the global second-hand context (see also Smith 2010; Boli and Elliot 2008; Giulianotti and Robertson 2007, 2006, 2004; Martinelli 2003b; Giulianotti 2002). The second-hand market at present takes the form of a vertical economic and social connection between the developed world and the developing world (Hotta, Elder, Mori and Tanaka 2008; Beuving 2006; Czaga and Fliess 2005).

Largely lacking productive industries, the developing world depends on the developed world for most of its imports. With increasing economic depression in the developing world, new imported goods have become less and less affordable to a large spectrum of the population. Used goods from the developed world have therefore become viable alternatives for consumers in the developing nations (Greenwood and Uysal 2005; Thomas 2003; Porter and Sattler 1999). Research has shown that the second-hand market has become a huge industry, employing a large labour force and providing goods to places where Western-style items might otherwise have been unaffordable (Pelletiere and Reinert 2010, 2006, 2004; Buchert, Hermann, Jenseit, Stahl, Osyguß and Hageluken 2007; Hawley 2006). Estimates show that, while the value of second-hand automobiles was globally worth about $70 billion in 2003 (Czaga and Fliess 2005), turnover from the global second-hand textile trade is greater than $200 billion per year (Baden and Barber 2005).

These figures attest to the vibrancy of the second-hand market which is directly related to the durability of the goods on sale within it. The durability has both economic and social dimensions. Within this construct of durability are goods with resale value. These are goods that have been acquired brand new but are resold after a while by the original owners to secondary consumers who can find use for them, second-hand. A vital attribute of durable goods, therefore, is their re-sale value (Yokoo 2010; Esteban and Shum 2007; Kumar 2002; Biehl 2001; Huang, Yang and Anderson 2001). The second-hand market provides, as it were, an alternative and thus a competitor for the primary producer. At the same time, however, the second-hand market provides the primary producer with an avenue for comparing the quality of the new product with that of the used. Hence the primary producer is able to attract surplus profit by emphasizing the high quality of a new product vis-à-vis that of a used one. Alternatively, the primary producer may attempt to kill off the second-hand market by reducing the durability of new goods, thereby eliminating their resale/secondary value (Licandro, Puch and Sampayo 2008; Orbach 2004; Waldman 2003, 1996; Dhebar 1994; Anderson and Ginsburgh 1994; Rust 1986).

Irrespective of the potential and real capabilities of used durables as alternatives, a potential threat to consumers' interests is the possibility of adverse selection and anti-trust practices. This is because used durables may be defective even when they look neat and attractive. Since buyers/consumers may be unaware of the true condition of such durables, the cost of repair and maintenance gets transferred to buyers (Waldman 2004, 2003; Hendel and Lizzeri 1999).

Nevertheless, it is equally important to note that anti-trust practices and adverse selection can also pose grave consequences to the business of second-hand sellers. According to Buskens and Weesie (2000), trust and social embeddedness are important in transactions over used cars. Buyers will only decide to purchase a used car if they are certain of the likelihood of getting proper value for the money spent. However, their decisions are dependent on the level of trust that has been constructed between themselves and the seller over time and through social embeddedness. In such situations, where social embeddedness exists and is respected, a seller who trades a used vehicle that is not worth its price would be sanctioned by the loss of would-be customers who would soon be informed through the embedded social network system. The second-hand market is, therefore, a social context where sellers and buyers mutually interact and socially construct values for goods (Aspers 2008; Fourcade 2007). The values that are constructed determine the price that is attached to the goods. The post-purchase utility value the consumer enjoys, along with the price paid, potentially impact on the construction of trust between the seller and the buyer. This relationship has implications for the buyers' continual patronage and the sellers' profitability and business survival.

From the foregoing discussion, it is possible to deduce the social construction and meanings attached to second-hand goods. First and foremost, it should be noted that, contrary to the assumption that the second-hand market is a market of inferior goods (Porter and Sattler 1999; Sherry 1990), it in actual fact satisfies the consumption needs of those who make use of it. The market, hence, conveys meanings other than inferiority: it conveys meanings affirming the satisfaction of socially constructed vital needs and is thus a centre for securing viable alternatives at minimal cost. It serves as an avenue for the practice of modernity among the population of the Third World, who would otherwise find new essentials unaffordable and too much of a luxury. In addition, the second-hand market conveys symbolic meanings of access gained to good quality modernity, and thus, at cheaper rates, makes it rationally possible to satisfy and/or acquire socially constructed symbolic elements of the modern 'good life' worthy of an elite class (Williams and Paddock 2003; Crewe 2000).

For example Besnier's (2004) study on the second-hand marketplace in Tonga reveals the impact of stratified society on the consumption of second-hand products. Imported new products such as shoes, clothes and household utensils are particularly expensive and beyond the reach of the poor lower classes, who are in the majority. The second-hand market allows access to cheap imported goods that are seen as a reflection of modernity and are used to practise it. Thus, the poor lower classes are able to have the kinds of imported goods the upper class use, but at a lower cost. Likewise, Omobowale (2008) has shown the popularity of second-hand *tokunbo* vehicles among members of the middle class in Nigeria who are unable to acquire the new vehicles popularly referred to as *tear rubber*. Both *tokunbo* and *tear rubber* are status symbols. *Tokunbo* on the one hand indicates the second-hand value of the vehicle as an imported used item, which still carries the glamour of the privileged among the masses who would otherwise find cars unaffordable. On the other hand, *tear rubber* indicates that the polythene seat cover is still in place. The polythene cover indicates the newness of the car; thus many new car owners leave the polythene cover on for as long as possible, to show off the car's newness and to make it a status symbol. The ability to afford *tear rubber* indicates success, comfort and riches, even if the purchaser has taken a loan to purchase it. This notwithstanding, the ownership of a *tokunbo* vehicle goes some way towards levelling the gap between classes because the mere ownership of a vehicle signifies status, irrespective of the state of the vehicle at the time of purchase and whether it is new or imported second-hand. Locally used vehicles, however, do not carry the same level of symbolic prestige: they tend to be socially derided and considered of lower quality – as *aloku*.

The continued growth of the second-hand market and economy in the Third World is associated with the waste management and recycling policy of the developed world. According to Hotta et al. (2008: 27):

> Early studies documenting the trend of increased transboundary movement of recyclable materials showed that (a) recycling of secondary materials (recyclables materials) is increasing in both developed and developing countries, (b) international trade of secondary materials grows at an even faster rate, and (c) developing countries tend to import recyclables from the developed countries.

Recycling preserves the developed world's landfills while it also indirectly promotes increasing productivity. As new products are released in the developed world, old ones drop into obsolescence and they then become potential valuable goods in the developing world. This is because the problem of the disposal of old goods is mitigated by the option of recycling them for potential users in the Third World.

The recycling industry in the developed world creates employment for low grade workers in both developing and developed countries; it also converts what might have been disposed of as its own waste into valuable goods for the developing world. Confirming this, Soderman and Carter (2008: 22) describe the salvage yard as 'a space where the souls of objects are saved'. The scrap-yard serves as a place where supposedly disused automobiles and vehicle parts acquire a re-use value among customers. The Third World remains a viable destination for such goods. Though they are described as 'scrap' in the developed world, a little repair reconfigures the vehicles and spare parts into valuable goods made ready for sale.

Likewise, used items of clothing from the developed world are readily accepted and purchased in the developing world. Of all used products, imported second-hand clothes are the most popular there. Used clothes are not just recycled for waste management and environmental preservation, but are sent as humanitarian efforts to provide clothing where it might otherwise have been unaffordable (Larney and van Aardt 2010; Hawley 2006). The value and importance of second-hand clothing is shown by Baden and Barber (2005) who claim that the trade in used clothing has grown since the 1990s to a value of about $1 billion per year. Likewise Peck and Pinto (2003) submit that between 80 to 90 per cent of Angolans wear second-hand clothes.

Similarly, there is a huge market for used electronic items in the Third world: it satisfies the quest of Third World consumers for modern e-technology at affordable prices. There are growing concerns about the impact from the toxic nature of used electronic equipment (popularly described as 'e-waste') on Third World populations. According to Greenpeace (2005), disused electronic items – including mobile telephones, computers (both desktops and laptops), printers, scanners and television sets – account for between 20 to 50 tons of global hazardous waste. Most 'e-waste' ends up in developing countries, endangering the lives of the already pauperized population, who tend to see used electronic items as affordable alternatives to new equipment (Yoshida and Terazono 2010; Osibanjo, Nnorom and Ogbona 2008; Osibanjo and Nnorom 2007). However, the consumption of imported second-hand goods, even when they amount to hazardous waste, is influenced by modernity diffusion. Modernity diffusion, in turn, structures consumer behaviour in the Third World: to consume second-hand goods, as a symbolic rational alternative to buying expensive new products, in the practice of modernity.

CHAPTER 5

The Social Value of *Tokunbo* in Human Naming

As in many African societies, and as hinted above, the naming of human beings among the Yoruba of South-Western Nigeria is not just a process of identification. It is an act imbued with meanings derived from the immediate social environment. The names given indicate the social world of the named person and the circumstances of his/her birth. Name thus constitutes a whole gamut of social history surrounding the birth and immediate family experience of an individual. Among other indices, names indicate social status, the form of birth, the family profession, religion, place of birth, lineage and hoped-for destiny. As much as family social history and experience play an important role in naming, the Yoruba also mythically believe that a child's name configures his/her destiny. Hence, reflecting the general beliefs of the society, three Yoruba proverbs on name say: *Ile la n wo ka to s'omo l'oruko* – 'the condition of the home determines a child's name' (see Akinnaso 1980: 279 and Ekundayo 1977: 57); *Oruko omo ni n ro'mo* – 'a child's name conditions his/her destiny'; and *Oruko omo ni ijanu omo* – 'a child's name is his/her caution' (Fasiku 2006).

All three proverbs indicate Yoruba beliefs as regards names. The first gives the social context of name: it indicates that a child is not named in isolation from the context of his/her background. For the Yoruba, therefore, the overt process of socialization starts with the act of naming (Akinyemi 2005). The second proverb indicates the power of name in the process of socialization. A child is expected to live according to the values attached to his/her name; doing so will attract positive rewards that should last a lifetime. To ensure this, as seen in the third proverb, a child's name cautions him or her. The Yoruba place a high value on names. Every child is socialized to comply, in order to protect his/her name and the family name. Thus, the social value attached to names cautions an individual and socially guides and configures him/her within socially acceptable limits. A child who does not live up to this expectation gets both his/her name, and the family name, devalued and dishonoured. Hence, the Yoruba believe *Oruko rere san ju wura ati fadaka* – 'a good name is better than gold and silver'. A child is thus expected to sustain the good name he/she has been given by maintaining a good character, because riches and wealth are worthless without a good name. The name, given on the eighth day after birth, must be consciously sustained through good conduct.

It is within this context that this study discusses 'Tokunbo' as a Yoruba name with meanings rooted deep in Yoruba social history and culture. As already explained, *tokunbo* means 'from across the seas', and this has special significance for the Yoruba as they are bounded on the southern flanks by the Atlantic Ocean[1] (see Figure 2).

Just like their eastern neighbours, the Edo,[2] the Yoruba attach mythical and supernatural beliefs to the ocean's vast splendour and natural spread. The ocean (*okun*)[3] represents supernatural powers, wealth and magnificence (Drewal, Pemberton III and Abiodun 1989; Nevadomsky and Rosen 1988; Ben-Amos 1973).[4] Among the native population of pre-colonial Nigeria,

1 Following the colonial partitioning of Africa, the Yoruba communities of Ketu and Sabe eventually became part of French Dahomey (Republic of Benin), while the rest of Yorubaland became part of the British colonial territory of Nigeria (Asiwaju 2003–2004; Asiwaju and Adeniyi 1989; Asiwaju 1985; Hargreaves 1985).

2 Both the Yoruba and the Edo share similar cultural and historical links. Until the early 1960s, when the Mid-Western Region was carved out of South-Western Nigeria, the Edo speaking people were largely regarded as being of Yoruba extraction. It is on record that Oranmiyan, a frontline Yoruba-Oyo prince ruled Edo and created the Oba dynasty in Benin (Bondarenko and Roese 2004; Bondarenko 2003). Recent identity disputes and reconstruction have, however, created an independent identity for the Edo. Nevertheless, both the Yoruba and Edo shared similar cultural traits till the contemporary era (see Ogundiran 2002, 2001).

3 The *Olokun* (goddess of *okun*) is worshipped by adherents among both the Yoruba and the Edo. Furthermore, in contemporary times, some Christian religious groups (especially 'White Garment'/Aladura churches such as the Celestial Church of Christ and the Cherubim and Seraphim sects) hold the *Okun* as a centre of high supernatural power and essence. Both sects conduct religious services by the seaside (see Larmie 2008; Meyer 2004; Ray 1993; Crumbley 1992; Probst 1989).

4 Yoruba social thought further alludes to the supernatural power of the *okun* (sea) through the myth telling how the Owa (a grandson of Oduduwa, the progenitor of

it was uncommon and, in fact, usually unthinkable to transverse the sea between continents. Although the local technological know-how could sustain survival, it could not develop a means of crossing to the European, American or Asian sides of the ocean.

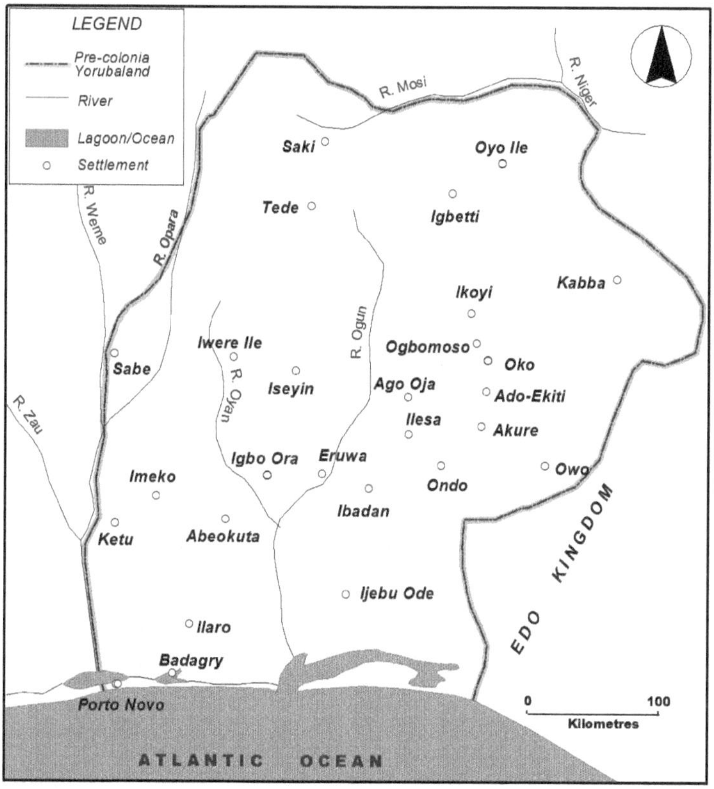

Figure 2 *The pre-colonial Yoruba nation, showing the southern border with the Atlantic Ocean*

---

the Yoruba, and later the King of the Ijesha, a Yoruba sub-ethnic group) performed the extraordinary feat of fetching water from the sea to heal the aging Oduduwa, the projenitor of the Yoruba race, from his blindness. Even today, the Owa's appellation is *Owa Obokun* – 'Owa the fetcher of sea water'. (See Dixon 1991; Peel 1984, 1980 a and b, 1979; and Law 1973 on Owa and the Ijesha.)

Boatcraft was limited to the construction of canoes, which were utilized for sailing along the coastline and for fishing. Since this was the limit to indigenous technology, the *okun* (or ocean) was regarded as an insurmountable barrier, making other continents unreachable.

The arrival of Europeans along the coast of the Yoruba nation in the fifteenth and sixteenth centuries marked a new era in Yoruba civilization and culture. For the first time, the indigenous people could interact with the people of *oke okun* – 'the upper end of the sea'. These people were, of course, of a different stock in colour, language and culture. The Europeans were admired especially for their technology and the splendour and magnificence reflected in their goods. Consequently, European merchandise acquired, locally, the prestige of valuable goods from *oke okun* through which class and honour could be symbolically expressed. In the mindset of the indigenous population, these goods conveyed an impression of awesome wealth, and of the prosperity and magnificence of those on the other side of the sea.

This primary contact and the subsequent colonization of African lands opened up chances to some of the indigenous population to make the transatlantic crossing themselves. They went in search of education and the 'good life' available across the sea. Colonization, by this time, had particularly exposed the indigenous population to the Western lifestyle, which thenceforth came to be regarded as the standard culture even for Africans. An ability to speak English created a special status and a supposed connection with the Europeans; whoever could manage to transverse the high seas and travel to Europe was very highly valued. Once a person had migrated to Europe (and much later, to North America), he/she was looked up to as being part of the privileged class. The adulatory perception of the society and culture across the sea was momentarily transferred to the migrant, who was therefore viewed as a privileged elite member of the modern class, wealthy and having a deep understanding of Western culture. Though exposed to Western lifestyles, the native migrant elite did not entirely abandon the local culture. In fact, those aspects of the local culture that advanced their privileged status were both actively and passively accentuated. Consequently, the migrant elite accepted the value of giving meaningful Yoruba names to their offspring, even in the midst of deep exposure to modern/western culture in Europe and North America.

Keeping to the local custom of giving meaningful names, the early migrants, alongside their kin in Africa, created the name 'Tokunbo'. It indicated not only the place of birth but also socially constructed elitist values, emphasizing a transatlantic transcendence and worth that seemed far superior to the 'native born'. Whereas in the early stage only children born in the West were christened 'Tokunbo', over time it became (and remains) quite common to name individuals born outside Nigeria (but not in the West) 'Tokunbo' too. However, since, for the sake of easy identification, no two siblings can bear the same first name, even if more than one child was conceived and/or born abroad, only one of them would be christened 'Tokunbo'. Usually this was the first-born, but, of course, for personal or contextual reasons, the parents might decide to give the name to one of their other children.

Research respondents who have a good knowledge of Yoruba and who have known people called 'Tokunbo' as kin, friends or associates attest to the social value attached to the name. A grandparent in Ibadan, recounts that:

> If a man travelled abroad and on his arrival to Nigeria, his wife delivered a baby; such a child would be named 'Tokunbo'. I have a grandchild that is named 'Tokunbo'; the parents are based in the United Kingdom. Just as people name a child that was delivered on the way 'Abiona', so also a child that was given birth to abroad is named 'Tokunbo'. People usually appreciate children that are called 'Tokunbo'. A good example is my grandchild. (KII/Male/Ibadan/19 August 2010)

This key informant gives insights into 'Tokunbo' as a human name. The data confirms the Yoruba's preference for meaningful names, due to the deep socio-cultural value they attach to them.

Another interviewee supports the view expressed above thus:

> In the olden days, there was the prestige attached to 'Tokunbo' as a name of a person … In the past, when a child is called 'Tokunbo' one will quickly realize that the parents of the child must have given birth to him or her overseas. At that time, there was a prestige attached to the name 'Tokunbo' because people saw overseas countries as *ilu oba* (the Monarch's country).[5] Overseas was seen as a special place … When

5 In colonial and immediate post-colonial South-Western Nigeria Great Britain was known as 'the Monarch's country'. This was an indication of the natives' acceptance of the sovereign overlordship of the United Kingdom and its monarch over themselves as colonized people.

> someone said he or she was travelling overseas, such a person was seen as travelling to heaven. Travelling overseas at that time was appreciated in the society ... In the past, out of one hundred families, one might not see a person who had travelled once before. Even as rich as some people were, they never had the privilege to visit an airport. (IDI/Male/Abeokuta/30 August 2010)

Yet another respondent states that:

> People that were born abroad are called 'Tokunbo' when they come back home, even if the person was not named 'Tokunbo' when he or she was given birth to abroad. Those who are called 'Tokunbo' are happy with the name because they are seen as important people in the society, by the virtue of their places of birth. (IDI/Male/Ibadan/25 August 2010)

A further respondent has this to say:

> *Tokunbo* are children that were born outside the country. When such children are brought home, their parents name them 'Tokunbo', for people to know that they were not born in Nigeria. People bearing [the name] 'Tokunbo' usually feel they are superior to those that were born in Nigeria because the way they speak and dress will signify that they were not born in Nigeria ... When I was young, I used to look at people bearing [the name] 'Tokunbo' as special people ... (IDI/Female/28 Augusts 2010)

Data from the in-depth survey relayed above affirm the social prestige attached to 'Tokunbo' as a human name. It is (was) indeed a symbol of social elitism commonly appreciated within Yoruba society and culture. Focus group discussion (FGD) data also corroborate the IDI findings. Discussants in a FGD in Ibadan concurred that:

> People see those who bear the name 'Tokunbo' as important and prestigious persons, especially because they exhibit distinct character and physical appearance. The way people behave overseas is different. A child that has just come back from overseas will definitely be superior to the local children. The child will be different in the way he/she speaks and in character. Even when such children come to Nigeria, they stay in some of the best environments where mosquitoes cannot sting them. The food they eat is different from the ones we eat. For instance, here in Nigeria, we fry egg with vegetable oil but abroad they do not do such. Nigerians believe that whoever comes from overseas should be respected, irrespective of the kind of job he/she is doing there. (FGD/Ibadan/1 September 2010)

Likewise, discussants in Abeokuta agreed that:

> Many of those who bear [the name] 'Tokunbo' derive pleasure in being called 'Tokunbo' because they are not associated with Nigeria alone but with the country other than Nigeria where they were born. They are proud to be called 'Tokunbo'. They feel honoured ... The person named 'Tokunbo' knows he or she holds dual citizenship and this boosts their ego. This is why they are proud of bearing the name 'Tokunbo'. (FGD/Abeokuta/3 September 2010)

The adoption of 'Tokunbo' into human nomenclature indicates rational symbolism in how the new born is presented to society at large. With the meaning of 'the foreign born' attached – and especially in Yoruba culture that so much admires Western culture – the name 'Tokunbo' potentially, and practically, creates elitist notions around the child bearing the name and around his/her family. The social creation of *tokunbo* superiority has its foundation in the colonizing of Nigeria. The ensuing 'civilization' process cut across the whole spectrum of society including family, educational, religious, economic and political groups. It was indeed a process of cultural reconstruction of the native – from the indigenous, to the Western. This was achieved through a deep socialization process, publicly advanced through educational, political, religious and economic institutions. The socialization process was, of course, readily accepted by the family unit, whose children and adult members were subject to influences already under the firm control of the colonial system.

Westernization symbolized comfort and modernity. Comfort and modernity were symbols of social wealth and development, which could only be brought about through the adoption of Western culture. As recipient subjects, the local population became dependent on the meanings of modernity values as defined by their colonial masters. Access to modern resources and possible sources of wealth and development germane to class mobility were restricted to those able to internalize Western culture; and this was achieved through the socialization processes anchored by institutions dominated by colonial officials. It thus became rational to choose to become 'modern' by internalizing Western culture. Becoming 'modern' afforded access to resources capable of enhancing class mobility and of ensuring cross-generational development.

Thus, local interpretation of the individual and social development potentials inherent in Western culture created values of superiority around it. Of course, the process was started by colonial officials and the missionaries who worked in conjunction with them; it was, however, socially spread and sustained through the family system that saw its survival and development as having to come through the social re-creation of its members along Western cultural lines.

The quest to be 'like the Europeans' by internalizing the totality of their culture for social and class mobility (Adejunmobi 1978; Guite 1962) became a motivating factor impelling many people of Yoruba extraction to travel to Europe, from the late nineteenth century onwards: Europe, for them, was the centre of civilization. Thus, despite British colonial efforts at providing basic and – much later, in 1948 – tertiary education (Adejunmobi 1978; Asiwaju 1975; Guite 1962), a prime ambition of many families who could afford it was to migrate to Britain for education and vocational training (Coleman 1971).[6]

A person's physical presence in the country of the colonizer was a status symbol. For example, newspaper adverts in the 1950s used to publish congratulatory messages from friends and family for those who had travelled to England for professional education or even technical training – such was the extent of social appreciation for those who went to Europe for any reason whatsoever. For example, the *Daily Times* of 6 January 1950 published a report on a certain 28 year-old, Mr Adebayo Soyemi, who made the voyage to the United Kingdom to learn brick-making. Likewise columns in the *Daily Times* editions of 26 January 1950 (p. 1) and 13 February 1950 (p. 9) announced the departure of Miss Sweetie Olayinka Williams and Miss Adefunke Ojo to the United Kingdom to study men's tailoring

6 The University College, Ibadan was established in 1948. It was affiliated to the University of London. Hitherto, Nigerians who aspired to gaining university degrees had the sole option of migrating to Europe (usually Great Britain, due to the colonial link), the United States of America or Sierra Leone, which admitted many Nigerians for degree programmes at the prestigious Fourah Bay College, which was established in 1827 (see Adejunmobi 1978).

and nursing respectively.[7] Another edition of the *Daily Times* published on 21 April 1950 (pp. 6 and 7) also gleefully published news on Nigerian tailors who had been trained in London and were returning home.[8] Yet another paid announcement published in the *Daily Times* of 26 May 1951 (p. 3) publicized the successful completion of a Law course by Mr I. A. S. Adewale and his return to Lagos, Nigeria to practise. On 2 June 1951 (p. 6), the *Daily Times* also reported on Mr Babatunde Jose, a 25 year-old news editor who had received a three-month scholarship to study journalism in the United Kingdom. A photograph published in the newspaper shows Mr. Jose in a handshake with his wife, on board the *Mary Kingsley*, a ship bound for the UK.

It is on record that Mr. Babatunde Jose later became a dominant figure in the Nigerian media after his return: he became editor of the *Daily Times* in 1957, managing director of the newspaper in 1962, and chairman in 1968. Mr. Jose remained an accomplished and regal journalist right up to his demise on 3 August 2008 at the age of 82 (Whiteman 2008).

Furthermore, many editions of the *Daily Times* published in the 1950s also contained paid advertisements sponsored by the producers of Star Lager Beer proclaiming brand approval of the beer by Nigerian returnees who had studied in Europe. One, in particular, published in the edition of 14 April 1951 (p. 4), showed a certain Mr. Ogungbe celebrating his return with family and friends, all drinking the brew. Mr. Ogungbe reportedly claimed that in all his trip round Europe 'he could find no substitute to Star Lager Beer'.

These reports and advertisements attest to the prestige the public accorded to those who had travelled to Western nations and the celebration of such migrants and returnees as privileged elite. The newspaper

7 These editions of the *Daily Times* were accessed from the collections of the National Archives, Ibadan, Nigeria.

8 Vocational training in the United Kingdom was especially prized in Nigeria at this period. Up until the 1980s, many tailors who had been trained in England proudly announced that they were 'London Trained' to indicate their superiority. They usually displayed the inscription 'London Trained' on plaques or signs installed in and/or near their shops.

reports were therefore a medium for announcing the 'new elite' while the Star Lager Beer advertisements also accentuated the privileged status of returnee migrants by selecting them specially (in lieu of professional models) to present the beer as their preferred drink: their opinions could be respected, because they had been to Europe.

Migration to Europe indicated class and social prestige and also impacted on the social standing of the migrants' offspring. In line with local tradition which transferred social honour and appreciation to the newborn through ascription, local society and culture constructed a nomenclature to ascribe a perceived honour to those conceived or born in the West.

The rationality of adopting 'Tokunbo' as a newborn child's name is also subsumed in wider *tokunbo* symbolism. *Tokunbo* indicates, sustains and advances the notion of being elite. The name thus momentarily gives the child elitist status which then projects the values of the privileged class onto the child. Furthermore, through the ensuing social interaction, a *tokunbo* child develops a self-concept predicated on his/her perceived status as 'foreign born'. The child is, of course, expected to internalize Western culture, and be appraised through it by his/her peers and society at large. Coupled with what Western culture the family may have internalized while in Europe, consciousness of the societal expectation (especially an expectation of 'modern values') motivated a *tokunbo* child to live up to his/her name, in the immediate social environment.

Hence, in the colonial time and the post-colonial period up to the 1990s, merely bearing the name 'Tokunbo' lent a person sufficient charisma to attract admiration within the Nigerian social environment. As a classifier (Charmaz 2006), the name 'Tokunbo' symbolically marked out bearers as privileged. It kept alive the memory and significance of their foreign birth within the local culture and also represented the social value of the family of the bearer. It indicated that the parents of the bearer were part of a class of privileged migrants who had 'surmounted the seas' to reside in Europe or North America. Unlike the Anglophone Creole Bastimentos islanders in Panama (Aceto 2002) who adopt non-official English names to indicate identity and family history, certain Nigerians received the name 'Tokunbo' as an indigenous construction to indicate the family's sortie abroad, and the bearer's foreign birth, in expectation of social honour.

The people bearing the name 'Tokunbo' who were the subjects of some of the field interviews readily acknowledged the attention the name drew to them within the local culture – especially prior to the advent of *tokunbo* goods. Below I relay a few of their experiences designating them Tokunbo 1, Tokunbo 2 and Tokunbo 3.

Tokunbo 1 is a female in her late 40s. At the time of her conception, her parents were working and residing in England. Her father was an engineer, while her mother was a practising nurse. Both parents were successful in their professions. In the seventh month of her mother's pregnancy, Tokunbo 1's parents returned to Nigeria and she was delivered a day after their arrival, apparently early because of the stress of the flight. She was subsequently christened 'Tokunbo'. Tokunbo 1 revealed that, when she was young, bearing this name was something she was proud of. The name attracted attention to her and her peers saw her as a person 'born with a silver spoon in her mouth'. Indeed, they perceived her as one of the elite.

Tokunbo 2 is a woman now in her late 20s. She was born in France. She revealed that whenever she introduced herself as 'Tokunbo', people, irrespective of their ages, always asked where she was born. They always wanted to know what part of the developed world she originated in. Tokunbo 2 said that, though she was not accorded preferential treatment within her family, she noticed that friends liked to be acquainted with her, just by the virtue of her name. In fact, she claimed her friends liked introducing her to as many people as possible: 'Meet Tokunbo!'

The case of Tokunbo 3 is a little different. He was not born in the West; he was born in Ghana. His parents must have named him 'Tokunbo' because people by then realized the potential of *tokunbo* to convey symbolic meanings of deep social worth and had begun to adopt 'Tokunbo' as the name for children conceived or delivered in any place other than Nigeria. Tokunbo 3 is a male artisan in his mid 40s. Though he was named 'Tokunbo', his parents were not really of the elite class. However, he acknowledges the fact that, despite being born in Ghana, a West African country, and despite his relatively low socio-economic family background, the name 'Tokunbo' has attracted attention and brought him popularity. Tokunbo 3 succinctly describes his experience thus:

> When I was still in secondary school, my fellow students used to acknowledge me because of the name. Several school mates would like to identify with me just because my name is 'Tokunbo'. I had the same experience where I learnt how to repair fridges. In the house where my family was living when I was a small boy, many of the adults liked playing with me ... At times, whenever the female adults were going out to visit their boyfriends, they took me along. They usually showered me with gifts, all because my name is 'Tokunbo'. It got to the extent that people started identifying our house with my name ... (*Tokunbo* 3/Male/Abeokuta/31 August 2010)

The life experiences recounted above of people named 'Tokunbo' attest to the potential of the name to confer prestige. Irrespective of the real socio-economic background of its bearers, the name 'Tokunbo' elevated them not only in the perceptions of individuals but also within the totality of the local social structure and society. For people in the immediate social environment, *tokunbo* denoted comfort, prestige and an apparent inclusion in elite realms. A person bearing that name was a sure candidate for friendship and companionship because the relationship would impact positively on the social perceptions of those looking on. Subsequent social interactions and perceptions of the person named 'Tokunbo', his/her family and acquaintances and friends might in turn be conditioned by these lookers-on outside the immediate relationship. Acquaintance with a 'Tokunbo' potentially transferred its glamour to the acquainted, who might be regarded as privileged and perhaps members of the elite class as well. Hence, the name 'Tokunbo' had a value attracting social networking from members of the immediate environment, who realized that close association with a 'Tokunbo' would positively affect their social worth within the larger social system.

In recent times the value attached to the name 'Tokunbo' has exhibited phenomenal dynamism. The dynamism is not unconnected with the globalization process that attracts larger numbers of Nigerians to the Western world, both legally and illegally, and with Nigeria's socio-economic depression throughout the last twenty years, which has made imported second-hand goods worthy alternatives for consumers. In contrast to the past, when very few could afford to migrate to the West, many Nigerians currently strive to get there. Migration to the developed world is no longer the exclusive preserve of the elite class. In a quest to survive at all costs, and with a belief that the developed world is a place of unlimited opportunities, many Nigerians try all possible means to migrate. It is not uncommon to see long queues of Nigerians in front of the embassies of the major developed nations (including the USA, Canada, Germany and Britain) waiting to process their visa applications.

For many who migrate successfully, return is hardly an option. Successful migration is an indication of socio-economic upward mobility and success; and assistance can be offered to kin and associates back in Nigeria in the form of remittances (Omobowale, Omobowale and Ajani 2010).

The research for this book has revealed that – aside from Mufutau Lanihun's pioneering efforts at importing second-hand vehicle spare parts – low- and middle-class Nigerian migrants with entrepreneurial competences were the first sets of people to ship second-hand goods with appreciable re-sale value to Nigeria.[9] They dealt especially in second-hand vehicles and electronic equipment. They found that what people in the West considered waste was good enough for repackaging, export and re-use in Nigeria. This last finding was confirmed by a returnee from England who now sells imported second-hand fridges and freezers. She said she was shocked to see functioning fridges simply being disposed of while she was in Britain:

> All these products are just wasted in their country. If you get to a street like this, you may find up to seven refrigerators discarded on the street and they would be carried away and destroyed. There was a day I was going to my workplace, and I saw one *Oppress* [a big fridge]; if I want to sell that *Oppress*, I cannot sell it [for] less than N45,000 ($300). As I was looking at the fridge, the people that take care of their sanitation just came and took it away. It was on a Thursday and they collect rejected goods on Thursdays. As they took the fridge away, they went to destroy it. As I walked further, I saw many other ones in adjoining streets. (IDI/Female/Ibadan/25 August 2010)

In the 1990s, it was a common practice for migrants to open second-hand shops for kin and associates back in Nigeria. Many actually owned

9 Imported second-hand clothes had been in the South-Western Nigeria markets for several decades. They were popularly called *bosikoro* ('go to a hidden place'). *Bosikoro* was largely patronized by people at the rough end of the socio-economic scale. It was not a practice to be proud of. The term *bosikoro* indicates that consumers tended to patronize the market covertly, avoiding known faces as much as possible.

the shops and had trusted people managing them. An interviewee revealed how his family first got into the second-hand vehicles business:

> [The] second-hand automobiles trade has developed within the last twenty years. Twenty years back, only two people were selling vehicles in the whole of Oke Ado. Even my father was working under the current chairman of Motor Dealers Association as at that time. It was when my older brother travelled to Germany for further studies that he started sending vehicles down to Nigeria to sell. He also has a place at Ojoo where he sells trailers. We, his brothers, are just managing with him here in Oke Ado. For instance, if I have vehicles I want to sell I can come down to his shop and display the vehicles. (IDI/Male/Ibadan/21 August 2010)

This confirms that the economic migrants of the 1990s served as catalysts for massive importation of second-hand goods into Nigeria. While one of the interviewees describes the experience of seeing seemingly functioning refrigerators in Britain being discarded as the thing that motivated her venture into second-hand imports, the other recounts that it was his older brother who set up a second-hand automobile business for his Nigerian family after he had the opportunity of travelling to Germany. The experience of the first set of desperate Nigerian economic migrants to the developed world, seeing goods that could still function being disposed of and discarded, served as an incentive for redirecting goods with potential re-use value into the Nigerian economy.

At this stage, *tokunbo* started to gain a new meaning. Just as the 'Tokunbo' name for people conveyed social respect, so imported second-hand goods gained a prestige value within the local society: they were from the West. Once again, the transatlantic experience (Ogundiran 2002) was behind it; in fact, popular brands were provided at relatively affordable prices to economically deprived Nigerians who ordinarily would not have been able to afford them. Though the goods had already been used, the social system reconstructed a meaning for them that made them superior to simple 'used goods' (i.e. *aloku* – a derisive term in local parlance). The imported second-hand thus acquired the nomenclature *tokunbo* (as is further discussed in the next two chapters). Paradoxically this social adoption of *tokunbo* for imported second-hand goods has rather devalued 'Tokunbo' as a human name in recent times. A woman named 'Tokunbo' relayed her experience thus:

> … nowadays second-hand goods are called *tokunbo*. That was why my husband renamed me Seunfunmi. Calling second-hand goods the *tokunbo* has reduced the value attached to the name as a name of a person, so I would not like to be called 'Tokunbo' any longer. For instance, when I was younger, 'Tokunbo' was a name one would be proud of, but these days I do not think people still name their children 'Tokunbo' even if they were born abroad. (Bearer of the 'Tokunbo' name/Female/Ibadan/4 September 2010)

Another bearer of the 'Tokunbo' name who grew up in the 1990s relayed her experience thus:

> As I grew older, I began to understand that *tokunbo* could also mean fairly used goods such as bags, shoes, cars and so on. So many people have called me 'second-hand'. It is not a pleasant experience at all. At the time, I was in South-Southern and Northern parts of Nigeria. Many people in those places believe *tokunbo* is associated with second-hand goods alone because the name did not originate from their cultures. They did not believe people could be called 'Tokunbo'. Once they saw me, they always called me 'fairly used'. This upset me. I tried to explain to them. Some got it, while others just never got it. (Bearer of the 'Tokunbo' name /Female/Ibadan/22 November 2010)

It is interesting to note how the same 'Tokunbo' name that recently conveyed high social value and elitism on those that bore it is now something to be avoided: parents hardly ever name newborn children 'Tokunbo' today. This is an indication of a change in the value attached to the name. In recent times, the transfer of the term *tokunbo* to second-hand goods has brushed off onto human bearers of the name, especially among friends and associates who may want to tease. The new reality is that one does not have to belong to the elite class to migrate to the West, even though such migration still bestows some elitist glamour on a successful migrant. The elitist status of the migrant tends to be measured by the perceived wealth he/she has attained in the Western country of settlement and the remittances he/she sends home, rather than by a 'Tokunbo' name given to his/her child. Hence, 'Tokunbo' as a personal name no longer carries the high prestige it used to convey. It is outdated in the contemporary globalized age, when, through cultural diffusion aided by modern technological and communication transformations, the modernity of the developed world seems closer to the population of the developing world than ever before.

Nowadays neither migration nor utilization of modern goods remains the exclusive preserve of the rich and wealthy elite class. Through remittances, the lower class also accesses goods, and it is this that shows that their kin and other close associates are in the developed world. Remittances convey meanings of modernity and elitism even when the beneficiaries are not part of the elite class in a real and material sense.

Besides, through regular imports of second-hand goods re-named *tokunbo*, modern goods have become relatively easily accessible – more often than not as used goods with appreciable re-use value. Thus, the social translocation of *tokunbo* from humans to goods has indeed transferred the values attached from the one to the other.

CHAPTER 6

Tokunbo Dynamism and the Second-Hand Economy in Context

In order to examine the dynamism of the *tokunbo* concept, it is important first to examine the history of Nigerians' preference for imported goods contextually. This throws more light on how the preference came about. Going beyond economics, it explains the rapid expansion in Nigeria's second-hand market.

In colonial Nigeria, both the colonizing authority and the local population viewed the country's growth in terms of the volume of imported goods consumed. The local population rationally symbolized European merchandise as being of higher quality and an indicator of class. Hence, European merchandise largely replaced locally produced goods, especially among those who could afford them. Colonial records show that, by the 1930s, some of the favourite goods in Nigeria were cotton piece goods, bags and sacks, spirits and items of clothing. Table 1 shows some of the most sought-after imported goods and their values in pounds sterling (£) between 1935 and 1936.

Table 1 *Most sought-after articles imported to Nigeria, 1935–1936*
Source: CSO 26 File No. 11772 Vol. IX: 4

Goods	1935: value (£)	1936: value (£)
Bags and sacks	269,596	226,076
Cotton piece Goods	2,534,216	4,038,243
Apparel	155,196	206,318
Motor lorries and parts	112,687	138,710
Motor cars and parts	106,847	138,710

The imports were on a huge scale. Cotton piece goods had the largest value of all for both years. Moreover, the value of cotton piece goods increased from £2,534,216 in 1935 to £4,038,243 in 1936, representing an increase of about 60 per cent within a year. The colonial official who prepared the 1936–1937 Customs Department *Annual Report*, from which these figures were extracted, described the increase in glowing terms, as an indication of wealth coming to the local population. He concluded: 'No healthier sign of the increasing prosperity of the native population could be found ...' (CSO 26 File No. 11772 Vol. IX: 7) than in the increasing value of imported fabrics. Colonial records also show the high value of imported cotton piece goods continuing between 1932 and 1937. This is shown in Table 2.

Table 2 *Total value of cotton piece goods, 1932–1937*
Source: CSO 26 File No. 11772 Vol. IX: 7

Year	Value (£)
1932	2,559,788
1933	2,076,552
1934	1,304,860
1935	2,534,213
1936	4,038,243
1937	4,827,227

Although the value of imported cotton piece goods dropped from £2,559,788 in 1932 to the lowest value of all at £1,304,860 in 1934, it quickly bounced back, making a progressive increase from 1935 (with value of £2,534,213) and finally reaching the peak of £4,827,227 in 1937.

This progressive increase in the value of imported goods (and especially cotton piece goods) between 1932 and 1937 was particularly significant because this was the period of the Great Depression, when the global economy was at its lowest ebb (Anari, Kolari and Mason 2005; Linehan 2003). That the local consuming population could consume well over four million pounds' worth of imported cotton piece goods was not just an indication of increasing prosperity, as the colonial official quoted above claimed, but showed an unquenchable thirst for Western goods, which symbolized the 'good life' even in the midst of deep-rooted poverty.

Once the social system had developed a taste for imported goods, it was difficult to switch back to the consumption of local alternatives, even when they were available. Subsequently, in the 1940s, the British government imposed import controls on its colonies, due to the shortages of goods in the world market caused by World War II (CSO 26 File No. 39439/S.295, DCI 1/1 File no. 4032/C.7). Colonial records show that, in spite of the imposed import control, the local population still preferred imported European goods. A 1948 memorandum prepared by the Nigerian colonial administration to the West African Council clamoured for the easing of import controls on British goods.

The document reads:

> Throughout Nigeria there is a strong preference for goods of British manufacture. The reason for this is that in the course of the long trading connection between the United Kingdom and Nigeria the goods supplied by British merchants have become known to the people. It would be untrue to say that the goods are bought simply because they are British: they are bought because through the years they have gained the confidence of the essentially conservative African. (DCI 1/1 File No. 4032/C.7: 40)

This document clearly shows the continuing preference for British imports among the local population. Imports from Britain were preferred by local consumers not only because Britain had a long trading history with Nigeria but also because it had a vantage position due to its imperial authority. Among the community of Western nations, Britain was seen as the primary nation, whose material and non-material culture set standards for Nigerians. The modernity and development of the local population was measured by the volume of British goods they consumed. Essentially, these goods served the vital purpose of transmitting British culture to Nigeria, and the locals could only look to Great Britain as the source of essential goods of high quality. Import control carried with it the risk that the local population might turn to goods from other countries, potentially leading to an economic loss for Britain and a possible cultural shift amongst

Nigerians to other European and non-European nations (such as France, Germany, the USA and Japan) that could supply the same goods at comparable standards. Hence the memorandum to the West African Council further stated:

> If such a state of affairs should arise, the economic results are obvious: at the best Britain would recover only part of her pre-war market, at the worst she would have lost it almost entirely. But there is a political aspect, far less tangible but in the long-run, even from the economic point of view, far more important. The fact that Nigeria has in the past looked, and indeed still looks, to Britain as the source of her supplies has formed a vital link in the chain that has bound Nigeria to the United Kingdom. Should Nigeria form the habit of looking elsewhere for her essential goods, as she inevitably will if Great Britain forces her to look elsewhere now – that link, and with it the political and cultural links, will be weakened and the United Kingdom will cease to be looked upon as a source of political and economic inspiration and will sink to the insignificant position of being no more than one of the many shopkeepers in the world's commercial thoroughfare. (DCI 1/1 File No. 4032/C.7: 41)

It is evident that the colonial administration understood the significance of material goods in the propagation of British culture cum Western values among the local population. Imported goods, as material culture, served the purpose of subtly transferring the culture of the exporting country to the local population. In this case, the major supplying nation, Great Britain, was also the colonial authority. According to Hudson (1984), people's material culture represents their values and reflects their society (see also Fletcher 2001); and material culture is indeed a physical representation of non-material culture, especially as regards norms, values and expectations. The consumption of European imports also meant the adoption of European norms and values, which then made the 'local' look 'modern' in physical appearance even when non-material aspects of modern culture were yet to be fully internalized.

Under the new restrictions, the controls notwithstanding, European goods were imported into Nigeria through smuggling (Asiwaju 1976). Colonial records indicated an increase in smuggling during this period, especially around the Lagos-Dahomey border at Idi-Iroko (Western Frontiers). Whereas the Customs Department records had indicated that smuggling was not rife in 1937 (CSO 26 File No. 11772 Vol. IX), by 1942 the

Western frontiers (the Idiroko route especially) were becoming smuggling routes for both new and second-hand goods (see CSO 26 File No. 10260, Federation of Nigeria 1955). In that year, for the first time, the Customs Department recorded large numbers: 226 seizures, 314 convictions, £211 in court fines, and £473 proceeds in sale/auction of seizures (CSO 26 File No. 11772/S.3).[1] By 1954 and 1955, the department was describing the western frontiers as a major smuggling route (Federation of Nigeria 1955; Nigeria 1954) and it increased its expenditure on the suppression of smuggling by 121 per cent, from £2,596 in 1951–1952 to £5,734 in 1953–1954 (Federation of Nigeria 1955; Nigeria 1954). The goods that were principally smuggled were spirits, cigarettes and fabrics, along with other items from Europe. This smuggling was indeed a testimony to the local demand for imports despite restrictions. The demand had been created by local internalization of Western culture, as practised through the consumption of Western material things.

By the early 1950s, the value of goods imported into Nigeria had significantly increased from what it had been in the pre-World War II years. Between 1950 and 1952 the value of imports to Nigeria increased from £61,868,104 (in 1950), to £84,568, 863 (in 1951), and further to £113,113,039 (in 1952) (Federation of Nigeria 1953). A more detailed breakdown shows that Britain remained the leading nation from which Nigeria imported the goods (see Table 3).

Table 3 also shows that between 1950 and 1952, more than 50 per cent of all imports to Nigeria were from the United Kingdom.

1 Page 249 of CSO 26 File No. 10260 contains a protest, dated 26 September 1951, from a certain Mallam Mustapha of 66 Palm Church Street from whom the Customs Department had seized 303 second-hand bags he was attempting to import from Dahomey (now the Republic of Benin). In addition, the document also contains a protest dated 17 July 1954 from the chambers of Nonyelu and Adeoba (Solicitors) in respect of a client's 100 bales of second-hand clothing confiscated and auctioned by the customs department. These accounts show that the history of smuggling second-hand goods into Nigeria dates to the 1950s.

Table 3 *Value of imports by countries of origin, 1950–1952*
Source: Federation of Nigeria (1953: 7)

Country	1950		1951		1952	
	Value (£K)	% of total	Value (£K)	% of total	Value (£K)	% of total
United Kingdom	37,026	59.0	43,467	51.0	58,207	51.4
India and Pakistan	3,755	6.0	4,943	5.8	6,471	5.7
Southern Rhodesia	199	0.3	345	0.4	403	0.3
Other Commonwealth countries	955	1.5	1,786	2.1	1,496	1.3
Belgium	454	0.7	1,530	1.8	2,024	1.7
France	613	0.9	1,236	1.4	1,457	1.2
West Germany	1,422	2.2	4,493	5.3	6,459	5.7
Italy	1,242	2.2	3,846	4.5	3,883	3.4
Japan	5,863	9.4	7,524	8.8	11,345	10.0
Netherlands	1,648	2.6	2,382	2.8	3,783	3.3
Netherlands possessions	2,967	4.7	3,006	3.5	4,558	4.0
Norway	592	0.9	1,507	1.7	2,668	2.3
USA	2,502	4.0	3,709	4.3	5,181	4.5
Other countries	1,741	2.8	3,430	4.0	3,867	3.4
Parcel Post	916	1.4	1,365	1.6	1,311	1.1
Total	61,868		84,569		113,113	

Imports from other nations ranged from 0.3 per cent to 10.0 per cent. More particularly, most of the imports were from Western nations, including the United Kingdom, Belgium, France, West Germany, Italy, Japan, the Netherlands, Norway and the United States. Though Japan is an Asian country, its imports, including equipment, automobiles, and electronic wares were regarded within the local culture as 'Western'. This is because Japan did not export its indigenous culture into Nigeria but merely material goods of a type Nigerians viewed as coming 'from the West'.

The apparatus of colonial rule had successfully presented modern values as represented by Western culture as the standard. The local culture that had internalized this conception had the opportunity of physically practising modernity through consumption of imported Western goods. Hence, the imported goods formed the structure within which the transformation of the 'local' to the 'modern' could be appreciated. Peel (1978) describes this transformation among the Yoruba as the *olaju*. The *olaju* is the modern man with western etiquette and values, who utilizes modern goods – and modern goods stand for the 'good life' and for development. Among the Yoruba, the saying *Oyinbo ti so aye di ero* ('the European has made life easy') was a succinct description of the local culture's experience of machinery and other products that seemingly made life more comfortable.

The distinction between the 'local' and the 'modern' translated itself into an inferiority-superiority dichotomy, with 'modern' culture, along with its goods, taking the 'superior' part. Modern materials became active ingredients of the taken-for-granted everyday life (Money 2007; Appadurai 1986). The materials were therefore imbued with meanings that somehow made their absence unthinkable for a 'modern' man or woman. Hudson explains this (Hudson 1984: 34): as goods, material culture 'represents the cognitive expression of [a society's] social organization and ideology ... The sum total of a society's artefacts, therefore, function as a mirror of its patterned values, beliefs, and social structure.' Modern goods indeed reflected the nature of the social organization that Nigeria had come to adopt with colonization.

It was a modern culture dependent on Great Britain, which of course supplied the bulk of the material goods imported into Nigeria. The local society depended on Britain for standardization of its values: modernization could not be indigenous. Nigeria's dependence on Great Britain also ensured that the old colonizing country determined and provided the modern material culture that became an integral part of everyday life. Broadly speaking, it was a political economy of development (Ake 1982) but, more particularly, it was a political economy of cultural transformation and internalization of modern values, overtly and physically represented in imported material culture – that is, goods imported from Great Britain and other Western nations.

Modern Western culture dictated and defined acceptable practices, ethics and etiquette in the formal public (colonial) and private sectors. The formal sector, and indeed the bureaucracy, determined public policy and acceptable conduct for the larger society. It determined which goods could be consumed and which could not. It determined which material culture could be imported and where it could be imported from. Modern bureaucracy under the control of Great Britain, the colonial and imperial power, therefore, controlled the penetration of material culture both into the social structure and into culture at the level of individuals. The utilization of European culture was the 'cognitive expression' (Hudson 1984) of modern culture. It was a social reflection of modern ideology presented as a compulsory replacement for the local culture, without which development was supposedly impossible (Inglehart and Baker 2000; Joas 1999; Pieterse 1996; Olutayo 1991).

Since independence, Nigeria has not changed much: the foundations laid by the British have stayed in place. Nigeria still imports most of its basic and essential needs from the developed world (Kraus 2002; Egwaikhide 2000; Byerlee 1987; Gutkind and Wallerstein 1985; Onimode 1978).[2] The only difference is that the British share has been reduced significantly. Notwithstanding, goods with meanings depicting modernity and, by extension, Western culture, dominate imports. According to Global Finance (2011), Nigeria's major import trade partners are (as at 2007): China 10.6 per cent, the Netherlands 7.9% per cent, the USA 7.8 per cent, South Korea 6.6 per cent, Great Britain 5.7 per cent, France 4.3 per cent, Brazil 4.2 per cent and Germany 4.1 per cent (see also National Bureau of Statistics 2012). The small amount of progress Nigeria was able to achieve in local production had largely collapsed by the late 1980s, due to the devastating economic effects of the Structural Adjustment Programme (SAP) and maladministration by successive governments.

2 World Bank (2010) statistics show that Nigeria's merchandise imports increased from US$8,721,000,000 in the year 2000 to US$39,000,000,000 in 2009 (search.worldbank.org) (see also Federal Republic of Nigeria 2006a).

The SAP was adopted by General Babangida's regime in 1986, following pressures from the World Bank and the International Monetary Fund (IMF). The World Bank and IMF specialists opined that the SAP could bring Nigeria back on the path to economic prosperity following the country's huge economic decline occasioned by the fall in oil prices and the corruption that had eaten deep into Nigeria's public spheres (Omobowale 2009a; Eweje 2006; Omeje 2006; Ukeje 2006). SAP demands entailed the rolling back of government from the provision of social services. It also entailed the privatization of public enterprises, an embargo on employment, the freezing of salaries and the devaluation of Nigeria's currency, the Naira (₦) (Walker 2000a, 2000b; Logan and Mengisteab 1993; Ezeala-Harrison 1993). Unfortunately, the Nigerian economy did not experience any rebound at all. Rather, inflation increased astronomically (see Table 4), industries collapsed, unemployment increased and up to 70 per cent of the population was left in absolute poverty by the year 2000 (Olutayo and Omobowale 2007, 2006; Walker 2000a, 2000b; Odulana and Olomajeye 1999; Olutayo 1999).

Table 4 *Inflation rate in Nigeria, 1986–1996*
Source: Central Bank of Nigeria 2002

Year	Inflation rate (%)
1986	5.4
1987	10.2
1988	38.3
1989	40.9
1990	7.5
1991	13.0
1992	44.5
1993	57.2
1994	57.0
1995	72.8
1996	29.3

Table 4 shows the disastrous increase in the inflation rate from 5.4 per cent in 1986 to 40.9 per cent in 1989. It decreased to 7.5 per cent in 1990. This decrease was not unconnected with the SAP Relief Package that the government implemented following violent anti-SAP riots in 1989 (Omobowale 2009b; Shettima 1993). Subsequently, the inflation rate increased to 13 per cent in 1991 and reached a peak of 72.8 per cent in 1995. It declined to 29.3 per cent in 1996, the year the SAP was officially discontinued.

The SAP and the poverty that resulted from it affected every aspect of the socio-economic life of Nigerians. The United Nations Development Programme's (2010) statistics indicate that Nigeria's Human Development Index (HDI) has been low over recent years. The values for 2005, 2006, 2007, 2008, 2009 and 2010 are 0.402, 0.410, 0.412, 0.416, 0.419 and 0.423 respectively (United Nations Development Programme 2010, 2008). Though HDI values between 2005 and 2010 show relative increases, they remain rather low. Hence, as at 2010, Nigeria ranks 142nd out of 179 countries, with 63.5 per cent of the population living in poverty (United Nations Development Programme 2010, 2008).

A consequence of high levels of inflation and widespread poverty among the population is a significant reduction in people's purchasing power. This has affected Nigerians across all classes. Many who were in the upper and middle classes have dropped into the lower classes, while others who have retained their class positions have had their purchasing powers significantly reduced (Ismail 2009; Lee, Nielsen and Aldersen 2007; Mberu 2007). Of course, imported goods, especially those from Western nations, have remained in high demand in Nigeria, but reduced purchasing power has resulted in a preference for imported second-hand items, since imported new goods are unaffordable for the large majority of the population. Though these items are second-hand, the local culture and/or society symbolically places 'standard and high quality' values on them because they facilitate the practice of modernity.

The importation of second-hand goods to Nigeria has been boosted over the last twenty years due to landfill shortages in the developed world and the re-use value of imported second-hand items in Third World countries (Yoshida and Terazono 2010; Larney and van Aardt 2010; Hotta et al. 2008; Omobowale 2008; Soderman and Carter 2008; Osibanjo, Nnorom and Ogbonna 2008; Osibanjo and Nnorom 2007; Hawley 2006; Baden and Barber 2005; Greenpeace 2005; Besnier 2004; Peck and Pinto 2003; Williams and Paddock 2003; Crewe 2000). Figure 3 below shows the flow chain of second-hand goods into and in Nigeria.

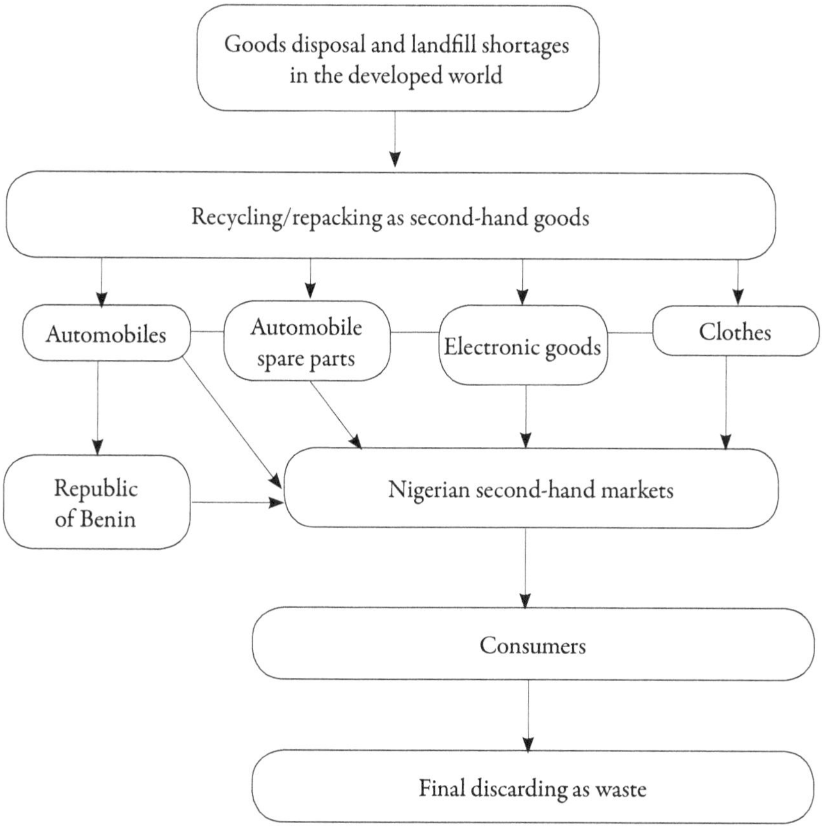

Figure 3 *The second-hand goods flow chain into and in Nigeria*

The figure shows that the supply of second-hand goods to Nigeria from the developed world is a direct consequence of shortage of landfills for used (discarded) goods, on the one hand, and the ready demand in Nigeria, on the other. Used Western goods are recycled and/or repackaged as second-hand goods for the Nigerian market (and the markets of other Third World nations). Consumers therefore purchase their preferred goods from the second-hand market and, when the lifespan of the goods is exhausted, they are finally discarded within the Nigerian environment.

It is important to be aware that second-hand goods are transferred to Nigeria by both legal and illegal means. Those that are not included in the prohibition list can be imported through legal channels by land, sea and air. Unscrupulous importers, seeking to evade payment of stipulated customs duties or to import prohibited items, smuggle second-hand goods into Nigeria with the aid of professional smugglers called 'crossers'. In order to investigate this activity, I visited the Seme border and also crossed over to the Republic of Benin, along with my research assistant and a guide. On the Nigerian side of the border, I employed the services of a Benin national who operates as a driver between the two countries. At the crossing post, each occupant was required to alight from the vehicle and walk over to the Benin side. We found that Benin agents collect bribes from people wanting to cross, ranging from ₦200 to ₦500 (US$1 to US$3).[3]

The operational base of crossers is close to the Nigerian-Benin border on the Benin side; the crossers call it the Old Soldier Park. The crossers are predominantly Nigerians and they operate in a special network as syndicates. Crossers claim they network with security agents on the Nigerian side of the border to ease the safe passage of contraband goods. My informants claim that some Nigerian policemen and customs officials also work as crossers. The primary responsibility of the crosser is to ensure safe delivery to the buyer at an agreed location in Nigeria – usually Mile 2 at Lagos or any other place that both parties agree on. Crossers also make use of numerous unofficial land routes to convey smuggled goods into Nigeria, especially when they have failed to strike a deal with the Nigerian border security agents or do not want to be bothered with this formality.

One of my informants was a former crosser named Musa. He had worked as a crosser for over a decade until he opted out in 2008, due to the risks involved. Musa informed me that crossers belong to a network

3 ₦ is Nigeria's currency unit, the Naira.

of professional smugglers who understand the channels of smuggling into Nigeria through the vast unofficial forest routes along the Nigeria-Benin border. Crossers are paid up to ₦25,000 (US$167) per vehicle. Musa claims that crossers rely on *juju* (local magical medicine) and drugs as stimulants, as ordinary alcohol would not provide the degree of confidence and assurance of success that such a risky venture demands. Besides agents in the Old Soldier Park, crossers have their agents in the numerous second-hand auto marts managed by Lebanese businessmen in the Republic of Benin. If a buyer does not have a crosser, one is quickly introduced to him at the auto mart. Crossers move in convoys. A convoy can range from ten to a hundred vehicles at a time. If the convoy uses the legal route, it goes through the border and either pays customs duties or bribes customs and security officials on the way. Alternatively, the crossers' convoy may take one of the numerous largely unsecured and unofficial forest routes. Musa says the forest routes are channels created by crossers so they can evade paying duties. Crossers are sometimes intercepted by customs officials in the forest routes, however.

Musa disclosed that crossers may negotiate, but if both parties fail to agree on the amount of bribe to be paid on each vehicle, the leader of the crossers' team will give the order to move on. At that point, the crossers drive off and speed recklessly through the forest, while the usually armed customs officials follow in hot pursuit, often aiming to shoot and kill. In such instances, many crossers are killed either by the customs officials' bullets or through accidents. Musa showed me the wounds he had received on his own body as a result of customs onslaughts when he was working as a crosser. He has a big lump on his head, which he claims was inflicted by a customs official who hit him with the butt of his gun. In spite of the real and potential risks involved, Musa stated that crossers value the vehicles they smuggle into the country more than their lives. Comrades may be killed in the course of a crossing but, if humanly possible, vehicles must be delivered to the customers (dealers) regardless. This is so that future deals are not jeopardized. As some sort of terminal compensation, crossers contribute between ₦40,000 (US$ 266) and ₦50,000 (US$333) to the families of each of their number who is killed in the process of a crossing.

Illustration 1 shows some crossers repackaging second-hand clothes procured by a small-scale trader for the Nigerian market. (The faces of the men have been hidden to conceal their identities.) [4]

Illustration 1 *Crossers repackaging second-hand clothes at Cotonou, Benin Republic*

The border is a hub of smuggling activities ranging from small-scale to large-scale transactions. Long hauls of trailers carrying contraband goods, along with some smaller scale smugglers, are clearly to be seen on the Benin

4 Large-scale importers do not have to repackage their bales before importing them into Nigeria. They are able to devise means of conveying the bales through the organized system of crossers and conniving security agents.

side of the border.[5] My informants told me that the trailers were queuing while they waited for feedback from their agents and crossers who had gone over to the Nigerian side to strike deals with customs officials and other security agents so that the vehicles might pass. Each truck received a signal to move into Nigeria once the deal was struck. Without these precautions, the trucks might be impounded and have huge fines imposed.

In the meantime, since Nigeria's consumer culture is partially dependent on imported second-hand goods, Nigerian society has symbolically redefined and recategorized its perception of 'used goods', ascribing differing meanings on the basis of their origin and supposed quality. Consequently, second-hand goods are now classed as 'domestic used' (*aloku*) or 'imported used' (*tokunbo*). In earlier times, *aloku* was the nomenclature for all used goods irrespective of their source. *Aloku* was culturally considered low in value and was patronized largely by the economically disadvantaged. With the economic downturn in Nigeria, middle-class people have, over the years, become ardent consumers of imported second-hand items as well. Retaining the term '*aloku*' for such imported second-hand goods would symbolically represent them as being substandard and inferior, incapable of achieving the modernity befitting the middle class elite. So local culture, through the underlying social relations it contains, has transferred the more prestigious nomenclature '*tokunbo*' to the imported second-hand. This term imparts meanings of high standard and good quality to imported second-hand goods while locally used goods have retained the description '*aloku*' (Omobowale 2008). This name change has been confirmed by interviewees. An interviewee stated:

5 Small-scale traders resort to all kinds of ingenuities to smuggle goods into and from Nigeria. My informants disclosed that many handicapped beggars at the border actually serve as smugglers (crossers), concealing contraband under their specially designed tricycles. Another set of small-scale smugglers operates on remodelled Vespa motorcycles, smuggling petroleum products from Nigeria into Benin. Likewise, at a beach close to the Nigerian border on the Benin side, I witnessed local boatmen transporting petroleum products allegedly illegally unloaded from ships some distance away in the Atlantic Ocean.

> *Aloku* simply means something that has been used to its utmost and is now condemned. Unlike *tokunbo* goods, *aloku* are more or less useless. Many *tokunbo* goods are still of very good quality. Many of them would still be used for a long time by the prospective owners and so they are completely different from *aloku*. *Aloku* are thoroughly useless ... (Female IDI/Second-hand Consumer/Lagos/31 August 2010)

Similarly another interviewee said:

> Second-hand goods are called *aloku*, which means someone in Nigeria had used them before selling them to some other persons. Used goods imported from abroad are called *tokunbo*. They are both *aloku*. It is just that the wear and tear on *aloku* is worse than that of the *tokunbo*. Over there [in the developed countries], they have better facilities, good roads, better maintenance culture and they take proper care of their goods. These are the major differences between the *tokunbo* and *aloku* (second-hand) goods. (Male IDI/Second-hand Consumer/Abeokuta/1 September 2010)

A seller also corroborated these assertions from the *tokunbo* consumers:

> The truth is that *tokunbo* goods are *aloku* (used goods) but the way *tokunbo* goods were used by the whites are different from the way we [Nigerians] would use the goods. Poverty has eaten deep and some people will use something as if that thing (maybe fridge, television or vehicle) should not be useful again to any other person. But in the countries from where the *tokunbo* goods are imported, the goods are used in such a way that they will still be useful to other people. *Tokunbo* goods are usually in better condition than *aloku*. (Male IDI/Second-hand Seller/Ibadan/25 August 2010)

The statements presented above show the opinions some interviewees hold on *aloku* and *tokunbo*. The social reconstruction of meanings attached to imported used goods further reveals the value attached to the developed world. '*Aloku*' represents the poor state of Nigeria's economy and widespread impoverishment. With as many as 63.5 per cent of the population being poor (United Nations Development Programme 2010), and with a general low purchasing power, it is perfectly understandable that Nigerian consumers should use the goods at their disposal to the full. Nigeria's own economy largely lacks the productive and manufacturing capacity to cater for local needs, and proper maintenance and prompt replacement are scarcely available to keep old utensils and appliances in their best condition. Goods are therefore used till they are completely worn out; economically disadvantaged consumers like to extract the maximum utility from everything they purchase before they even think of reselling or discarding it. Passed on at this stage, *aloku* is largely useless and is ready for disposal, except that people at the lowest end of the socio-economic ladder may still be prepared to try to find a use for them.

Aloku, therefore, contrasts strongly with the imported second-hand goods that come in in a fairly new state. The relatively good condition of imported second-hand items, at least as seen locally, is directly related to the affluence of the exporting countries, which have very productive and lucrative economies. Consumers in the developed economies have easy access to ever-changing new products whose enhanced features make the previous ones redundant within a short while. The disposed goods are directed to the Third World market, as otherwise they could pose an environmental challenge at home, where there is already a shortage of landfill sites (Smith 2010; Hotta et al. 2008; Hawley 2006).

In the Third World in general, and in Nigeria in particular, consumers tend to find the condition of imported second-hand items quite good. A documentary broadcast on *Aljazeera* reported on the conveyance of used goods from the developed countries and the degree of appreciation of the goods in Africa. It showcased the export and sale of second-hand clothes, locally called *mitumba* in Tanzania. *Mitumba* means 'dead-man's clothes', because local consumers find it difficult to understand how anybody living could dispose of such relatively new clothes (*Aljazeera* 27 July 2010). This shows the degree of impoverishment that lies behind the social reconstruction of the imported second-hand as 'new'. Since alternatives in the form of genuinely new goods are barely affordable, the poor populations of the African countries and of other regions in the Third World simply make use of available goods, and infuse them with symbolic notions of good quality, as judged from their relatively good state in the local context. When the developed world's disposed-of goods reach the Third World markets, they momentarily attract consumer preference and, once bought, they are consumed until they become virtually unusable.

In Nigeria, where there is a general perception that 'used goods' should look really old, wrinkled and battered, the progressive importation of second-hand goods still in conditions the local consuming population considers more than adequate makes the term *aloku* inappropriate. The symbolic and real interpretation of *aloku* is demeaning to the status of members of the middle and upper classes and to public and private institutions, who are forced to make use of imported second-hand goods (especially automobiles and equipment) for rational reasons. This is why the *aloku* terminology hitherto attached to all second-hand goods has been withdrawn from these ones. A differentiation between the *aloku* and the *tokunbo* has rationalized the patronage of the imported second-hand among the more affluent classes. There is no longer any stigma attached to having imported second-hand possessions; rather, these can attract admiration from the public, most of whom have also become consumers of one imported second-hand item or another. *Tokunbo* imports thus afford access to essential and luxury goods that ordinarily would have been unaffordable to the consuming public. This finding supports the conclusions of several scholars – Pelletiere and Reinert 2010, 2006, 2004; Buchert et al. 2007 and Hawley 2006 – who all state that the second-hand imports to the Third World provide essential goods to places where they would otherwise be unaffordable, while at the same time creating a burgeoning economy employing a huge segment of the population. The finding agrees too with Besnier's (2004) study on the second-hand marketplace among the Tonga. In this study, Besnier posits that the second-hand market serves as a class leveller, since it provides access to 'elitist' goods that would otherwise be out of the reach of the lower classes and those on low incomes.

To sum up, this study submits that the social values surrounding *tokunbo* symbolism attach meanings of superiority, high standards and good quality to imported second-hand products. Just as *tokunbo* symbolism used, until recently, to confer prestige on human bearers, so, transferred to imported second-hand goods, it now gives popular appeal to a booming market attracting huge patronage in South-Western Nigeria right across class boundaries. *Tokunbo* when used to describe goods, thus signifies a commodity which, though used, is imported and is of a better quality than the new locally produced and/or Asian goods available. In fact, the notion of the 'imported' in turn evokes provenance from lands 'across the seas', where goods are produced at high standards and assured quality (Okechuku and Onyemah 1999). Again, the local population assumes that, though the *tokunbo* products they buy are used, the sustainable quality of production of the Western world makes re-use viable to the extent that the items can be almost appreciated as 'new'.

Consequently, the imputation of good quality, together with relatively affordable prices and easy accessibility, puts *tokunbo* goods high in the preferences of Nigerians. The *tokunbo* maket provides access to modern goods which the local pauperized population would once have assumed to be luxuries affordable by the wealthy class alone. Thus, the combination of second-hand automobiles, essential spare parts, electronic goods and clothes make a near-perfect combination for the consuming public.

CHAPTER 7

The *Tokunbo* Second-Hand Economy: Automobiles

In this chapter and the following three, I discuss the second-hand economy of South-Western Nigeria. I pay particular attention to imported used automobiles, automobile spare parts, electronic goods, and clothes. These are the imported used items that dominate the second-hand market of the region. The present chapter is about *tokumbo* automobiles.

The United Kingdom introduced automobiles into Nigeria in the early twentieth century. In 1925, a group of commercial corporations announced to the colonial government, via a letter dated 12 January, the formation of the Nigerian Motor Traders' Association with their office at 200, Broad Street, Lagos. The association comprised six member corporations: Nigerian Motors Ltd, John Holt and Co (L'pl) Ltd, Lagos Stores Ltd, Niger Company Ltd, African and Eastern Trade Corp Ltd, and Miller Brothers (of L'pl) Ltd (CSO 26 File No. 50753). For many years, and in fact up to the eve of Nigeria's independence, importation and acquisition of automobiles was controlled, with the Governor having the sole authority of approval (see DCI 1/1 File No. 195 C/7, DCI 1/1 File No. 195C/S.45, DCI 1/1 File No. 195/S.6, DCI 1/1 File No. 195C/S.65, DCI 1/1 File no. 195D/S.19, DCI 1/1 File No. 1043/S.2, DCI 1/1 File No. 1043/S.5). Automobiles were largely out of the reach of the vast majority of the local population when they were first introduced to Nigeria. If and when some members of the local population could afford to purchase an automobile, getting the Governor's approval could prove a Herculean task. Vehicle ownership, hence, became a status symbol at this initial stage in Nigeria, just as it was a symbol of power and class when first introduced to Europe and North America in the late nineteenth and early twentieth centuries (Gartman 2004; Alber 2002; Newcomb 2000).

During the post-independence period in Nigeria automobile ownership was liberalized, though it remained something of a status symbol. Following the indigenization programme of the 1970s and the policy reorientation favouring import substitution and self-reliance, the Nigerian government attempted to make automobiles readily available locally and to reduce importation through the establishment of vehicle assembly plants.[1] These plants included Peugeot at Kaduna, Volkswagen at Lagos, Leyland at Ibadan, the Anambra Automobile Manufacturing Company (ANAAMCO) at Enugu and Steyr-Nigeria, Bauchi (Munkirs, Braunfeld, Carter, Kuester and Myart 1993; Bangura 1987). The nation was encouraging local production in order to reduce foreign control of its economy. Joseph (1978: 223), however, describes the efforts as amounting to 'little more than a ritual for exorcizing the devil of dependence'.

In the late 1970s and early 1980s, Nigeria appeared to be making some progress at achieving supposed self-reliance in local production. However, whatever progress was initially achieved was drastically reversed during the SAP years by economic downturn, corruption and the policy maladministration of successive governments. Nigeria's automobile assembling industry, along with other manufacturing industries (especially fabrics), had substantially declined or totally collapsed by the 1990s. For example, for the former, Okechuku and Onyemah (1999: 612), quote the 1997 records of Nigeria's Federal Office of Statistics, which noted the reduction in 'the domestic assembly of Peugeot 504 automobiles from 100,000 units in 1986 to about 4,500 in 1996, and the closure of [the] Volkswagen assembly plant in 1994'. The other assembly plants suffered similar fates. By the late 1980s and early 1990s, most Nigerians could no longer afford the vehicles assembled by these plants. Attention was then directed to imported second-hand vehicles (Omobowale 2008; Ajayi and Dosunmu 2002) and, consequently, most of the plants eventually closed down. Only Peugeot and ANNAMCO still maintain some minimal production.

1 Following the Indigenization Decree of 1972, Nigeria's federal military government forced multinational corporations to sell majority shares to Nigerians. Nigerians were to take up top management positions in the companies. Except for a few, such as UAC, Cadbury and Lever Brothers, most of the companies eventually collapsed with the departure of their original owners.

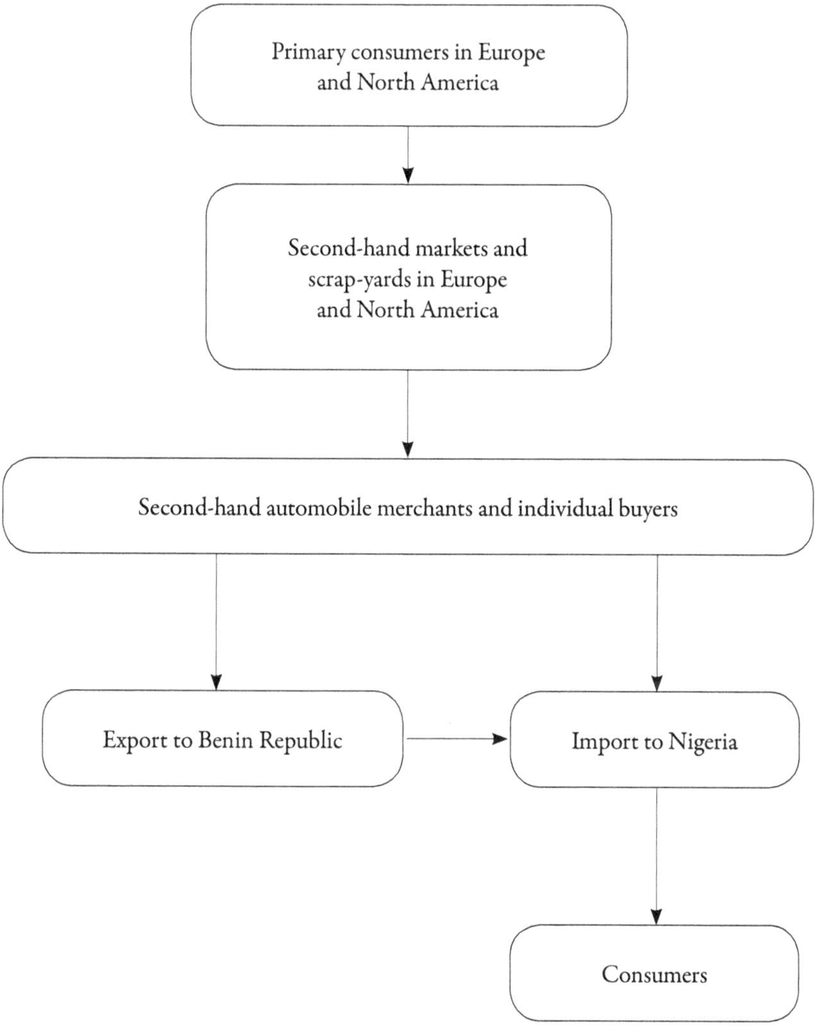

Figure 4 *Second-hand automobiles flow chain*

Tokunbo automobiles provide the alternative with comparable utility and symbolic value for consumers across class boundaries.[2] About 95 per cent of the vehicles in Nigeria are imported second-hand ones. The *tokunbo* automobile inflow into Nigeria has a peculiar flow chain. The vehicles are either imported legally or make an illegal entrance through points on the Nigeria-Benin border. Figure 4 (p, 75) shows the flow chain of *Tokunbo* vehicles to Nigeria.

The flow chain of second-hand vehicles to Nigeria starts with primary consumers supplying used vehicles to the second-hand markets and scrap-yards in Europe and North America. From these markets and scrap-yards, exporters of second-hand vehicles, along with independent or individual buyers from Nigeria, ship the second-hand vehicles meant for the Nigerian market over the sea. The vehicles may be good[3] or bad.[4] They go either

2 Inasmuch as the upper class are able to afford new vehicles, they, more often than not, buy expensive vehicles such as the Hummer Jeep from the *tokunbo* second-hand market. Likewise, upper class entrepreneurs purchase *tokunbo* automobiles for the operation of their businesses and/or welfare packages for staff.

3 Automated vehicles attract high consumer interest in Nigeria. Automatic transmission, automatic gearboxes and power windows (locally known as 'tapping glass' because of the operation by buttons) are great selling points for the marketers to use to persuade potential buyers. Automated vehicles usually cost more when compared to those with manual gearboxes and windows. The cost difference could be between ₦100,000 ($666) and ₦300,000 ($2,000), depending on the brand, model and year of production.

4 Vehicles damaged by flood and accident are also frequently shipped to Nigeria as second-hand (*tokunbo*) cars by the auto importers and/or marketers (see White 2011 for a related article). Such vehicles may be superficially repaired to give the semblance of being in good repair to unwary buyers. Observations at mechanics' workshops and interactions with consumers show that vehicles produced from the late 1990s on, with automated facilities (including automatic transmission, automatic gears, power windows and injector and/or high tech engines, as in the V5, V6, and V8 and above), develop electronic faults that the local maintenance experts are incapable of repairing or that consumers consider too expensive to repair. Mechanics and consumers alike suspect that such vehicles are accident and/or flood vehicles. Such faulty vehicles, initially acquired as *tokunbo*, are either subsequently abandoned in mechanics' workshops or resold as supposedly 'neat' *aloku* to unwary consumers who desire 'posh' cars conveying symbolic elitist values.

directly to Nigeria through its various ports, or via the Republic of Benin. If they go to Benin, the vehicles are usually transported into Nigeria illegally by 'crossers'. Vehicles are illegally 'crossed' from Benin either because they are older than ten years, and thus, officially prohibited from the Nigerian market or because the importers and/or crossers want to evade paying duties (see Nigeria Customs Service 2011 for a list of prohibited items).[5]

Due to the smuggling in of used automobiles, there are two types of *tokunbo* vehicles in the Nigerian market. One is called *Cotonou* while the other is called *Lagos cleared*. The former, *Cotonou tokunbo*, is a smuggled *tokunbo* automobile without valid customs papers. It is so called because most of such automobiles, smuggled into Nigeria by land, are from Cotonou in the Republic of Benin. During the last five years, the customs service has been deploying its men at strategic locations on Nigeria's major highways to confiscate and impound such vehicles. Owners of *Cotonou tokunbo* are thereafter expected to pay duties or have their impounded vehicles auctioned. The auctioning is usually not open to the public but only to customs officials and people with powerful links to the customs service.[6]

This has become a nightmare to many *Cotonou tokunbo* owners. They either have to go to the customs office to pay duties or must restrict their vehicles to intra-city routes. *Lagos tokunbo*, on the other hand, is imported through any of Nigeria's land, sea or air ports. The customs papers of *Lagos tokunbo* are supposedly up-to-date and genuine. As marks of authenticity and overt confirmation, many users of *Lagos tokunbo* leave paint marks and paper labels showing 'Lagos, Nigeria' on their vehicles' windows. This is done in order to avoid incessant customs scrutiny and the risk that the vehicles may be seized from their owners.[7] This practice is also emerging as

5 This was increased to fifteen years in 2011. Government officials have, however, been indicating that this policy may soon be reversed to ten years.

6 Due to the non-transparent nature of the auctioning, members of the public often speculate that customs officials receive orders for particular types of 'posh' cars from powerful politicians and the economic elite, who buy these cars at give-away prices after paying some bribe money.

7 It should be noted that *Lagos tokunbo* is not entirely immune from customs scrutiny and possible seizure – especially when the clearance papers and details of customs duties presented by owners appear to be fake.

a way of enhancing a vehicle's monetary value, as pointing to '*Lagos cleared*' is a current selling and bargaining strategy the *tokunbo* auto marketers employ to encourage consumers to pay a higher price than they would for *Cotonou tokunbo*. The price difference between *Cotonou tokunbo* and *Lagos tokunbo* for the same brand and model is between ₦200,000 and ₦500,000 (US$1,333 and US$3,333), depending on the make.

Tokunbo vehicle marketers have an umbrella association called the Motor Dealers Association of Nigeria (MDAN), which regulates the *tokunbo* automobile market and protects members from harassment from security organizations (especially customs agents).[8] Entry into the *tokunbo* auto enterprise is semi-closed; an intending *tokunbo* auto-dealer must belong to the MDAN. Each new member undergoes one to two months' training under the supervision of a senior member, usually a successful dealer. During the training period the new entrant is introduced into the nitty-gritty of the trade. The training period also serves as a process of socialization for the imparting of the Association's values.

The Association seeks to internalize in members the value of 'cooperation-in-competition'. Members are expected to protect one another's interests and not to take competition in the market place to its limits. They are to see one another as partners in progress for profit-making and the protection of the trade from unfavourable government policies. 'Cooperation-in-competition' is therefore, an important value for auto dealers as otherwise the *tokunbo* auto trade would be adversely affected.

There is hardly a *tokunbo* auto dealer who does not have *Cotonou tokunbo* in his or her stock. The Association has been able to protect its members from harassment from customs and police agents by lobbying and bribing. It lobbies the government against policies that may be inimical to

8 Though most *tokunbo* automobiles sold in Nigeria were smuggled in, the customs service does not raid second-hand auto-shops to confiscate and impound such vehicles. Instead customs officials confiscate vehicles without valid customs papers from hapless consumers on the highway. That auto-marts displaying *Cotonou tokunbo* are not raided is an indication of the protection the Motor Dealers Association of Nigeria (MDAN) provides for its members. The 'protection' is, of course, secured through negotiations and financial inducements to the relevant security agencies.

tokunbo auto sales. An auto dealer from Ibadan informed me that one of the Association's achievements through lobbying was to stop the customs impounding *tokunbo* vehicles from dealers' shops. He claimed they had been able to achieve this through a representation to the Comptroller General of Customs. In spite of the strong hold of the Association on members, wealthy individuals with clout and power could easily engage in *tokunbo* auto-marketing without having to go through the Association's protocols. Such marketers would open up shops in places outside the major *tokunbo* auto-marts.

In all the three major Nigerian cities – Ibadan, Lagos and Abeokuta – there is no formal auto-market. Auto sellers simply display their vehicles by the side of the road. In Ibadan and Lagos, however, there are places especially known for *tokunbo* auto sales. In Ibadan the major *tokunbo* auto-marts are located at Oke-Ado and Sabo while in Lagos they are at Maryland and Berger. *Tokunbo* sales are not, however, limited to these locations. Some *tokunbo* auto marketers display their wares in any location they find convenient by the side of the road. In Abeokuta, there is no major *tokunbo* auto-mart as such; marketers display *tokunbo* vehicles anywhere where a potential customer could be attracted (see Illustration 2, p. 80).

Qualitative data collected in the field revealed consumers' preference for *tokunbo* vehicles. A marketer of *tokunbo* vehicles at Abeokuta stated:

> People can hardly afford new vehicles but *tokunbo* second-hand vehicles are affordable. It is the government and its officials that usually patronize places where new vehicles are sold. The places where new vehicles are displayed for sale are not common in Abeokuta but *tokunbo* vehicles are sold everywhere ... A *tokunbo* vehicle cannot be compared to a second-hand vehicle used in Nigeria [*aloku*] due to the state of Nigeria roads. Also by the time a new car is used in Nigeria for two years, it would not be in a good shape like a *tokunbo* vehicle that has been used overseas for five years. Cars that have been used in Nigeria start having problems right from the very day they are bought and put to use. There are potholes on the roads which domestic second-hand vehicles have to battle with ... Consumers usually enjoy *tokunbo* vehicles after purchase. *Tokunbo* second-hand vehicles are durable, cheap and affordable because with ₦350,000 [US$2,333], one can become a car owner. Many people cannot afford the new vehicles. (Male IDI/*Tokunbo* Automobile Seller/Abeokuta/31 August 2010)

Illustration 2 *Tokunbo automobiles on display at Oke-Ado, Ibadan*

Supporting this, a *tokunbo* automobile seller in Lagos revealed that:

> *Tokunbo* cars are good because of the good roads in the originating countries. You cannot compare the state of their roads with our own roads. And that means that you cannot compare their cars with the ones we use here ... We appreciate their culture because we are following their footsteps in civilization ... *Tokunbo* cars are in high demand in Nigeria because they are cheap and they have higher quality than the new Chinese and Korean brands in Nigeria. You cannot compare a *tokunbo* vehicle with Chinese and Korean cars. White men ensure high standards and the cars sold in their markets are of good quality; better than our own, because their systems are working. The authorities who are in charge of inspecting the qualities of goods do their jobs well. But in Nigeria, standards are not followed. Sometimes when I go to Tin Can Island to clear vehicles from the port, I go through the back door [bribe]. I know how much I pay customs officials so that they would release the vehicles without inspection. So that is the problem with Nigeria. (Male IDI/*Tokunbo* Automobile Seller/Lagos/31 August 2010)

A female respondent in Ibadan opined thus:

> There are some vehicles that were used in Nigeria and they were called *tokunbo* so that they would be marketable. Imported second-hand vehicles are appreciated because of the maintenance culture overseas. It is economic recession that has made people to go for *tokunbo* cars. If people really have the money they will not go for such cars. In the long run, a *tokunbo* car will develop one or two mechanical problems. It is better to go for a brand new vehicle. It is not even advisable to use a *tokunbo* vehicle if one has the money to buy a new car. The reason why I have said *tokunbo* is not advisable is that a brand new vehicle I bought years ago did not develop any fault until I had used it for four years. (Female IDI/*Tokunbo* Automobile Consumer/Ibadan/28 August 2010)

Finally another interviewee who has been involved in *tokunbo* auto selling since 1990 stated that:

> *Tokunbo* goods are also used goods but they are a lot different from goods used in Nigeria. There are second-hand goods that are fairly used, as well as the ones that are roughly used. *Tokunbo* cars are fairly used and they look like new cars, but they are not new. It is the government that makes people to patronize *tokunbo* vehicles. Most of the domestically used vehicles in Nigeria cannot be used elsewhere except Agodi Gate spare parts market where the vehicles will be dismantled and sold as scrap. Imported second-hand vehicles and the domestic second-hand vehicles [*aloku*] are incomparable. The conditions of most of the domestic second-hand vehicles are bad: the very worst and majority of them are not road-worthy because they have been worn out substantially. *Tokunbo* vehicles look more or less like new vehicles when they are put side by side the ones that have been used locally. Customers are satisfied with the *tokunbo* vehicles because they are the vehicles they can afford, but nothing can be compared to a new vehicle. Customers are satisfied with *tokunbo* vehicles because of the situation of Nigeria's economy. Nigeria's economy does not allow people to purchase new vehicles. Nigerians cannot afford to buy brand new cars which may be sold for nothing less than ₦2 million [US$13,000]. Many Nigerians do not even earn up to ₦2 million [US$13,000] annually. (Male IDI/*Tokunbo* Automobiles Seller/Ibadan/21 August 2010.)

Car ownership is a class symbol in Nigeria. It indicates success at work and momentarily takes the car owner out of the realms of the underprivileged low-income earner to at least that of the elite middle class, even if this is only in symbolic terms. In reality, the car owner may neither belong to the middle class nor the elite class. The mere ownership of a car symbolically conveys a certain amount of honour in relative elitism on the owner, irrespective of the owner's actual socio-economic status.

Additionally, it is expected that a middle-income earner, either in the public or private sector, should have at least one car as an indicator of career success. Ownership of a car is a cause for celebration with close friends. Since many potential car owners are unable to acquire new cars, the second-hand automobile market provides the best source of affordable cars. In comparison with domestic second-hand cars (*aloku*), *tokunbo* automobiles attract customers because they look relatively new and seem to be in good condition. *Aloku* automobiles do not convey the prestige of the *tokunbo*. This is because vehicles wear out quickly in Nigeria because of the very poor road infrastructure. Most of Nigeria's roads are damaged, with huge pot-holes contributing to auto wear and tear. Hence, after a short period of being driven, a vehicle has visible 'Nigeria use': there is damage to the body and chassis, and other parts show signs of wear.

The price of a *tokunbo* automobile depends on its make, its features, the year of production, the country of production, and the port of clearance. Japanese brands are very popular – particularly the Toyota, Honda and Nissan brands. This is because of the availability of local maintenance expertise, the perceived durability of the vehicle, the fuel efficiency and the supposed second-hand value even after the car has been domestically used and become *aloku* second-hand. Other Japanese brands, such as Suzuki, Mazda and Mitsubishi, also attract huge patronage in relative terms. Depending on the condition of the vehicle, *aloku* models of Toyota, Honda or Nissan could cost as much as 60 per cent of the price of a *tokunbo* auto of the same type while other *aloku* (domestically used) Japanese cars would cost just 20 to 30 per cent of the cost of the equivalent *tokunbo* car. Non-Japanese cars in *aloku* condition cost far less than other Japanese brands. Consumers and auto repairers often claim that Japanese brands are preferred because they have similar technologies and this makes it easy to cannibalize parts and keep up maintenance. Consumers also claim that Japanese vehicles are stronger and more fuel-efficient than most other brands.

Toyota models are more expensive than the other vehicles, with Camry, Corolla, Rav 4, 4Runner and Avalon as the most popular Toyota models.

These cars exude a symbolic aura even in their *tokunbo* forms. Likewise, the different models of Honda Accord attract huge patronage, especially in Northern Nigeria.

Tokunbo autos produced in the late 1980s cost between ₦350,000 and ₦450,000 (US$2,333 to US$3,000); they are contraband goods smuggled in through the Republic of Benin. They usually lack customs papers but they are at least affordable to many low-income earners. The cost of *tokunbo* autos of the 1990s, especially those of 1990–1997, range from ₦500,000 to ₦700,000 (US$3,333 to US$4,666), while those manufactured between 1998 and 1999 range between ₦800,000 to ₦1 Million (US$5,333 to US$6,000).[9] The vehicles of the 2000s are generally more expensive. Depending on the make, their prices range from ₦1.5 million to ₦5 million (US$10,000–US$33,000). Virtually all brands are smuggled in and are cheaper than those cleared at the Lagos port. Constant seizures of smuggled *tokunbo* cars produced in the late 1990s and 2000s by officers of the customs service make many consumers who could afford *Lagos tokunbo* wary of purchasing them. In spite of the threat and possibility of seizure by customs officials, *Cotonou tokunbo* vehicles are still commonly driven on Nigerian roads. Owners of such vehicles, lacking valid customs papers, try to evade possible seizure by avoiding federal and intercity roads and highways, which are the focal points of customs special task force operations.

Most of the new brands that are locally available and affordable are Korean and Chinese cars. Very few can afford to buy new Japanese cars. Hyundai and Kia are popular Korean brands in Nigeria; Hyundai made its debut in the 1990s while Kia became relatively well known from the year 2000. Chinese vehicles such as Brilliance, Hydra, Cherry and Geely are new entrants. These Korean and Chinese cars are already frequently seen on Nigerian roads, driven especially by the middle classes who can afford them. They cost between ₦1.5 to ₦4 million (US$10,000-US$26,000) and are yet to be as popular as Japanese brands. This does not necessarily

9 Nigerian laws prohibit the importation of vehicles whose dates of production are above ten years. Such vehicles are, however, smuggled in through Nigeria's borders or shipped in through Lagos. Importers ship in such vehicles by falsely declaring the years of production within acceptable limits and, of course, with active connivance from the customs agents and officials.

mean that they are inferior. Nigeria's conservative consumers nevertheless regard them as 'second generation' automobiles, good enough to be used as new (though definitely not on a par with Japanese brands) but with little or no second-hand value.

Many consumers still do not consider new Korean and Chinese vehicles to be as good as imported second-hand vehicles of Japanese origin. The present author believes that, rather than being about standards, consumer apathy may be connected with the fact that the service expertise of these brands is scarce and spare parts are hard to come by and extremely expensive. Chinese and Korean brands therefore lack domestic second-hand value – quite unlike Japanese *tokunbo* cars that can still be easily re-sold profitably. Irrespective of this, however, it should be noted that many middle class professionals and public and private organizations desirous of having new cars as status symbols or of furthering organizational competitive strategy, opt for Chinese and Korean brands, which are also cheaper than most new Japanese cars of equal capacity and capability.

It is important to note that even though Japanese brands are the most popular, Nigeria hardly imports any *tokunbo* automobiles from Japan itself. One reason for this is that Nigerians drive on the right-hand side of the road while Japanese cars are built to be driven on the left. Use of right-hand drive cars is illegal in Nigeria, even though some consumers still drive them without being sanctioned.[10]

Tokunbo vehicles are mostly imported from Europe and the USA. The supply countries in Europe are Germany, Belgium and the Netherlands. *Tokunbo* auto imports from the USA are more appreciated than imports from the other countries. They are called *American Specs*.[11] *American Specs* look a little bit different from the European models of popular Japanese automobiles. Marketers and consumers believe they really are made to a better quality to meet American standard specifications. And since the

10 Left-hand drive vehicles are designed for countries that drive on the right side of the road while right-hand drive vehicles are for countries which drive on the left side of the road.

11 '*American Spec*' is the local parlance for American Standard Specification. Nigerians believe that the *American Spec* is equipped with better features and facilities, and also has higher standards than the European models of Japanese automobiles.

USA is seen as the most advanced country in the globalized world, consumers and sellers alike believe that *American Specs* are the best automobiles around. This assumption may not necessarily be valid – especially in terms of quality and durability. The assumed superiority of *American Specs* is not unconnected with the dominance of American material and popular culture in the modern 'tech age' which has been globally transmitted through the mass media. While Japanese *American Specs* are popular and appreciated, American vehicles such as GM, Chevrolet and Oldmobile are not popular brands in Nigeria due to the scarcity of maintenance expertise and spare parts. Lately, Ford cars have been coming onto the roads more than ever before. Nonetheless, Japanene *tokunbo* autos imported from Europe and North America remain the more popular brands because they serve as rational alternatives, satisfying consumers' demand and symbolically conveying elitist and modern status on their users.

In summary, *tokunbo* automobiles serve consumers' practical needs and also a need for ostentation, both depending on the car type and the consumer's social class. A basic feature of Nigeria's auto culture is that vehicle ownership still remains a status symbol, even in the twenty-first century. Car ownership indicates a degree of affluence and membership of the privileged class. In a country where up to 70 per cent of the population live in poverty, it is only those who have extra funds not directly tied to basic needs who can own an automobile, especially as, besides the buying price. The owner must be able to afford the added costs of fuel and maintenance. Many families with working adult members in the public and private sectors just cannot afford a car.

Those who can afford one would often rather go for a *tokunbo* model, which may cost as little as 10 per cent of the price of a new vehicle (depending on the brand). Older models are cheaper, while more recent models are dearer. Nigerians have developed a trust for Japanese cars such as Toyota, Honda and Nissan, especially because of the general availability of repair expertise and the low fuel consumption of these brands. New Korean and Chinese brands are now readily available, sometimes at even cheaper prices than the popular brands of used Japanese automobiles. Consumers, however, are sceptical about Korean and Chinese automobiles. The unavailability of spare parts and the limited repair expertise in Nigeria weighs against them and there are doubts regarding their general quality.

Instead, consumers put their trust in brands such as Toyota Camry, Honda Accord and Nissan Altima (among other Japanese brands). The vehicles tend to be described in superlative terms, reflecting the awe consumers feel towards them. The 2007 and 2010 models of Toyota Camry are called *Muscle* and *Big Daddy* respectively while newer models of the Honda Accord are called *End of Discussion* (2003–2005) and *Discussion Continues* (2006–2010).[12] These names also indicate that the vehicles are the exclusive preserve of the wealthy and the upper classes. As new models are released, automobiles hitherto socially perceived to be available only within the realms of extreme elitism drop in price and prestige; thus they become part of the priced material culture within the reach of consumers who may not necessarily be part of the top echelon of the elite class, but are financially capable of acquiring such cars. As the years go by and new models are released, auto prices and the attached symbolic values drop, leading to consequent acquisition by members of socio-economic groups who hitherto could not afford them. For example, the 1995 Toyota Camry which was seen as an exclusive possession of wealthy members of the upper class is now commonly acquired by middle-income earners. To the consumers, what matters most is that the car they drive is the symbolically and culturally priced Toyota Camry, irrespective of the year of production (Omobowale 2008). The consumers can proudly say, 'I drive a Camry.' This boosts their egos and they enjoy considerable social appreciation from the immediate public. Of course, both new and imported second-hand versions of the latest models of the popular brands are readily

12 Nigerians have constructed various appellations for automobiles over the years. A new appellation evolves at the release of a new model of a popular brand. Some other appellations for some popular models still used are: *Orobo* ('big', used to describe the 1992–1996 models of Toyota Camry); *Pencil* (the 1997 Toyota Camry model); *Pen* (the Toyota Camry 1998–1999 models); *Bulldog* and *Bullet* (American and European models respectively of the Honda Accord 1996–1997); *Babyboy* (the Honda Accord 1998–1999 models); *End of Discussion* (2003–2005); and *Discussion Continues* (2006–2010). This list is not exhaustive. New appellations emerge as new models catch the popular imagination.

available in Nigeria, as Nigeria attracts a relatively large auto market, due to its high population and more expansive economy, compared with its West African neighbours. Many consumers would however, rather invest ₦3 million (US$20,000) on a 2008 *tokunbo* Toyota Camry than on a new Chinese or Korean model at the same price. This is because, even though the *tokunbo* vehicle is second-hand, it conveys a greater symbolic aura and sense of class than the Chinese or Korean brands.

Korean or Chinese models may be new; yet they would fail to convey these things or attract honour and prestige to an equal degree. Most of the Nigerian imports come from Europe and the USA. American brands of Japanese cars (*American Specs*) attract a higher economic and social worth: consumers generally believe that they are of the highest quality and will attract greater prestige.

Some body features make *American Specs* stand out. A recent feature that further increases their value is the daytime running light (DRL) that automatically turns on and remains on as long as the engine is running. Scandinavian countries were the first to introduce the DRL system in the late 1970s, due to low winter light levels experienced there even during daytime. The DRL is meant to ensure that a vehicle is seen even during such poor daytime visibility (Williams and Lancaster 1995; Elvik 1993). The DRL system is currently common in Europe and North America (Farmer and Williams 2002; Tofflemire and Whitehead 1997). In Nigeria, the DRL system tends to announce a 'posh' *American Spec*, even though the vehicle might have been imported from a country other than the USA. Nigeria does not experience poor daytime visibility; yet, owners of such vehicles would not think of disabling this facility, since it is an indication of status and a proof that the vehicle owner drives a real *American Spec*. Finally, it is important also to note that, under military rule in the 1990s, it was common for high-ranking government officials not entitled to siren-blaring pilot vehicles to have their headlamps on full and hoot loudly to proclaim their right of way. Other motorists usually then gave way to such vehicles. The popularity of the *American Spec*'s DRL system among motorists may actually stem from this elitist idea of 'day-time-full-lamp' from the 1990s. Thus the *American Spec*, with its DRL system, gives a symbolic impression of the 'elite in motion'.

CHAPTER 8

The *Tokunbo* Second-Hand Economy: Spare Car Parts

In any country the availability of spare parts is vital for maintaining automobiles on the roads. Luthar (2006), for example, has shown how, under the former socialist regime in Yugoslavia, Yugoslavs travelled all the way to Trieste, a border town in Italy, to purchase essential spare parts and other scarce resources for their cars. Likewise, an article by Lazarev and Gregory (2002) reveals how, due to scarcity, vehicle-owners in the former Soviet Union used to cannibalize spare parts from disused vehicles to keep their current cars on the road. Rau's (2002) research gives insights into the ingenuity of the East Germans too in repairing damaged disused parts as spares for vehicles and other pieces of machinery. Continued automobile maintenance in this way underscores the value of spare parts for the sustenance of the automobile industry (Nestorović and Vale 1991).

Within the Nigerian cultural space, where vehicle ownership serves as a status symbol and sign of belonging to the elite, availability of spare parts has direct implications on the symbolic class representation of automobiles. Capability of maintaining a car and ensuring it is in good service condition is a major factor in the social construction and appreciation of the status of the owner. It is therefore not enough to own a car; it must be maintained. A car owner who is unable to keep his/her car in good condition is ridiculed as a person trying to belong to a class he/she is economically incapable of really joining.

In South-Western Nigeria, *tokunbo* automobile spare parts gradually came into popular demand in the mid 1990s. My informants disclose that Alhaji Mufu Lanihun pioneered their importation. He started with a massive importation of motor engines. With these available to fit, many people who had been forced to depend on public transport were able to get vehicles they had thought too expensive to repair back on the roads. This made *tokunbo* auto spare parts very popular.

Mufu Lanihun himself was very popular too in the 1990s: he built up a multi-million Naira (₦) business empire and a huge client base. His enterprise spawned many of today's spare parts sellers, especially in Ibadan and Abeokuta. A craver for recognition, while he reigned in the auto spare parts business, Lanihun used to invite the public, through radio and TV adverts, to go to designated places to receive cash gifts, in accordance with his Islamic religious belief of *Zakat* that emphasizes alms-giving to the poor and downtrodden (see Kochuyt 2009; Al-Krenawi and Graham 2000). Lanihun openly praised himself, and he was popularly called *Olowo ti o n f'owo saanu* ('the rich man who is graciously benevolent'). He also received many 'honorary doctorate degrees' from supposed 'American and European universities' and claimed to have been awarded an 'honorary professorship' in recognition of his business acumen. The ceremonies were usually conducted in rented halls in Nigeria with supposed representatives of the universities conferring the degrees on him, with academic gowns, hoods and caps to match.[1] The authenticity of these 'degrees' and the 'professorship' is of course in doubt.[2]

Lanihun's success prompted other investors to go into the *tokunbo* auto spare parts trade. In Lagos, the trade is at present dominated by the Igbo, a major ethnic group associated with successful investments and business enterprise in Nigeria (Ismail 2009; Olutayo 1999; Meagher 1997). Mufu Lanihun's influence has largely declined, but his landmark achievement and contribution to *tokunbo* automobile spare parts merchandise is widely recognized and acknowledged.

1 There was mad rush for honorary doctorate degrees from Western universities in the 1990s and early 2000s. Many people who had never seen the inside of a high school, least of all a university, became 'doctors' overnight. This craving for doctorates is a manifestation of the cultural worth of titles, which are believed to catapult bearers into higher realms of social appreciation and elite status.

2 In Nigeria, many affluent people crave titular recognition. The frenzy stretches from traditional chieftaincy titles, to political titles (of 'Honourables' for elective and appointive political offices, and 'His Excellency' for governors and the president) and honorary doctorate degrees from tertiary institutions in Nigeria and beyond. Whereas some of the titles are well deserved, it is common knowledge that many affluent men and women in Nigeria actually 'purchase' titles. In the case of political titles, elected officials often cling to the titles long after their tenures have lapsed.

Both low quality counterfeits and imported second-hand spare parts are available in Nigeria's automobile spare parts markets. The low quality counterfeits give value to *tokunbo* spare parts as customers regard the *tokunbo* parts as superior on the basis of their origin in the developed world. The major auto spare parts markets in the study areas here are: the Agodi-Gate spare parts market in Ibadan (*Iso paati* in local parlance), the Ladipo spare parts market in Lagos; and the Ijaye and Isale Igbeyin spare parts markets in Abeokuta. Figure 5 below shows the flow chain of imported second-hand automobile spare parts in Nigeria.

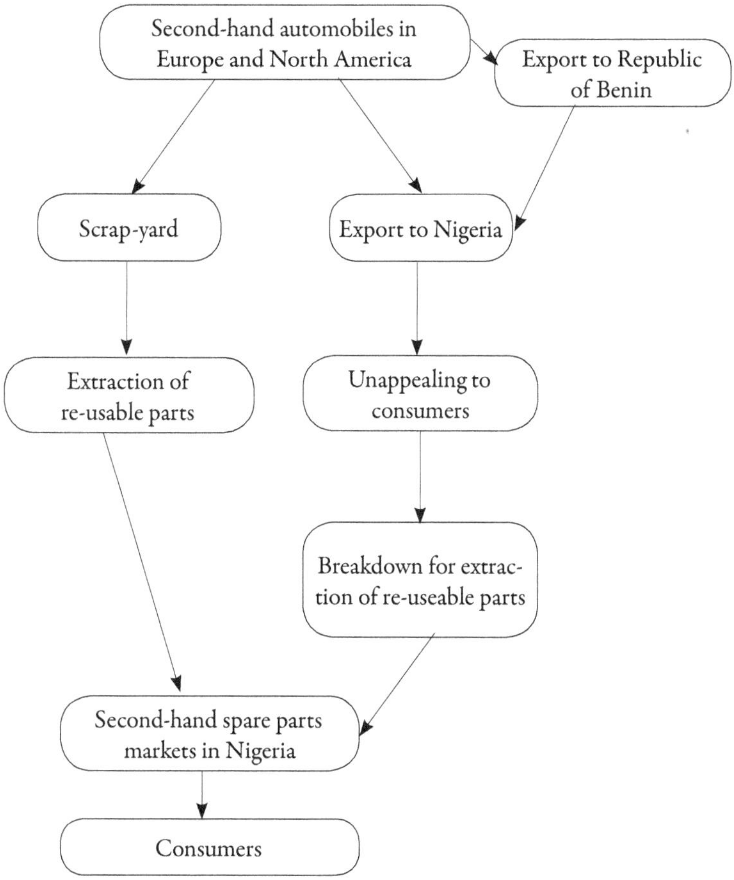

Figure 5 *Second-hand automobile spare parts flow chain*

With the collapse of automobile assembly plants in Nigeria and the consequent heavy reliance on imported second-hand automobiles, vehicle owners in Nigeria currently rely on *tokunbo* spare parts to keep their vehicles running. Figure 5 shows that auto spare parts are sourced either from direct imports or from used vehicles dismantled in Nigeria. The sourcing of *tokunbo* automobile spare parts starts from the points of disuse, with vehicles then dispatched to the scrap-yard. At the scrap-yard, re-usable parts are extracted (Soderman and Carter 2008) and shipped to Nigeria and other Third World nations. In addition, there are vehicles that are shipped directly to Nigeria or via the Republic of Benin, which, as they could not readily appeal to consumers, are dismantled in Nigeria for the extraction of re-usable parts. Finally, the used spare parts from both sets of scrap-yards are displayed at spare parts markets where consumers eventually purchase them.

Just as *tokunbo* vehicles have transformed car ownership in Nigeria, *tokunbo* automobile spare parts have transformed vehicle maintenance and, in the long run, the status of the vehicle owners. Ikporukpo (2002) has shown how *tokunbo* vehicle spare parts have revolutionized the motor mechanic trade in Nigeria with auto artisans and vehicle owners preferring *tokunbo* to new spare parts, whose genuineness is suspect. Thus, not only do *tokunbo* spare parts provide a vital means of keeping vehicles on the road, they have also contributed to the flourishing of the local motor repair business, employing a good number of Nigerians.

Increasing consumption of imported automobiles has also meant increasing demand for *tokunbo* automobile spare parts. Though *tokunbo* vehicles have re-use value, they often have weak and worn-out parts, whose quick collapse is accelerated by Nigeria's deplorable roads and harsh environmental conditions. In fact, a basic assumption among many *tokunbo* vehicle buyers is that some vital parts must be checked and/or changed immediately after purchase. These parts include the tyres, fuel pumps, radiators and brakes. Other parts may be changed as they become faulty and incapacitate the vehicle. Tyres are changed because of the assumption that those that come with *tokunbo* vehicles are weak and made for cold weather as opposed to the harsh hot weather in Nigeria. Ironically, more often than not, *tokunbo* tyres are procured to replace the old ones (see Ayinla 2011; *Nigerian Tribune* 2010). The quality of the *tokunbo* tyres is judged by the grip threading on them. Little or no attention is given to the validity period, which is a four-year period from the date of manufacture as inscribed on the tyre. The tyres are simply assumed to be good, once the supposed 'experts' (who are also the tyre merchants or their agents pretending to be 'advisers' to consumers) confirm the quality.

The widespread use of *tokunbo* tyres partly accounts for the high incidence of fatal motor accidents in Nigeria, though this is coupled with deplorable roads pitted by huge pot-holes, reckless driving, and faulty vehicle parts. Between 2006 and 2008, Nigeria recorded a total of 79,409 road accidents, 16,278 resultant fatalities, and 63,206 injuries (Omobowale, Akinade and Omobowale 2011; Adeoye 2009). Many of the accidents were due to burst tyres, which, more often than not, were imported second-hand.

Likewise, radiators may be changed to bigger ones due to Nigerians' experiences with imported second-hand vehicles whose engines quickly reach high levels of heat, especially when there is traffic congestion. Along with the installation of bigger radiators, consumers are also advised to install fans to keep engines cool. Brakes are checked to ensure they are in good condition, or if they need to be replaced with another braking system, probably *tokunbo* too. A vehicle owner will subsequently patronize the second-hand market to replace the other parts as they develop faults, one after another. Typical replacements include camshafts, clutch discs, engines, gear boxes, doors, 'brain-boxes', side mirrors, fuel pumps, water pumps, lighting, key starters, valves and propellers. Illustration 3 shows some *tokunbo* spare parts.

As mentioned earlier, consumers tend to patronize second-hand automobile markets by proxy, relying on 'experts' or, if they go themselves, they go in the company of such an 'expert'. The experienced 'expert' is usually an auto mechanic who is either asked to carry out the purchase or to accompany the primary consumer to the market and advise. Car owners hardly ever go to the automobile spare parts markets without an accompanying 'expert' for fear of purchasing defective parts. Even when an automobile part is good, an unscrupulous auto artisan may claim it is bad in order to spite and cheat a car owner who has gone to the market alone to make an independent purchase. Hence, vehicle owners are virtually obliged to employ the services of 'experts' in order to forestall the possibility of being cheated, or of purchasing deficient auto parts, or of having the parts they buy rejected by the mechanic. In many instances, however, the 'expert' makes some economic gain out of the transaction. If he goes alone, he inflates the purchase price and keeps the balance. If he goes accompanied, he still gains, for even in the presence of the unwary and uninformed consumer who has gone along to forestall cheating, auto-artisans and automobile spare parts merchants exchange coded messages to strike a deal over the commission assured for the 'expert'. Both the merchant and the 'expert' enjoy good informal relations and seek as much as possible to protect their mutual interests in economic gain and to strengthen their business partnership. Hence the loyalty of the 'expert' tends to lie primarily with the automobile spare parts seller. The presence of the primary consumer notwithstanding, auto mechanics and automobile spare parts vendors share a concealed subculture and sign language and roundly defeat a purchaser who aims to control: the price is not likely to go below an amount that will pay the 'commission' of the wily 'expert'. Unknown to the accompanying consumer, the 'expert' encourages purchase by affirming the quality of the goods while he goes back to collect some tip and/or commission (usually 3–5 percent of the value of purchase) from the merchant. Of course, the purchaser will give the 'expert' a tip for his services as well. The irony of it all is that, despite paying for the services of the 'expert', the consumer may well be deceived into purchasing faulty goods – especially if the loyalty of the 'expert' is basically with the seller because of the payment he will get from him.

Consumers buy imported second-hand automobile spare parts because they generally believe they are of better quality. The numerous low-quality new spare parts emanating from China are a consumer's nightmare. A respondent explains:

> Customers neither request for the locally used spare parts nor the new spare parts. Customers rather demand for *tokunbo* spare parts for their vehicles because the *tokunbo* spare parts are more reliable. For example, if a *tokunbo* headlamp is sold for N300 (US$2) and new headlight is sold for N50 (US$0.3), consumers will still demand *tokunbo* headlamp because, if the new headlamp lasts for one month, the *tokunbo* headlamp will last for one year or more. Most of the new vehicle spare parts are imported from China and Taiwan, and the *tokunbo* spare parts are from United States of America, Germany and United Kingdom. The products of Western countries are known for good quality. (Male IDI/*Tokunbo* automobile spare parts seller/Ibadan/20 August 2010)

Illustration 3 *Unloading imported second-hand automobile spare parts in Lagos*

Corroborating the position above, a motor mechanic who has practised for twenty-five years affirms that:

> *Tokunbo* second-hand vehicle spare parts do not give me much trouble whenever I am fixing any part of a vehicle. *Tokunbo* second-hand spare parts were removed from a vehicle, so it has already been tested and made fit. Fixing it to another vehicle of the same model will not be a problem. Most of the new vehicle spare parts may not fit in properly. It is either the new vehicle spare part is bigger or smaller than the original part of the vehicle ... I have been on the job for the past twenty-five years. Since the time I have been doing this job, I have noticed that *tokunbo* spare parts are patronized in the market more than the new vehicle spare parts. Due to the demand for *tokunbo* spare parts, dealers have been importing *tokunbo* spare parts the more ... The huge volume of imported second-hand spare parts confirms this ... Imported second-hand sales are growing because car owners are satisfied with the functioning of *tokunbo* spare parts. One can guarantee the quality of *tokunbo* automotive spare parts ... (Male IDI *Tokunbo* automobile spare parts buyer/Abeokuta/1 September 2010)

Another respondent states that:

> Most of the new automotive parts in Nigeria are Chinese products. Nigerians are very cautious of the new spare parts because of their default rates. Original new spare parts are unaffordable to many Nigerians, hence they go for *tokunbo*. *Tokunbo* performs better than most of the new ones available in the market. The original spare parts from Japan last longer than the *tokunbo*, while the *tokunbo* lasts longer than the Chinese ones. (Male IDI/*Tokunbo* automobile spare parts seller/Lagos/1 September 2010)

Again, these testimonies reveal that the presence of low-quality automobile spare parts and counterfeits in the Nigerian market fuels customers' preference for *tokunbo*. *Tokunbo* spare parts are highly appreciated vis-à-vis the counterfeits. In the field, my research team met a man bargaining for a *tokunbo* windscreen at Ladipo market in Lagos. He emphasized that he was buying the windscreen because he was sure that, though used, it would be better than a new counterfeit. The customer claimed that, at 40 per cent of the cost of a brand new windscreen, the *tokunbo* one would still give the expected use value. This typifies popular opinion. In essence, *tokunbo* spare parts sustain both *tokunbo* vehicles and those bought new. Within a short while of the release of new car models popular in Nigeria, used spare parts for them become available in the spare parts markets.

Counterfeits last for shorter periods of time, and cause problems for hapless low-to-middle-income earners who want to ensure that their vehicles remain on the road. Any damage or fault that deprives a vehicle owner from having a comfortable ride attracts the attention of people in the neighbourhood, kin, acquaintances, colleagues and even friends. The first question they ask is, 'What has happened to your car?' A quick explanation may dissuade further probing. Failure to put the vehicle back on the road attracts sympathy and/or empathy but, eventually, if the vehicle remains at the auto workshop while the owner 'walks the street', he/she gradually loses social prestige among compeers.[3] He/she becomes just like any other 'commoner' and/or 'disadvantaged fellow' unable to afford a car or maintain one on the road. The person may be jeered at. Thus, it is not enough just to own a car; being able to put it on the road symbolically reinforces the owner's social status. The socio-psychological impact of a car owner's inability to maintain his or her car potentially brings social stigma, leading to feelings of social exclusion and of being disadvantaged. Productivity, efficiency and punctuality may be affected and, in extreme cases, the person may be forced to withdraw from social circles so that comments about his/her 'missing' car do not get raised. This is because taking public transport to social engagements is prone to attract unfavourable attention from elite colleagues and may damage the social status and prestige of the former car owner. *Tokunbo* auto spare parts therefore offer a 'reprieve' to vehicle owners, ensuring that their social status as car owners is maintained. Attached to *tokunbo* spare parts, therefore, are meanings of affordability, good quality and the ability to keep up appearances.

The social organization of the spare parts market comprises shop owners, apprentices (*omo ikose* among the Yoruba and *sales boys* among the Igbo who dominate the Lagos spare parts market), and also touting agents. Shop owners are the retailers who display their wares in shops; they get their wares from wholesale importers. The apprentices are usually school drop-outs and young secondary school leavers who are put under a master (the shop owner) to learn the 'nitty-gritty' of the trade (see also Akinwale

3 'Walking the street' in local parlance is used to describe the movements of a person who hitherto had a car but currently relies on public transport.

2009; Olutayo 1999). The apprentice undergoes training for about five years, perhaps more, during which period he also attends to the master's errands and other assignments. He is expected to be absolutely loyal to the master. The apprentice helps the customer to carry his purchase to his car, while the customer is expected to give him a tip of as little as ₦50 to ₦100 (US$0.3 to US$ 0.6).

As an apprentice gains his master's trust, he is exposed to the ins and outs of the trade. He learns the sources of *tokunbo* spare parts and is allowed to bargain with customers independently and manage the shop in the absence of the master. Of course, the apprentice is made to pay for any losses or under-priced items that may be sold in the absence of the master. To avoid such sanctions, an apprentice naturally tends to sell at a price higher than the basic reserve price. The apprentice may keep the surcharge while he remits the rest to the shop owner. Thus, an apprentice gains experience through direct participation in the *tokunbo* trade – so long as he has earned the master's trust. If he fails to please the master, he might be forced to leave, or remain a subordinate in the master's service until he is allowed 'freedom' from *ikose* (apprenticeship).[4] Gradually, the apprentice 'collects and gathers' his own wares, for which he may get potential buyers, testing and perfecting his mercantile capabilities as a future automobile spare parts trader.[5]

The touting agent presents himself as a shop owner to the would-be customer – especially if such a person is an unwary primary user who has visited the market for the first time or comes without an 'expert'. The touting agent guides the customer to the shop of his preferred seller and

4 'Freedom' is the local term for an apprentice's 'graduation' once he has thoroughly learned his trade. Unless he has been 'freed' by the master and certificated, the artisans' guild will not allow an apprentice to practise. 'Freedom' is celebrated with family and friends, and on some occasions the 'freed' graduands are made to wear academic gowns with cap and hood to match. For them, wearing the academic gown is a symbol of graduation just as with university graduates.

5 The act of collecting and gathering spare parts may be through legal or illegal means. Legally, the apprentice/trader might collect and gather from disposed items or *gratis* gifts from friends, associates, the boss, and sometimes customers. Sometimes it could also be through deliberate acts of stealing from vehicles parked in isolated and/or dark places.

conducts and/or negotiates the transaction, acting as a co-shop owner or the boss while the real shop owner watches. The touting agent emphasizes the good quality of the goods and encourages the customer to buy. Once a deal is made and the customer departs, he collects his commission from the shop owner. As the cost of the touting agent's commission gets transferred to the customer (without his knowledge), touted goods are usually more expensive. It is very difficult for an outsider to differentiate a touting agent from the apprentice or from the shop owner. All three work together for the common purpose of ensuring sales. Touting agents are called *onibaranda* (trickster), the name capturing their extraordinary ability to persuade customers to purchase goods, even at higher prices. An unwary customer may pay as much as 40 to 50 per cent more than the real price of the goods.

The teeming population of youths in spare parts markets provides labour for lifting and carrying and for dismantling. They carry heavy loads of metals with wheelbarrows or on their heads. Of course, these services are provided to customers at a fee. If the load is not too heavy and can be carried by the customer, the apprentice in the retailer's shop is asked to carry it, as an act of goodwill; but, in actuality, the customer is expected to tip the apprentice. Should the customer attempt to leave without tipping, the apprentice will respectfully ask for his tip.

Lacking modern technical skills, the teeming population of young artisans and apprentices in Nigeria's spare parts markets provide the dismantling 'expertise' for de-commissioned vehicles. The activities of these human dismantlers are a sight to behold. Armed with simple tools, such as screw drivers and hammers of varying sizes, the young artisans, numbering up to twenty or more, descend on the vehicle to be dismantled, each working on a particular part, and within minutes, the vehicle is split into parts to be marketed as spares.

Both locally used second-hand cars and *tokunbo* automobiles are dismantled in this way. Wily marketers display parts extracted from the locally used vehicles as '*tokunbo*' in order to achieve sales at a higher price. This further attests to the symbolic efficacy of the term '*tokunbo*'. Unless buyers are experienced and can distinguish between domestically used spare parts and *tokunbo* spare parts, they may, to their dismay, purchase domestically used and faulty service parts at the cost of the *tokunbo*; and the goods cannot be returned, because they are covered by neither guarantee nor warranty. They are therefore purchased at the consumer's risk. This partly explains why consumers either send 'experts' or request that the 'experts' go with them: they are anxious that the spare parts they buy will be valid.

In summary, there is a symbiotic relationship between the *tokunbo* auto sector and the automobile spare parts sector. The spare parts sector plays the strategic role of supplying vital automobile spare parts. Correspondingly, vehicles from the *tokunbo* auto sector that do not get ready buyers are dismantled to complement the spare parts that are sourced from discarded vehicles in the developed countries. Virtually all parts of the popular brands are available in the spare parts market. Availability, however, is also dependent on the brand and the year of production. Parts for more recent models are scarcer than those for the old models. Over time, though, parts for new brands trickle into the market. Initially, the parts may be expensive but, as supply increases and the parts become readily available, the prices crash. Unlike other goods, *tokunbo* spare parts are not necessarily cheaper than the available new spare parts (particularly the substandard spare parts popularly called '*Taiwan*'). Standard new spare parts are largely out of most customers' reach. They are available only in a few top class shops that service high-income earners and the upper classes. Consumers, however, find *tokunbo* automobile parts better in quality than the *Taiwan*, and the cost difference is usually as much as 100 per cent or more. *Tokunbo* spare parts last longer; they fit easily into vehicles and they satisfy consumer confidence. Thus, in terms of preferred purchases, *tokunbo* spares are the first to be considered even when new spare parts are available. This is because the authenticity of most new automobile spare parts is suspect.

CHAPTER 9

The *Tokunbo* Second-Hand Economy: Electronic Goods

The electronics industry is one of the fastest growing industries in the world. According to Sodhi and Lee (2007), the global consumer electronics industry is worth US$240 billion. The major electronics producing countries are the United States of America, Japan and (as a new entrant) South Korea.

The history of Nigeria's consumption of electronic goods dates back to the colonial era. By the oil years of the 1970s, brands such as Panasonic, Sharp, Hitachi, Sony, Morphy Richards, JVC and Phillips had gained ground in the country. Though it is a huge electronics-consuming nation, Nigeria, with its low industrial base and inadequate technology, remains incapable of providing for its own electronic needs, and thus depends on imports. Following the economic downturn of the 1980s, the electronics market experienced a new trend. The Naira (₦), the nation's currency, was devalued; inflation was high; and purchasing power was generally at its lowest ebb. In these circumstances, most Nigerians could no longer afford the popular electronics brands that had become household names.

Hence, consumers submitted to substandard alternatives in the form of counterfeit clones, as the country started receiving cheap but poor quality electronic goods from Asia. The substandard alternatives were principally cloned counterfeits of the popular brands that had earned consumer loyalty. Their brand names were designed to mimic those of the popular brands in a general attempt at deception. Panasonic became *Parasonic*, Sony became *Sonic*, JVC became *JBC*, Sharp became *Shap*, Phillips became *Phillibs* and Hitachi became *Hitaci*.

At first, these counterfeit goods attracted consumers' patronage because they were relatively cheap, seemed affordable and looked just like the popular brands. Consumers simply 'bought' the idea that they were buying real alternatives at lower prices. The cloned counterfeits were, however, a customers' nightmare. They quickly tended to develop irreparable faults, causing huge losses to the consumers. Already squeezed by economic depression, the consumers lost the money they had invested, lost the product, and were further subjected to the psychological pain of trying to get a replacement in the midst of competing needs but meagre resources.

Nigerian importers sourced cheap electronic goods from Taiwan and, subsequently, Malaysia and Hong Kong among other Asian regions; but, despite this variety of sources, the goods were all referred to as '*Taiwan*'. They *looked* exactly like the original brands. An unwary customer could easily buy one without noticing that the brand name differed slightly from his/her real preferred choice. An honest vendor would take pains to explain the difference between *Taiwan* and the original to would-be customers, but many marketers preferred to make out that these were authentic products with slightly different brand tags, or were new releases from the parent company. In a short while, consumers came to realize that they were being sold fake and substandard products, but there were hardly any alternatives they could turn to, because the original products were out of the price range the great majority of the population could manage, since they had been economically disempowered by inflation.

Recently, *Taiwan* has been replaced by '*Chinco*'. *Chinco* are sub-standard electronic goods mainly coming from China. *Chinco* products are better than *Taiwan* goods, and to some extent, have provided an alternative to the expensive new electronic items from the developed world. *Chinco* goods are still very much substandard, however: they last only a little longer than *Taiwan* products. Informants claim that Nigerian importers deliberately specify very poor standards to Chinese manufacturers in order to make the products affordable to potential buyers.[1] In fact, the Nigerian standard is said to be 'lower than poor' in the international electronics market.

1 The Director General of the Standard Organization of Nigeria, Dr. Joseph I. Odumodu, has decried the importation of substandard electronic goods by unscrupulous importers, stating that substandard products have virtually taken over the market, while Nigeria loses over ₦500 million ($33 million) each year to substandard products (Adeloye 2011; Obinna 2011; Standard Organization of Nigeria 2009).

Unlike *Taiwan* goods, however, *Chinco* products are not deceitful clones of popular brands: they carry unique, distinctive brand names. The most popular *Chinco* products are mobile phones, iPods, radio sets, camcorders, television sets, DVD players, electric stoves and boilers, and digital recorders; but there are others too. Consumers' experience with *Chinco* products indicates that they overheat during use and develop faults quickly. The devices are usually irreparable and have to be discarded once they have become faulty. Having experienced substandard electronics for over twenty years, consumers expect *Chinco* products to develop irreparable faults at some point – and sooner rather than later. The common expression when a *Chinco* device becomes unusable is *o ti la'na* (which literally means, 'It has exploded'). The user gets a replacement either by buying another *Chinco* product or a *tokunbo* one, depending on his/her resources.

Certainly this type of experience increases customers' patronage of *tokunbo* electronics. Both consumers and marketers claim that, unlike *Taiwan* and *Chinco* products, *tokunbo* electronic devices have proved to be of reasonably high quality. And, once again, consumers can afford to purchase their preferred popular brands. Hence, within the last twenty years, the marketing and patronage of *tokunbo* electronic goods has increased tremendously, with a mounting demand from the consuming public, who see these goods as the only viable alternatives.

Meanwhile the structure of the global utilization and discarding of electronic products has profound consequences for Nigeria and other Third World nations, especially with respect to the management of e-waste. Figures 6 and 7 (p. 104) show the global chain of e-waste and the second-hand electronics flow chain in Nigeria.

Figure 6 shows the chain of e-waste to and in the developing world. Electronics companies produce both standard and substandard products. While the developed nations have stricter controls and safety rules and keep to standard and high quality products, both types of products are shipped to the developing world, where social disequilibrium creates a ready market for substandard goods. These substandard items are obsolete 'junk' for consumers in the developed world but are nevertheless prized in the developing world.

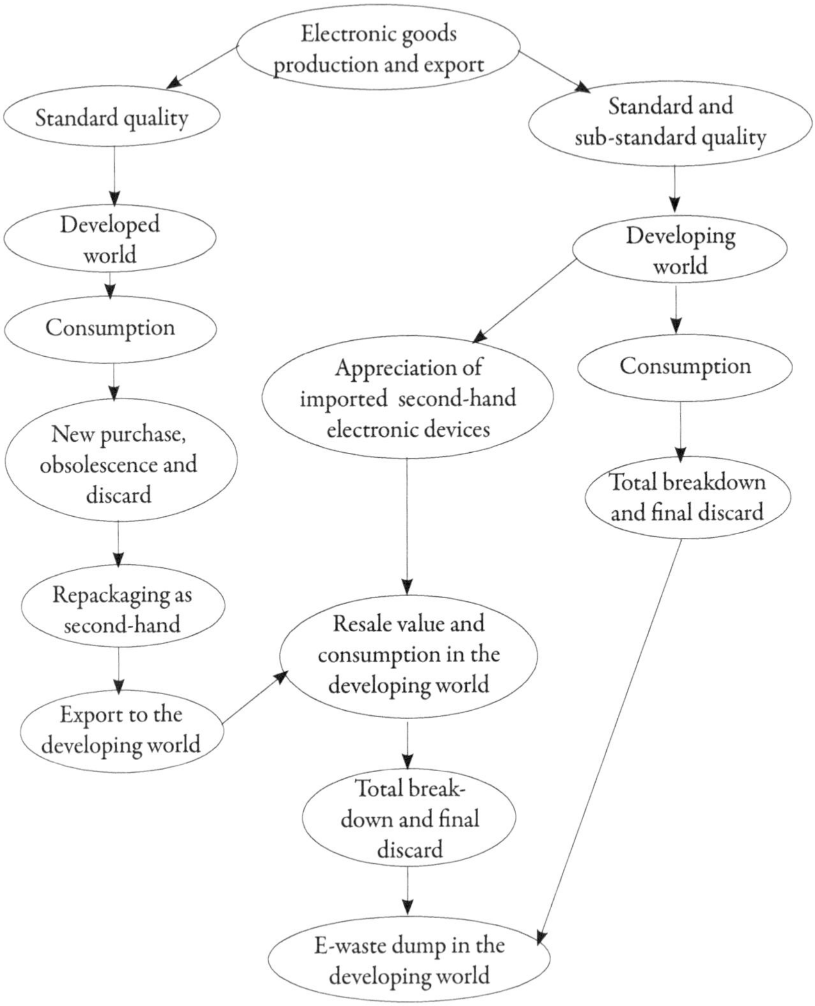

Figure 6 *The global chain of e-waste*

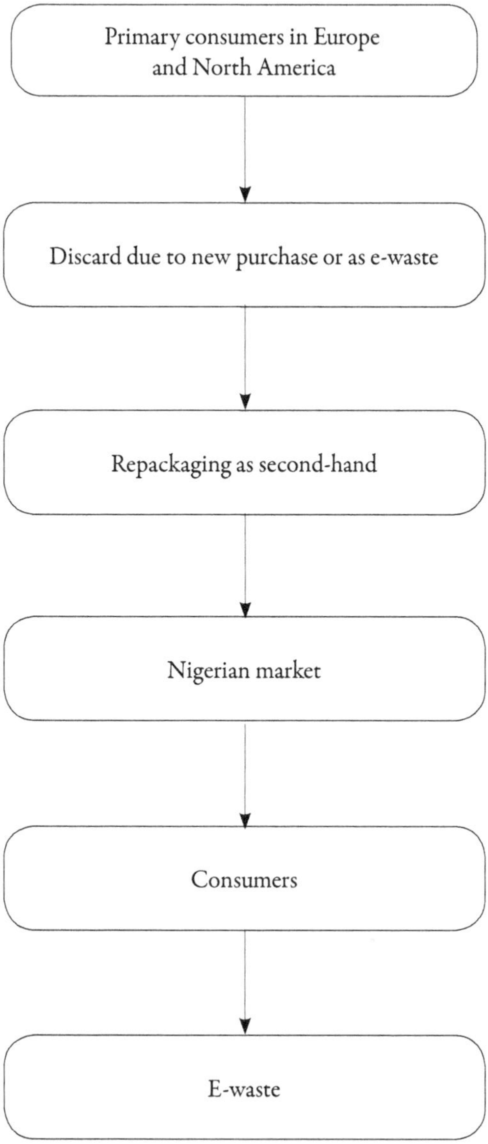

Figure 7 *The flow chain for imported second-hand electronic goods*

> The Standard Organization of Nigeria is lacking in its responsibility. It is not doing enough. Almost all new electronics sold in Nigeria are substandard Chinese products. Importers specifically demand poor quality jobs and Chinese manufacturers simply give them poor quality electronics that they display for sale in Nigeria. On the other hand, since *tokunbo* electronics were originally made for use in the developed nations, they are tested and trusted because they are of good standard. They use it for one year or thereabout and drop it off because they have better socio-economic conditions than we do. So when *tokunbo* electronics are eventually imported into Nigeria, they remain new and customers will still buy them and the electronics last for years without giving one problem. (Male IDI/*Tokunbo* electronic products seller/Lagos/3 September 2010)

Another interviewee said:

> The way the imported second-hand electronics were used abroad is better than the way we use electronics in Nigeria ... *Tokunbo* electronics ... lasts more than second-hand electronics that were used in Nigeria [*aloku*] and it is better than most new electronics ... I have many *tokunbo* electronics like television set and DVD player at home and since I have been using them, I have never repaired them, not even once. The pressing iron I am using at home has never developed any fault since I bought it. I bought all my electronics four years ago and they are functioning well ... I appreciate the electronics that are imported into Nigeria because they are functioning well. All my *tokunbo* electronics are satisfying me. Since I have been using *tokunbo* electronics, they have never disappointed me. In fact, I am very happy to use anything called *tokunbo*. (Male IDI/*Tokunbo* electronic products consumer/Abeokuta/3 September 2010)

Still another interviewee praised *tokunbo* electronic devices at length:

> *Tokunbo* electronics is no *aloku*. Overseas, an electronics gadget purchased today can be sold off next month to purchase a new one. Such electronics cannot be called *aloku*. It is more or less new ... The value of *tokunbo* electronics is much. *Tokunbo* electronics are stronger than the new ones ... *Tokunbo* electronics helps the common man like myself. Without *tokunbo* electronics in Nigeria, many people will not have electronics in their homes. The prices of new electronics in the market are high and besides getting original ones is always very difficult ... I have been patronizing *tokunbo* market ever since I completed my vocational training. *Tokunbo* electronics are good especially if you are fortunate to purchase the right ones ... The *tokunbo* electronics I use at home include television set, pressing iron and DVD player. These electronics help at relaxation after a hard day's job ... As long as I live, I will continue to buy *tokunbo*

> electronics ... *Tokunbo* electronics have displaced new electronics in Nigeria. They have also made electronics affordable and within reach. Years back, when someone buys an electronics gadget, people will come to celebrate and congratulate him. For instance if somebody bought a video machine in a house, almost all the neighbours will come to watch, but now *tokunbo* electronics are available everywhere ... (Male IDI/*Tokunbo* electronic products consumer/Abeokuta/3 September 2010)

Finally, another interviewee in Ibadan had this to say:

> People are patronizing *tokunbo* electronics and the importation of *tokunbo* goods has really helped our economy. But for *tokunbo* electronics, a lot of homes would have been without television sets. For instance, when I was a kid, only one person had a (black and white) television in the whole of my neighbourhood. People trooped to his house to watch his television set. With the advent of *tokunbo* electronics, the prices of new electronics have reduced and nowadays, new electronics are not even as durable as *tokunbo* electronics ... The electronics foreign manufacturers produce for their home countries are good quality products. This is why *tokunbo* electronics are more durable than most of the new ones ... The reason why people do not like to patronize new electronics is that the new electronics are not strong and durable compared with what obtained in the recent past. For instance, the black and white television my father has been using since I was a kid is still with him. In this contemporary time, I cannot give a year guarantee on any new electronic gadget. In other words, *tokunbo* electronics are stronger and their spare parts are readily available while the new electronics are weak and their spare parts are scarce. (Male IDI/*Tokunbo* electronic products seller/Ibadan/25 August 2010)

Just as in the case of car spare parts, consumers consider *tokunbo* electronic goods to be of better quality than the new ones, whose standards are doubtful. Aside from the perceived and real quality of *tokunbo* electronic items, which encodes the imported second-hand with connotations of superiority, electronic devices, as consumer goods, have symbolic meanings for users. Electronics represent an essential aspect of the modern world and its material culture. Current globalization processes transmit the cultures of the producing, developed nations (principally Europe and North America) to local milieux where they are admired as the ideal. Aspects of modern and/or Western culture that are transmuted into the local scene blend with the local experience. Consequently, the blended international-local experience uniquely transforms into a 'glocal' phenomenon, expressing the local interpretation of modern culture. Simply put, the 'glocalization' of diffused modernity presents unique elements of the local culture, conveying contextual and locally defined embedded meanings even when the diffused modern culture is dominant (Wagner 2011; Achterberg, Heilbron, Houtman and Aupers 2011; Krossa 2009; Roudometof 2005; Sheppard 2002).

The presence of electronic gadgets in everyday human relations, both within the house and in the outside world, accentuates particular culture-bound meanings (Money 2007). In Nigeria, electronic gadgets, as elements of the modern world, transmit meanings of being up-to-date, civilized and modern. Depending on social class and other factors, electronic gadgets confer prestige on their owners. The arrangement and furnishing of a home is not complete without television sets, DVD players and sound systems, especially in the living room. (Those who can afford air-conditioners also tend to install them in the living room).

The next point in the home is the kitchen, where an average middle-class family would want to have a blender, microwave oven, refrigerator, deep freezer, electric cooker and other necessary gadgets – not just for their functionality, but as social class indicators. It is expected that bedrooms should be equipped with some further electronic appliances ranging from television sets, radios and such other gadgets as may be deemed fit and affordable. The advent of the GSM mobile phone has democratized access and usage of the telephone, which was hitherto the exclusive preserve of the privileged class. Phones complement everyday fashion and interaction as means of communication and symbolic expression of class, wealth and power – and especially in Nigeria (Obadare 2006; Smith 2006).

Thus, as much as electronic items are essential gadgets for particular purposes and functions, they are also infused with meanings. It is not sufficient to have a television set; the brand, make and type matters. Whether it is a popular British, American, Japanese or Korean make indicates distinctions of class.[2] American, British and Japanese products are con-

2 South Korean television sets, DVD players and cell phones are quite popular in contemporary Nigerian markets. Consumers consider them to be of lower quality to most American, British and Japanese brands. In terms of relative quality, standard

sidered to be of very high quality and are very expensive in the electronics market.[3] Their prices range from as much as 50 to 200 per cent more than those of the Korean brands. Korean electronic brands, such as Samsung and LG, have gained relative popularity, especially among the middle class because they are relatively affordable and they carry features that many customers consider attractive. The features matter in the symbolic codification of the user as being modern, up-to-date and elite. For example, it is not enough to have a colour television set, the type says a lot about the owner too. Flat-screen television sets impressively hung on the wall of a living room with booming hoofer systems around them (or a complete 'home theatre') together with a split air-conditioner making the room cool give the successful professional an aura of dignity. The possessions represent success on the 'home front'.

Outside the home, mobile phones generally confer some respect on the owner. Phone aesthetics and extra features such as a camera, internet capability, a touch-screen, recording functions, a radio function, social networking and Bluetooth, among others, impact on the social value placed on a phone and the user.[4] Of course, the make also matters. Mobile phone brands that are popular in Nigeria are BlackBerry, Nokia, Sony Ericsson, LG and Samsung (both BlackBerry and Nokia attract consumer preference over other brands). These brands are considered to be original. Depending on the accompanying features, the prices of mobile phones range from ₦5,000 to ₦100,000 (US$33 to US$666) or even more.

---

and affordability, Korean electronic goods have gained great customer preference and loyalty, especially among middle-income earners who can buy them new. If the option is for *tokunbo* second-hand, consumers prefer European, American and Japanese brands, because of the general notion that brands of these developed countries have greater durability.

3 Japanese electronic goods are more popular than American and British ones. Nevertheless, because second-hand electronic items are mostly imported from North America, they are considered 'Western' goods, even though they have an Asian origin.

4 Lately, BlackBerry phones have gained popular consumer usage and are a status symbol in Nigeria (see Tade and Adekoya 2012; Akpan-Obong 2010).

On the other hand, Chinese phones are also readily available; and their prices range from just ₦1,500 to ₦12,000 (US$10 to US$80), depending on the features. The most expensive *Chinco* phones purportedly have the same features as the more expensive popular brands. The *Chinco* features are considered to be of poor quality, however. Though *Chinco* handsets provide mobile phone access and ownership to low-income earners who desire to have the features of the more expensive brands in their reach, the handsets are very much derided, and middle-class professionals would never want to be seen using *Chinco* phones because of anticipated slurs on their prestige, image, business and profession. Frequently supposed middle-income earners who use *Chinco* phones are taunted for being too stingy to spend funds on accessories that physically and materially denote their class. *Chinco* phones are primarily used for communication purposes and do not socially reflect class, power or a call for respect.

People's need to access modern electronic equipment and make a statement about their real or perceived class and status makes the imported second-hand electronics market a definite option to consider. This is especially so for customers who desire a particular electronic gadget with aesthetic features symbolically associated with class, status and power but who cannot afford it new. The imported second-hand electronics market serves as a melting-pot. It attracts customers across classes. In terms of utilization and accompanying social status, it serves as a leveller across class boundaries. A new BlackBerry phone could cost as much as ₦40,000 to ₦100,000 (US$266 to US$666). In the second-hand market, however, it can be acquired for as little as ₦8,000 to ₦12,000 (US$53 to US$80). Likewise a new 42-inch flat-screen television with a market value of between ₦120,000 and ₦200,000 (US$800 to US$1,333) can be bought second-hand for between ₦15,000 and ₦20,000 (US$100 to US$133). Irrespective of the difference in price, both the new and the used gadgets elicit a similar degree of social appreciation, so long as the source of purchase is not disclosed and the gadget itself looks new and is in a good working condition. A second-hand user wanting to bolster his prestige simply claims that 'a close relative abroad' sent the appliance to him.

At minimal cost, consumers are able to access goods conveying the desired messages about status. Symbolically the goods exemplify imaginary attainment to the class of the privileged. Outsiders, having no close or deep insight into particular consumers' real socio-economic status, view and assess them on the basis of the electronic gadgets in their houses and the mobile phones and equipment they carry around. These things boost the respect the consumers are accorded and their socio-psychological status, the assumption being that they are members of the privileged class.

Efforts of consumers to access good quality electronic goods capable of satisfying the primary function for which they are produced and to convey high social status, contribute tremendously to the growth of the electronics second-hand market. The principal second-hand electronics markets are located in Lagos. They are Alaba International Market, Westminster Electronics Market and the 'Computer Village'. Alaba International Market is the biggest of the three. Several tonnes of second-hand electronic appliances of various brands and makes are brought into the markets weekly. The scene in the markets is a crowded space strewn with second-hand computer desktops, laptops, printers, television sets, DVD players, electric irons, vacuum cleaners, washing machines and all sorts of household electrical appliances. The markets attract customers from across Nigeria and West Africa. In Ibadan, second-hand electronic goods are principally sold at Iwo Road. Other points of sale can be found around the Dugbe, Ring Road and Challenge areas of the city. The second-hand electronic goods markets in Abeokuta usually follow the periodic market systems in the city. Abeokuta markets periodically operate on a five-day-a-week basis. Illustration 4 shows *tokunbo* electronic gadgets displayed for sale in Abeokuta, Nigeria.

Illustration 4 *Imported second-hand electronic goods displayed for sale at a market in Abeokuta*

Second-hand electronics markets display both 'tested' and 'not-tested' gadgets. Tested gadgets carry more value and are costlier than the 'not-tested' ones. A marketer allows a would-be customer to test the functionality of a 'tested' model but does not allow this with 'not-tested' goods. In actual fact, the 'not-tested' gadgets are ones that the marketer has indeed tested, but he has discovered that they are irreparable or too expensive to repair. He therefore displays them as 'not-tested', hoping to sell them cheaply in order either to recoup the cost of purchase or add to the profit he can make on the tested gadgets. An unwary customer who opts for the 'not-tested' because of the cheap price bears the consequences. It is likely that he/she will be buying a non-functional, irreparable or expensive-to-repair bit of e-waste. Of course, once bought, the item cannot be returned and the money paid cannot be refunded. Additionally, it is important to note that the patronage of 'not tested' wares carries some social dimensions. The 'not tested' tends to attract customers who are unable to afford the more expensive 'tested' gadgets. Apparently they purchase the 'not tested' item in the hope that they will be able to fix it and find some use for it. Of course, if it is successfully fixed, the 'not tested' gadget adds to the social value of the consumer. Even if the gadget is irreparable, a wily consumer may still conspicuously display it as evidence of social relevance by leveraging class disparity, using the gadget 'carcass' as a symbol of prestige, especially when it involves an outsider who is unaware of the true state of the appliance. Should an inquisitive visitor ask about the condition of the gadget, a stock deceptive response would be to say that it had just developed some fault and will soon be fixed, or that a damaged part in it is very scarce and rather difficult to get hold of. Furthermore, it is also important to note that the 'not tested' items provide a handy source of spare parts for those who repair electronic appliances. That both 'tested' and 'not tested' goods attract patronage attests to the peripheral nature of electronics consumption in Nigeria, where even disused second-hand electronic items find buyers in the second-hand market.

Ultimately both the 'tested' and 'not-tested' contribute to the swelling e-waste in Nigeria. Full statistics of the amounts of e-waste in the country are as yet unavailable. A recent report, however, indicates that 40 million tonnes of e-waste are generated in Lagos annually (Echenim 2011; see also Greenpeace 2009b; and Schmidt 2006). This is indeed a huge quantity. It is even more worrisome that the figure is just for Lagos: the e-waste outlook would look worse if statistics were available for other big cities in Nigeria. What is really happening is that Nigeria, along with some other developing nations, is serving the developed world as the epicentre for the discarding of toxic e-waste. Schmidt (2006: A234) reports that 25 to 75 per cent of used electronic items shipped to Nigeria are 'irreparable junk'. He adds that shipping a 40-foot container of used electronic goods costs only US$5,000; so a few working gadgets in the whole container can pay for the entire shipment. Nigerian importers therefore pay the cost of the evacuation of the e-waste from the developed world to their country, and at the same time the challenge of managing the e-waste and the accompanying possible health implications is transferred to Nigeria as well. Of course, the shipment cost is transferred to consumers, while the populace also bears the economic and health cost of e-waste at its toxic end. In addition, the continual transfer of e-waste to Nigeria to supply re-usable alternatives to new products impacts negatively on the country's productive sector and its capability of producing electronic gadgets itself. Nigeria has simply become a dumping ground for e-waste at the expense of the country's productive economy and development.

In summary, Nigeria has always imported electronic goods. Two computer manufacturing (assembly) companies – namely OMATEK Computers and Zinox Technologies Limited – have opened up in Nigeria within the last decade. The products of these companies are not cheaper than the imported popular brands. Hence, most Nigerians are inclined to stick to the brands they have come to trust over the years. Unable to afford new products, they find that the imported second-hand is the rational alternative that satisfies their needs. Electronic goods, including household appliances, ICT gadgets and other electrically powered appliances convey varying degrees of comfort and status. The presence of a colour television set, DVD player, electric cooker and microwave oven in a household conveys the meaning that the owners live well. The same applies to individual ownership of cell phones and digital cameras. Though most middle-income earners could readily afford new brands of these appliances, low-income earners seeking access to them must normally turn to the imported second-hand markets. Significantly, both low- and middle-income earners acknowledge the quality of *tokunbo* electronic goods. Besides, the *tokunbo* markets parade the favourite brands Nigerians have popularly constructed as quality and status symbols. A Phillips, Sharp or Sony flat-screen TV that a consumer finds unaffordable at a shop selling new television sets is available at 10 per cent of the original price in the *tokunbo* market. Similarly, a consumer can purchase a BlackBerry phone there at 5 to 10 per cent of the price of a new one. Then, so long as the *tokunbo* substitute remains functional, it conveys a degree of social dignity and worth similar to possession of the new. Domestically and in public, *tokunbo* consumers are able to flaunt electronic gadgets that carry out their uses and are also capable of conveying socially constructed symbolic meanings, emphasizing a degree of elitism, whatever their real socio-economic position. Hence, though *tokunbo* goods are used, they are socio-psychologically reconstructed as 'new' and celebrated and appreciated as such. A major downside of imported second-hand electronic items, however, is that they are progressively swelling e-waste, even as Nigeria is fast becoming a major e-waste dump for the developed world.

CHAPTER 10

The *Tokunbo* Second-Hand Economy: Clothes

Along with the markets for used automobiles, spare car parts and electronic goods, there is a global trade in second-hand clothes, and this is also popular and profitable: it attracts huge patronage among low- and middle-income earners. The major supply countries are the United States of America, Great Britain, Germany and other states in Western Europe. Empirical evidence reveals that, lately, the Nigerian second-hand clothing market has also been receiving supplies (usually of lower quality) from South Korea. These come through the Republic of Benin. The USA alone supplies about US$1 billion worth of second-hand clothes annually to the global market (Czaga and Fliess 2005; Thomas 2003) and the whole global trade is estimated at being worth over US$1.4 billion (Baden and Barber 2005). In actual monetary value, this figure is just a fraction of US sales of new clothes, which amount to about US$150 billion per year (Czaga and Fliess 2005) and the global trade of about US$200 billion (Baden and Barber 2005). In real terms, however, the volume of used clothes exported to the global market is very considerable. Given the fact that second-hand clothing goes for just about US$80 (£50) per tonne (McVeigh 2009) and that, in the recipient countries, the clothes cost about 5 to 10 per cent of their original values, it can be asserted that the volume of second-hand clothing in the global market is really huge. Second-hand clothing is packaged in bales of 50–55 kg (Chris Carey's Collections 2010; Field et al. 2007). A tonne thus contains about 20 bales with each bale of clothing having a net cost of around US$4. Each bale contains between 400 and 500 garments of varying makes, sizes and colours. A ton could contain about 10,000 clothes.

The export of second-hand clothes from the supplying countries is usually accounted for as being a response to shortage of landfills, as well as a charity offering to make textiles available in places where there are shortages, and also a means of profit maximization (Hansen 2004). Hawley (2006) has described the second-hand clothing business as 'digging for diamonds'. This phrase aptly describes the economic benefit of second-hand clothing merchandise in both the supplying and recipient countries. He states (Hawley 2006: 262–263):

> The process of recycling and reclaiming textiles affects many entities and contributes significantly, in a broader sense, to the social responsibility of the textile and apparel industries ... textile recycling can contribute to larger profits because landfill costs are avoided. But the recycling of textiles also contributes to goodwill associated with environmentalism, employment for marginally employable labourers, charity contribution, disaster relief, and the movement of used clothing to areas of the world where it is needed ... Western lifestyle is a significant contributor to landfill waste. Not only are products consumed at high levels, but Western goods are often overpackaged, which contributes even more to the waste stream ... As landfill capacity continues to be scarce, the costs of dumping will continue to rise. These rising costs continue to be of concern for businesses as they seek ways to reduce the overhead cost.

Even though Africa receives the poorest quality second-hand clothing compared to other parts of the Third World (Hansen 2004), the importance of the trade there is underscored by the sheer popularity and high levels of consumption of imported second-hand clothing across the continent. Peck and Pinto (2003) estimate that about 90 per cent of Angolans wear second-hand clothes; Baden and Barber (2005) give the same figure for Ghanaians; and in Kenya, Mangieri (2006) reports that national dailies describe *mitumba* (second-hand-clothing) as the Kenyan national dress. In Senegal, Scheld (2007) describes how youths in the cosmopolitan city of Dakar use second-hand clothing to portray their urban identity and differentiate themselves from the 'backward' village youth. Finally, Velia, Valodia and Amisi (2006) have discussed used clothes trade dynamics in Durban, South Africa (for similar cases on video, see Aljazeera 2010; Youtube 2009 f and g).

The use of second-hand clothing in Nigeria dates back to the colonial era. It was a culture transferred from Great Britain, which had a second-hand textile industry dating from the seventeenth Century (Lemire

1988). Second-hand clothes gained popularity during World War II and the immediate post-war period, when the British government controlled exports of new goods to its colonies due to domestic shortages (see DCI 1/1 File No. 4032/C.7). The immediate post-independence period (especially 1960–1979) saw a period of boom and the preferred new textiles were once again accessible and affordable. With new imports readily available, imported second-hand clothes were derided as the clothes worn by low-income earners. The second-hand clothes market was termed *bosikoro* ('go to a hidden place'). This simply describes how uncomfortable people felt about buying second-hand clothes at this period. Of course, the market was still patronized openly by the poor and by low-income earners; but a consumer with a higher status to preserve would not want to be associated with second-hand textiles and would avoid being seen at the market by any acquaintances. The values around imported second-hand clothes began to change from the 1990s and the market is no longer described as *bosikoro*. Imported second-hand clothes are now called *tokunbo* and they attract consumers across class and socio-economic groups. Figure 8 (p. 118) shows the flow chain of second-hand clothes into and in Nigeria.

The second-hand clothes flow chain starts with the donation of used clothes by consumers in Europe and North America. The clothes are deposited in large bins, mostly provided by charities and not-for-profit organizations, which are placed in strategic places. When collected, the clothes are sorted and packaged into bales. Because existing laws in Nigeria class used clothes as prohibited items, the bales are shipped first to the Republic of Benin and then are smuggled into Nigeria by professional crossers. Once successfully over the border, the second-hand clothes get into the markets and are 'protected' from customs officials and other security agents. Retailers open the bales and sort the clothes into Grades A, B and C. Grade A looks quite new and unused. Grade B has been used but is still sufficiently good for re-use and may hardly be detected as used by the uninformed public. Finally, clothes that are torn and stained are categorized as Grade C. Consumers buy from virtually all the grades, depending on their purchasing powers.

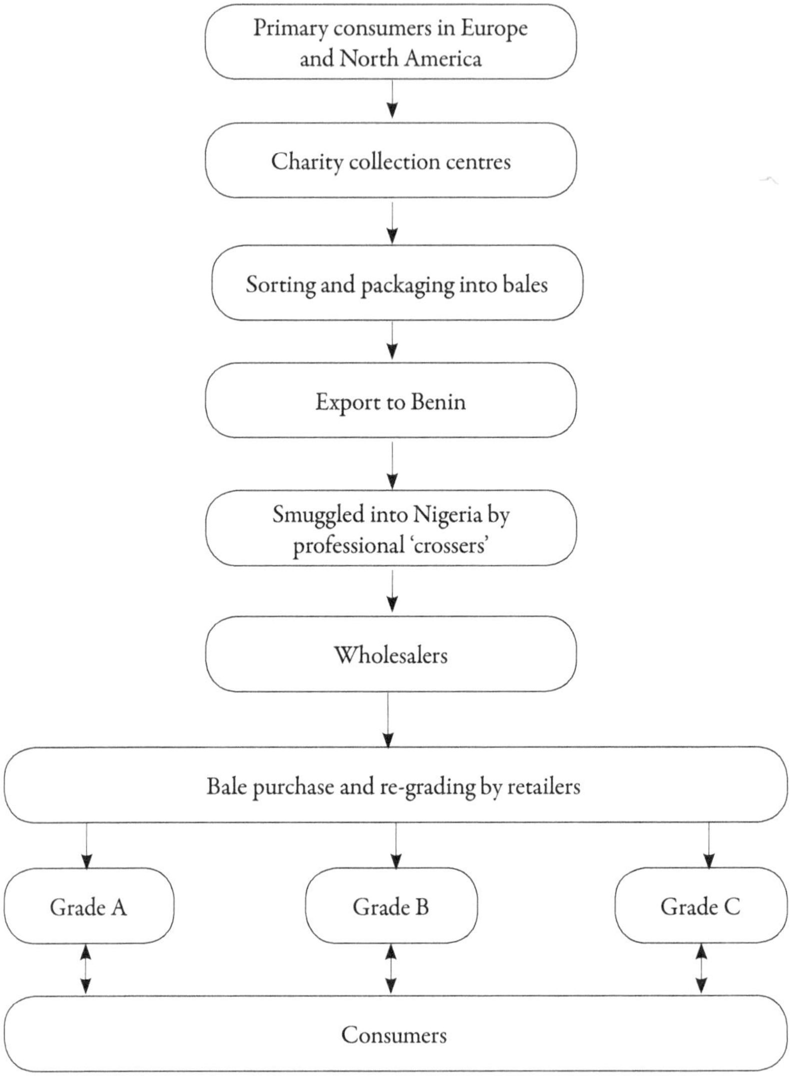

Figure 8 *The second-hand clothes flow chain*

The Republic of Benin serves as a major transit economy for second-hand clothes bound for Nigeria. Informants in Benin and Nigeria claim that 90 per cent of the second-hand clothes imported to Benin are smuggled into Nigeria. Transporting consignments to Nigeria is the responsibility of professional crossers who also have special networks to help them get past security agencies and border patrols. Crossers charge between ₦5,000 (US$33) and ₦10,000 (US$66) per bale. From Benin, crossers transport the goods to Mile 2 in Lagos, where consigned people collect them. From Mile 2, the second-hand clothes are taken to the various markets round South-Western Nigeria. In Lagos, the major second-hand clothes markets are Kotangora and Yaba. The major second-hand clothes market in Ibadan is located at Dugbe, while second-hand clothes markets move rotationally between the Lafenwa and Kuto markets in Abeokuta. Quite apart from the major markets, there are small-scale second-hand clothes markets dotted about in various parts of these cities.

The markets in Lagos are more structured and organized than those of Ibadan and Abeokuta. Both Kotangora and Yaba have wholesalers, retailers, touting agents and tailors. The wholesalers are the 'big time' second-hand clothes entrepreneurs; they control most of the lock-up shops in the markets. Wholesalers sell in bales. Each bale costs between ₦30,000 (US$200) and ₦45,000 (US$300) depending on the source, type and quality of ware. This represents 4,900 per cent to 7,400 per cent value appreciation from barely US$4 per bale at the point of initial export in Europe or North America. The wholesalers largely control the market. They hardly participate in daily market transactions as they have their own employees, ranging from accountants, store keepers and agents; but they do move from one shop to another supervising and observing sales.

John is a wholesaler who allowed me to interview him and observe his goods and transactions on condition that his voice would not be recorded, because (as he admitted) his goods are contraband. Aged forty-seven, John has been in business since 1993. He gets his goods from the United Kingdom and ships them via the Republic of Benin. He has thirty-seven people in his employment, including people with university degrees. (One of them, who serves as manager, holds a Masters degree in Public Administration; there is also a qualified accountant.)

I inspected the bales in John's shops. Labels on the bales show that they originated from popular second-hand exporters in the United Kingdom. John claims that he has contacts in the customs service, the police, the immigration service and the military: they all provide cover for his business. He claims that he does not fear or foresee any punitive action from security agencies. If any security agent should seize his goods, all he needs to do is to put a call through to the appropriate quarters, and all his goods will be immediately released with an apology.

Retailers source their goods from the wholesalers. They open the bales and regrade them on the basis of texture and quality; those that look very new, with tags still attached, are described as 'factory return' and are graded as A. Informants and retailers who were interviewed described 'factory return' as defective clothes (for example, ones with missed button holes, unequal sleeves, or dot stains) or clothes that were not sold at the end of particular fashion seasons. Such clothes are sometimes repackaged and displayed in boutiques as 'new'. The second category is Grade B, which includes clothes that have obviously been used but are still good. Depending on the quality, such garments can still be washed, ironed and repacked as 'new' in boutiques. The last category is Grade C, which consists of second-hand clothes that are stained or torn. Though damaged, Grade C clothes still attract customers. The wares are subsequently hung up in shops or spread on the floor for potential customers to make their selection. Retailers claim that they make up to 100 per cent of the cost of *tokunbo* clothing in profits and that already by the time a bale's grade A has been sold there is some gain.

Touting agents are strategically positioned at the market entrance to solicit customers. They plead with customers to patronize their shops, presenting themselves as shop owners. They then guide willing customers to their masters' shops, participate in the bargaining process, and later collect commissions from shop owners for their services. They are pivotal to the market processes because they serve as informal advertising agents and marketers to shop owners, and direct customers to the points of sale.

Finally, tailors have their stands at strategic locations in the market. They alter clothes to suit the customers and repair minor defects. Their services are vital in the market because they provide the strategic function of fixing and mending, to the wishes of customers, who can then happily take home clothes that fit perfectly, which they wear to the admiration of those in their immediate social environment.

The markets in Ibadan and Abeokuta operate at lower scales. When I visited, I did not notice wholesalers or touting agents at either of them. However, tailors, who perform similar functions to those at Lagos, were strategically located within the markets. Most of the sellers there are retailers and they source their goods from wholesale points in Lagos or directly from Benin. Interviewees from Ibadan and Abeokuta affirmed that they source their goods mostly from Lagos due to the risk involved in cross-border transportation. Dugbe second-hand clothing market is located in the heart of Ibadan's central business district; it is a sprawling place with shopping complexes up to three or four storeys high. Most of the shop lots are locked up because retail traders cannot afford the rent charges, which range from ₦100,000 (US$666) to ₦300,000 (US$2,000) per annum. So wares are spread under makeshift sheds and on the bare floor, or are hung on the walls of temporary shops within the premises of the shopping complexes. The few retailers who can afford lock-up shops in the shopping complexes display their wares inside. In Abeokuta, as stated earlier, the second-hand markets periodically move between the Lafenwa and Kuto markets. They do so on a five-day rotation. Most of the retailers come from Lagos, which is 77.66 kilometres distant.

Illustration 5 shows Kotangora market in Lagos and gives some idea of the colourful scene in these places.

Illustration 5 *A view of Kotangora second-hand clothing market, Lagos*

The imported second-hand clothing market allows access to popular fashion brands at very cheap prices. Consumers appreciate a good buy, especially if it is a grade A or a grade B item that is still sufficiently good. At prices 8 to 10 per cent of the cost of new garments (see Table 5), imported second-hand clothing stands as the rational alternative, symbolically conveying values associated with clothes of the same brand and fashion. Again, these *tokunbo* clothes are preferred over the low-quality ones from China that can be as much as 250 per cent dearer. Chinese fabrics may start fading and breaking almost from the first wash. In addition, second-hand clothing displays popular fashion names that command respect and appreciation in Nigeria's consumer culture. Brand names such as Atmosphere, Next, Cezani, St. Michael, Taylor and Wright and Dunnes serve purposes beyond ordinary brand identification: they serve as status symbols, especially among middle-class professionals whose jobs demand formal dressing. Employee fashion tends to represent an organization's success in the eyes of the public, and it has the potential of attracting customers (Veen, Bezemer and Karsten 2011; Fincham and Roslender 2004; Scarbrough 2002/2003; Benders and Veen 2001). Hence, second-hand clothing markets attract even middle- and high- income consumers desiring to buy, at minimal cost, the brands that reflect social appreciation within their working environments. Such consumers prefer the grade As, which can be described as 'unused', especially if a garment still carries the tag, even though the tag may have been attached by the retailer.[1]

In the course of the research for this book, I bought some samples of second-hand clothes and later enquired about the prices of the new versions from consumers and sellers who had a good knowledge of the trends in fashion. The reaction was that the labels were those of top-rated clothiers popular among middle- and high-income professionals who are very fashion-conscious. Table 5 shows how the prices compare between

1 As explained later, brand tags of popular fashion designs are commonly sold at second-hand markets in Lagos. A crafty (or unscrupulous) retailer simply purchases the tags, attaches them to neat *tokunbo* clothes and presents the clothes as 'new' or as 'factory-return'. Such clothes may also be displayed in boutiques as new garments.

used (*tokunbo*) samples and new samples of popular labels of shirts and blouses. The 'new' prices are estimates and these are only moderate, put generally on the low side. A search through the web pages of the popular brands shows that new clothes of similar design can cost as much as 70 per cent to 150 per cent more than these estimates!

Table 5 *Labels and their comparative prices – tokunbo and (estimated) new*
Source: Fieldwork 2010

SHIRTS			BLOUSES		
Label	*Tokunbo*	New	Label	*Tokunbo*	New
Dunnes Stores	₦200 (US$1.3)	₦3,000 (US$20)	Per una	₦300 (US$2)	₦2,500 (US$16.6)
William	₦300 (US$2)	₦3,000 (US$20)	Next	₦300 (US$2)	₦2,000 (US$13.3)
Cedarwood State	₦200 (US$1.3)	₦2,500 (US$16.6)	Atmosphere	₦300 (US$2)	₦2,800 (IS$18.6)
Easycare	₦300 (US$2)	₦2,000 (US$13.3)	Joanneh	₦300 (US$2)	₦2,500 (US$16.6)
Claiborne	₦300 (US$2)	₦2,500 (US$16.6)	Evans	₦300 (US$2)	₦2,500 (US$16.6)
Van Heusen	₦300 (US$2)	₦1,800 (US$ 12)	Jones New York	₦300 (US$2)	₦2,500 (US$16.6)
Wrinkle Free	₦300 (US$2)	₦2,500 (US$16.6)	Omega	₦300 (US$2)	₦2,500 (US$16.6)
Barisal	₦400 (US$2.6)	₦3,000 (US$20)	Augusta	₦300 (US$2)	₦2,500 (US$16.6)
Cezani	₦400 (US$2.6)	₦3,000 (US$20)	Dunnes Stores	₦300 (US$2)	₦3,000 (US$20)
Taylor & Wright	₦400 (US$2.6)	₦3,000 (US$20)	Marks and Spencer	₦300 (US$2)	₦5000 (US$33)
Dunnes Stores	₦400 (US$2.6)	₦3,000 (US$20)	Next	₦300 (US$2)	₦3,500 (US$23.3)
Dunnes	₦400 (US$2.6)	₦3,000 (US$20)	Jean-Marc-Philippe	₦300 (US$2)	₦2,500 (US$16.6)

Even though the price of second-hand clothing goes up hugely between the point of export and at the points of sale in the second-hand markets of Nigeria, the clothes are still very much cheaper than new clothes. Second-hand clothing still conveys the social standing that is attached to their brand labels. Popular fashion labels carry a high degree of social appreciation. For this reason, unattached label tags of popular designers are readily available in Nigeria's second-hand markets. Consumers buy label tags to attach to clothes that have been sewn, bought new or purchased from the market. The labels enhance the social value attached to the clothes and the wearer, even when they have only been added on later.

Consumers generally attest to the quality of imported second-hand clothing. According to an interviewee:

> I prefer imported second-hand clothing to the new clothes that are locally available. The quality of second-hand clothes is a lot better, while most of the locally available new clothes are substandard. The new clothes are packaged to deceive the customers. After the first wash, the texture and the colour of the clothes wane. *Tokunbo* clothing saves money especially if one cannot afford good quality new clothes. (Male IDI/ *Tokunbo* clothes consumer/Abeokuta/31 August 2010)

Another interviewee from Abeokuta states:

> The way people overseas use clothes differ from the way we use clothes in Nigeria. They use washing machines to wash clothes while the environments where they work and recreate are friendly, not damaging, to clothes. Abroad, children play on grass, while in Nigeria they play on sand. All these have implications for the clothing … *Tokunbo* second-hand clothing satisfies my need because they are cheaper. One could buy cloth [a garment] for as low as ₦100 (US$0.6) or ₦200 (US$1.3), depending on the type. *Tokunbo* second-hand clothes satisfy me because they last longer than most of the available new clothes that easily fade. *Tokunbo* second-hand clothing is good quality clothing. (Female IDI/T*okunbo* clothes consumer/Abeokuta/2 September 2010)

Information from other interviews corroborates the above. A female middle-class professional, who confided that she sold second-hand clothes to make extra income while at university, affirmed the quality of *tokunbo* clothes. She maintained that she still uses nice and beautiful *tokunbo* clothes, to the admiration of her colleagues. She states that:

> A lot of people patronize *tokunbo* clothes because of their high quality. People know that *tokunbo* clothes last longer than clothes manufactured in Nigeria. They are even more economical: you get more value for your money. For example, if you bought a *tokunbo* blouse for N700 (US$4.6), you would be surprised that a new cloth [garment] that is not as good will go for N3,500 (US$23.3). So, why waste your money? *Tokunbo* cloth is more valuable and you will get your desired result. It is nice, beautiful; you will be satisfied and you will use it over a longer period of time ... In fact, I have made up my mind that I will not buy all those so called China products that they bring to us, that do not have any quality, as long as I am doing my shopping in Nigeria. If I travel to a place like Dubai, or another country where I can get good quality cheaply, then I would buy new clothes ... Do not be surprised that even some people who run boutiques come for grade A, recycle them and display them as 'new' in their boutiques and sell each for as much as N3,500 (US$23.3) ... We females like going for nice things, ranging from clothes, shoes, scarves and brassieres. *Tokunbo* market allows access to all these at good prices and quality. (Female IDI/ T*okunbo* clothes consumer/Ibadan/28 August 2010)

All the data presented above confirm the consumer preference for *tokunbo* clothes. As far as the interviewees are concerned, as far as it is possible, the *tokunbo* clothing market is the place to get value for money. It is not an exclusive preserve of the poor but a melting pot for people across classes and socio-economic statuses. During the course of this study, I met professionals who prefer always to buy from the second-hand market. Ayo is a 26 year-old graduate student who admits that she has been using *tokunbo* clothes right from her pre-teen years. Ayo confirms that grade A is the best of all. She says she has many *tokunbo* clothes she has been wearing for more than four years, and they still look as though they are new. She affirms that she receives admiring comments from people when she wears them. She showed me a pair of Atmosphere combat trousers she bought in 2006 for ₦500 (US$3.3). She said that the quality – in terms of colour and texture – has remained intact. A new pair of trousers of the same type and quality would have cost her about ₦2,500 (US$16.6), while a cloned Chinese or Nigerian pair would have been about ₦1,200 (US$8).

Ayo notes that people can easily detect that the quality of new Chinese and Nigerian clones are substandard; and this attracts some social stigma among contemporaries. By contrast, *tokunbo* clothes are not stigmatized because the majority of people use them. They are considered clothes of higher quality. Ayo says that she meets a lot of her colleagues in the *tokunbo* market. Of course, these colleagues never openly disclose that they purchase their garments there. Everybody takes his or her pick, bargains, pays and moves on. Describing the quality of *tokunbo* clothes, Ayo says they are called *emi kan o loo tan* (meaning 'one life cannot exhaust its utility'). They are so described because, after prolonged use by a primary *tokunbo* wearer, they are given away or sold to someone else who can still find a use for them.

In summary, *tokunbo* clothes afford consumers access to popular fashion labels that ordinarily would be out of the reach of most of them. Popular fashion labels such as St. Michael, Dunnes, Atmosphere, Next, T. M., Calvin Klein, Easycare, Claiborne, Cezani and Taylor & Wright, among others, are at the top of the consuming public's preferences. Even when the clothes produced by these fashion labels are obviously worn, they are still very much appreciated because of the social value of good quality and because of the prestige attached to the labels among the consuming public and admirers within the immediate social environment. The value socially attached to the fashion designers and/or labels is transferred even to the label tags. Hence, such label tags are detached from clothes and openly traded in the second-hand markets, as is the case at Kotangora Market, Lagos. In fact, it is common practice for label tags purchased from the second-hand clothes markets to be attached to clothes that are produced by local tailors and such clothes are marketed to the unsuspecting public as 'new' garments produced by the designer on the fashion label. Besides, some customers, desperate to wear clothes with the highly valued labels, ask local tailors to make garments and attach one of the fashionable tags to them.

The general opinion of consumers is that the quality of *tokunbo* clothes, in terms of texture and colour, remains largely intact even after prolonged use and much laundering. *Tokunbo* clothes are a lot better than Nigerian and Chinese clothes, even when these latter are new. In contrast to other goods where consumers prefer European and/or American imports of used Japanese brands (as in the case of automobiles, automobile spare parts and electronic devices), the popular preference in clothes is for European labels (especially British) and American ones. This is largely due to the nation's colonial experience and the globalization process (aided by technological advances) that is dominated by the United States of America. The globalization process continually and effectively transfers reigning Western fashions and tastes to receptive consumers in Nigeria, who eagerly seek to satisfy their wish to keep in fashion through the second-hand market.

Recently, second-hand Korean clothes have gradually been penetrating Nigeria's second-hand market. Both sellers and buyers, however, affirm that used Korean clothes are lower in quality than those from other sources. Used Korean clothes largely come worn out, faded and torn. The entrance of low quality, damaged Korean clothing is a reflection of the pervasive and degrading poverty of many Nigerians. Korean bales are easily identifiable at the wholesale market since the bales bear the inscription and labels of the exporting organizations and countries; but once they get to the retail market, the Korean used clothes are mixed up with those from the West.

While used clothes of Korean origin usually fall into the lower strata of grades B and C due to their quality, they are part of the general *tokunbo* stock as far as the consuming public is concerned. This is because the consuming public (especially the poor majority) is hardly able to differentiate between the preferred *tokunbo* clothes imported from Western nations and the used clothes sourced from Korea: they all form part of the overall collection of *tokunbo* garments.[2] Inadvertently, the social value attached to *tokunbo* clothes in particular and *tokunbo* goods in general has created a market for poor, cheap and unpopular used clothes imported from Korea, which the consuming public ignorantly patronizes, thinking they are the valued *tokunbo*. That poor quality used clothes are bought and constructed as *tokunbo* reflects and confirms the social reality of poverty, especially among low-income groups and others at the most basic levels of survival, who find some use for torn and faded clothes and symbolically categorize them as *tokunbo* sufficiently good to wear.

Finally, middle-income professionals, whose corporate fashion normatively dictates Western formal wear, find the imported second-hand,

2 Most Korean clothes have Europeanized or Westernized nomenclature on their tags. The unsuspecting public is unable to differentiate them from Western used clothes without a close scrutiny of the tag. This is not often done at the point of purchase, as the buyer concentrates on picking and bargaining what seems an attractive choice.

especially grade A, a truly viable alternative. This is not to say that all, or most, middle-income professionals buy second-hand. Nevertheless, the fact that Nigerians across the social strata have their wardrobes stocked with *tokunbo* clothes and imported second-hand accessories (belts, shoes and even underwear) is a social reality that the interviewees for this research have also acknowledged and affirmed. Though these goods are used, they enhance the possibility of modernity in the contemporary globalized age. This is further discussed in the next chapter.

CHAPTER 11

The *Tokunbo* Economy and 'Glocalized' Modernity

The *Tokunbo* economy is a 'glocal' representation of the globalization process in Nigeria. It serves an essential purpose of ensuring access to consumer goods, for the working class and for many people from the middle and upper classes. It allows modernity practice across these classes, and bridges the gap between the elite and less privileged groups – especially as regards access to modernity. Modernity practice refers to the overt and covert expression and/or utilization of material and immaterial aspects of Western culture to denote a belonging to the contemporary scene and activity within it. In Global South countries, modernity as expressed Westernization is not indigenous, but diffused from the core countries of the Global North. As such, modernity practice in the Global South is 'imitated' (Schifirnet 2012) with the West setting the basic, ultimate standard, but it is also infused with elements of the recipient cultures.

Modernity is basically an embodiment of Western culture. It indicates a progression made from traditionalism and archaism to being contemporaneous and up-to-date. Of course, this 'contemporaneousness' and 'up-to-dateness' is defined by Western societies, the primary custodians of modernity (Schifirnet 2012; Smith 2010; Domingues 2009, 2002; Kaya 2004; Eisenstadt 2001). Eisenstadt (2010: 3) notes: 'Modernity has indeed expanded to most of the world and given rise to civilization patterns which share some central core characteristics, but which unfold differently even if with cognate ideological and institutional dynamics. Moreover, far-reaching changes, beyond the original premises of modernity, have also been taking place in Western societies.'

The globalization process has aided the spread of modernity and thus of Western culture universally.[1] Aided by advances in information and communications technology (ICT) (Ball, Dworkin and Vryonides 2010; Vogiatzoglou 2009; Abraham 2008; Lahlou 2008; Ya'u 2004; Shrum 2005; Thune and Welle-Strand 2005; James 2001), the globalization process has diffused modernity across the countries of the world, even as world cultures are increasingly fusing into one, though with Western culture taking the lead. Peoples and individuals fuse elements of the local culture into globalized modernity, forming unique cultural experiences and interpretations that have been defined in the literature as 'glocalization' (Achterberg, Heilbron, Houtman and Aupers 2011; Krossa 2009; Hung, Li and Belk 2007; Giulianotti and Robertson 2007, 2006, 2004; Roudometof 2005; Ritzer 2003; Giulianotti 2002, 1995; Bauman 1998). It is therefore imperative to understand the 'glocalization' of modernity in order to fully appreciate the local expression or dimension of globalized modernity. Stressing this, Martinelli (2003a: 292) states:

> Today globalization implies not only the emergence of a new object of study, the world as such, but requires that any specific study be framed in a global context, since each part of the world is increasingly interdependent with many others and the world as such is increasingly present in all of its parts. The contemporary world looks more and more like a laser beam hologram, where every point contains the information of the whole, since each human being increasingly tends to consume information and resources coming from everywhere. Hence there is the need to shift the level of analysis at the global level and to take a world system perspective in any study. The study of world society and its relations with national and local social realities should become a central theme of research. The higher the degree of interconnectedness of social relations at the world level, the greater the need to analyse the links between global social reality and multiple local social realities. 'Glocal' is an increasingly relevant neologism in our lexicon. At the cultural level we must analyse the many ways in which the unity and the diversity of the world combine and collide; at the social level we should investigate the many manifestations of complementarity and antagonism of social action in the global arena.

1 Africa was introduced into the globalization process right from the period of merchant capitalism and the slave trade (see Wallerstein 1980, 1976; Rodney 1973).

In Nigeria, the imported second-hand economy, popularly called *tokunbo*, represents a 'glocal' dimension of the modern economy and culture. *Tokunbo* sustains modernity practice, following its dynamic forms across classes in spite of Nigeria's dismal economic profile, which might otherwise have constrained modernity practice across the population, and have thereby confined it to the wealthy upper classes only. The 'glocal' picture of modernity in Nigeria cannot be dissociated from the social construction and reconstruction of *tokunbo*. Having shifted its meaning from a human nomenclature to a tag for imported second-hand goods, '*tokunbo*' depicts the standard people aspire to, and also perceived class, quality, affluence, power and, in the final analysis, modernity.

Due to the values attached to it, *tokunbo* conveys a degree of social consciousness that emphasizes its association with the Western world, and thus with modernity. When used as a tag for imported second-hand goods, *tokunbo* ensures a non-stigmatized access and utilization of these goods, which convey values associated with modernity. *Tokunbo* goods represent the material aspect of modernity and Western culture most accessible to Nigerians across social class boundaries and socio-economic groups.

When asked which aspects of Western culture they most appreciated, interviewees indicated that they appreciated above all: Western education, the English language, and dress, cars and electronic devices. Western education gives the foundation for social formation into the 'modern being'. It serves the purpose of equipping people with the skills they need to move up the social ladder or to secure and sustain at least a middle-class position. Education is in itself a status symbol, and is also potentially a springboard for social networking and integration into the privileged class, and a possible guarantee of access to modern material and immaterial culture.

Unfortunately however, public primary and secondary education in Nigeria is in a deplorable condition. Private educators have taken the centre stage for providing schooling. A casual observation indicates that private schools are socially structured in such a way that each socio-economic group has some sets of schools whose fees are more or less within parents' means. Simply put, the private school system represents social class positioning of parents. Irrespective of the parents' income levels, there is likely to be a school somewhere that can accommodate what they can pay. Hence, an average earner would rather put his/her ward in a private school than in a public school whose standard is largely bastardized. Nevertheless, it is important to note that public schools still attract patronage, especially among pupils and parents who cannot afford the fees charged in the private sector of education.

Though public schools are regulated by the government, people generally assume that private schools set standards that the public education system is unable to attain, due to the poor motivation of teachers and students, weak inspection of schools, and ineptitude and administrative corruption. All of these things, and others, bedevil the system. In this situation, many public pre-tertiary (both primary and secondary) schools in Nigeria turn out a class of poorly educated but literate young people who are recycled into the proletarian class, serving the interest of the privileged middle and upper classes as 'certificated' artisans, chauffeurs, commercial drivers, bus conductors, janitors, cleaners, messengers and so forth. The educational standards set by the private schools are measured by how much modern culture can be imparted to the student, along with academic learning. The 'modern' young person is the one who can speak good English, wear nice Western clothes and observe basic Western etiquette. The private school is expected to internalize modern culture in its students, both consciously and unconsciously, otherwise the fees paid would be considered a waste. Hence, along with socialization processes at home and across the social environment, the child grows up to become an adult with internalized modern values, yearning to be Western in outlook in order to escape the possibility of being grouped among the 'uncultured low class' who are thought of as exhibiting the so-called 'primitive' character of the 'native'.

Education places and sustains people in the middle class, irrespective of different income levels across sectors of the economy (Lehmann 2009; Kaufman 2005). The middle class consciously and unconsciously creates and re-creates the dominant values and cultural norms that sustain the status quo and/or bring about change (Polanska 2010; Thies 2007; Emmison 2003; Easterly 2001). The ingenuity of the middle class in generating and re-generating ideologies greatly impacts on the survival of an elite and on upward social mobility for both low and middle classes. Policies designed and implemented by the middle class, with the active support of the upper classes, determine the direction of the society to a major extent.

It might be practically impossible for the upper class to effect a transformative change without the active support of the middle class, who, as government officials and private sector managers, set the impetus going for the policy to be designed, adopted and implemented. The capability of the middle class to effect transformative changes makes it an essential structural element that can catalyse societal policy orientation and direction, and make or mar the interests of the lower and upper classes.

Bureaucratic structures are governed by meritocracy, impersonal relationships, specialization of duties, hierarchy and transparency – all supposedly ingrained elements of modernity and rationality (Courpasson and Clegg 2006; Casey 2004) – and the upper class appreciates the capability of the middle class to implement policy and manage the administrative technicalities and know-how it entails: it is well aware that the middle class can sustain or destroy its own (upper class) dominance and power. Wanting to maintain the status quo and remain the power elite and dominant group, the upper class takes special interest in the activities of the middle class, either subtly and/or aggressively constraining it through monitoring and sanctions and/or courting its support through material and immaterial rewards and social networking. By accommodating the middle class in upper-class networks, this ruling class appears to 'share' its power, allowing the middle class into the centres of power, even though in subordinate positions. And the middle class seeks to protect its interests too, through cooperation with the upper class, thus forming a seemingly broad-based 'elite group' with the middle class as the junior partner.

The middle class serves as the link between the upper class and the lower class. The lower class may not have direct access to the upper class but, at a distance, it aspires to the relative comfort of the middle class. Although the upper class may hold key infrastructures that drive the economy and societal development, it depends to quite a degree on the middle class for policy-making and management, letting the middle class strive to emulate the aesthetic and 'comfort' values it admires in their lifestyle. The middle class adopts these aesthetic and comfort values within the limits of its economic and purchasing power. Poised between the lower and upper classes, the middle class plays a major role in adopting the modern values that would put it in the 'comfort zone'. To do so with limited financial means, it has to improvise alternatives such as consumption of *tokunbo* goods (in the case of Nigeria) that can symbolically transmit these values. The capability of the middle class to acquire and utilize goods that reflect upper-class material culture, attracts lower class interest, and this class too seeks to emulate middle class taste. It wants to achieve some sorts of modernity, even when what is achieved does not, in the long run, depict modern standards in optimal forms. For example, focusing on the adoption of modern values among Thai villagers, Mills (2005: 386–387) states:

> Powerful ideals of progress, development, and modernity represent deeply desired standards of well-being for many people in today's world. Although the content of such ideals (as well as their diverse vocabularies) are always variously imagined and locally constructed, the desires they evoke can retain a powerful attraction for individuals and communities even when their achievement is continually frustrated or denied ... In Thailand these 'modernities' celebrate ideals of wealth, comfort, and commodified style that are encapsulated in part in the Thai phrase *khwaam pen thansamay*, 'being up-to-date'. The desirability of *thansamay* forms and practices reflects their links not only to privileged middle class and urban Thai standards of living but also to even more distant arenas of global authority and privilege. In Baan Naa Sakae, new forms of geographic mobility take place amid proliferating images of these attractively 'modern' ways of being, yet few migrants are in a position to achieve the material or symbolic benefits that these promise ... One consequence of these complex ideological and material entanglements is that migrants and others in Baan Naa Sakae confront a continuing gap between constructed desires for Thai standards of 'modernity' and 'progress' ... and at best the partial achievement of such desires in everyday life.

In Nigeria, though the middle class serves as the harbinger and transformer of modernity, it has been subjected to the impact of Nigeria's economic downturn over the last three decades. Material symbols of modernity have been largely priced out of the purchasing power of the middle class, just as they have for the lower class. The plight of these classes can be deduced from the disastrous decline in the real income of public servants between 1979 and 2003. (In the latter years it appreciated, but only a little. This is shown in Table 6).[2]

2 These values reflect the purchasing power of public sector income. I presume that US dollar values must have been accommodated to arrive at the values. It should, however,

Table 6 *Monthly (real) take-home remuneration for public servants in Nigeria, 1979–2003*
Source: Federal Republic of Nigeria (2006b: Chapter 13)

Year	Grade Level 01	Grade Level 08	Grade Level 15
1979–1983	₦244.00	₦737.22	₦1,947.70
1984–1988	₦164.29	₦427.64	₦1,064.06
1989–1993	₦149.23	₦272.64	₦576.14
1994–1998	₦82.10	₦198.20	₦369.70
1999–2003	₦139.40	₦340.30	₦728.90

The National Bureau of Statistics arrived at the rates of real take-home remuneration shown in Table 6 by deflating nominal salaries/wages with the Consumer Price Index (Federal Republic of Nigeria 2006b). Nigeria's public service is basically divided into two: namely, junior staff and senior staff. Grade levels 1–5 are junior, while grade levels 6–17 are the senior staff. The remaining senior position of Permanent Secretary is attained by political appointment, made from the ranks of senior civil servants (usually level 17). Junior grade levels represent the low class while senior grade (especially grade levels 8–17) represents the middle class. Hence Table 6 reveals that grade level 1 monthly real income declined by over 66 per cent from ₦244 in 1979–1983 to ₦82.10 in 1994–1998; that of grade level 8 decreased by more than 73 per cent from ₦737.22 in 1979–1983 to ₦198.20 in 1994–1998; and that of grade level 15 fell by 81 per cent from ₦1,947.70 in 1979–1983 to ₦369.70 in 1994–1998. Real wages subsequently increased by 69 per cent to ₦139.40, then by 71 per cent to ₦340.30, and next by 97 per cent

be noted that the value of the Naira (₦) has fluctuated from ₦1 to US$1 in the late 1970s to ₦ 10 to $1 in the late 1980s, ₦90 to $1 in the late 1990s and ₦150 to US$1 in recent times. Thus, though public sector workers may be earning more in currency quantity, their real income, paradoxically, has abysmally decreased over time. Private sector income varies across companies, and hence has not been represented here. Public sector income largely serves as the benchmark for the determination of wages in other sectors of the economy. The more vibrant sectors pay more than what is obtainable in the public sector, while some other sections of the private sector pay less.

to ₦728.90 for grade levels 1, 8 and 15 respectively between 1994–1998 and 1999–2003, without reaching 1979–1983 levels, despite growing inflation and astronomic increases in the prices of consumer goods.

The periods of steep decline, especially 1986 to 1996, represent the years of the Structural Adjustment Programme (SAP) when Nigerians experienced the steepest economic decline and inflation of all. The improvements between 1999 and 2003 reflect salary increases and relative stability, catalysed by democracy that was re-instituted in 1999 after almost three decades of military rule.

The data above represent only the real incomes of those employed in the public service. Employees of some segments of the private sector, especially the banking and oil sectors, fared a lot better; the worst off were those employed in struggling organizations and those who were unemployed. This period witnessed the regeneration of *tokunbo* values, first, through the migration of skilled labour to the developed world for economic reasons; and, secondly, through the sending of remittances to the emigrants' families and friends back in Nigeria (Omobowale, Omobowale and Ajani 2010; Hernández-Coss and Bun 2007; Larsen, Allan, Bryan and Smith 2005; Schuerkens 2005; van Dalen, Groenewold and Schoorl 2005; Reynolds 2002; Sako 2002).[3] New experiences in the lands of sojourn and the need to retain contact with home and show care through remittances have ensured continual transfer of immaterial remittances as well, especially in terms of 'ideas, behaviours, identities, and social capital …' (Levitt 1998: 927). This kind of social remittance has ensured cultural diffusion, which has also advanced and affirmed the primacy of modern/Western culture (both material and immaterial) as the dominant, standard culture that must be attained and sustained at all costs.

In the developed world, migrants are exposed to the culture of massive production and constant consumer purchases and the discarding of

3 The value of traceable remittances to Nigeria increased from a little over US$1 billion in 2003 to about $10 billion in 2010 (World Bank 2011; Oronsaye 2011; Hernández-Coss and Bun 2007). The value may be more because some other remittances are done through the informal sector, being sent through close associates visiting Nigeria and/or personally delivered by benevolent migrants taking the remittances to people's homes.

used goods that are still in a reasonable condition. Knowing the situation back home, migrants see these used goods as commodities with potential re-use value in Nigeria. Back in Nigeria, the Western used goods are different from the used goods (*aloku*) that the local population has passed on. They represent a high degree of quality, not just in comparison to *aloku* but also when compared with substandard new goods that have flooded the market from Asia. Once again, benefits have come from the developed world, in the form of imported second-hand goods. This time, *tokunbo* is not patronized by the lower class alone, but also by the middle class. The upper classes also patronize certain ostentatiously high-level second-hand goods, such as top-of-the-range cars like Mercedes Benz (especially the newly released luxury models) and BMW, which were once generally regarded as the exclusive preserve of the super-rich.[4] Thus, the social system has re-constructed the meanings attached to the second-hand. It is not all regarded as *aloku* any more; imported second-hand goods have been retagged *tokunbo*. The consuming public regards imported second-hand goods as things of the highest quality which have only been minimally used by Western consumers, who have discarded them merely in order to purchase new and better versions. What is discarded in the West is still highly valued by consumers in Nigeria.

Tokunbo goods have played important roles in the 'glocalization' of modernity practice in Nigeria since the 1990s. It started with automobiles: once again, the middle class, and later the lower class, could afford to purchase vehicles that would aid mobility and enhance status and prestige.[5] A middle-income earner could thus own a car, just as the high-income earners and the upper-class elite could, and this was done by opting for the imported second-hand (*tokunbo*). Vehicles such as Mercedes Benz cars, which were generally seen as a symbolic representation of wealth, became

4 Wealthy Nigerians have a penchant for luxury models of automobiles and they do acquire them shortly after release to the market. Those who cannot afford them new opt for imported second-hand.

5 It is important to note that government agencies also patronize *tokunbo* automobiles in Nigeria. *Tokunbo* vehicles serve as a major auto infrastructure for both the public and private sectors.

readily affordable and they quickly became common sights on Nigerian roads as from the mid 1990s.[6] Imported second-hand vehicles are generally celebrated as 'new', with the second-hand auto buyer announcing and celebrating a 'new' buy with family and close associates.

It is important to note that *tokunbo* vehicles announce the re-emergence of the Nigerian middle class, which many lay commentators saw as having disappeared in the years of the Structural Adjustment Programme (SAP). Of course, the middle class had not really disappeared. Composed of civil servants, the judiciary, academics, private sector professionals, police officers and officers of military and paramilitary forces, this class of public and private officials is central to the administration of Nigeria; it has remained active in the nation's administration and in the running of the economy, in spite of the economic downturn.

The middle class only seemed to have disappeared between the late 1980s and 1990s because it was so economically deprived. Symbolically and economically, it dropped to the level of the pre-1980 lower class, who earned low incomes and could not afford to own vehicles and other goods that symbolized middle-class standing in the understanding of the public. With the middle class economically transmitting the meanings of deprivation socially attached to the lower class in the 'boom years' of the 1970s, they were perceived to have dropped in status, hence the popular saying that 'the middle class has disappeared in Nigeria'. With the availability of *tokunbo* vehicles, the middle class is beginning to re-emerge in the public domain and in social consciousness.

Likewise, *tokunbo* spare parts have won consumer confidence as automobile service parts of high quality and standard. New spare parts are mostly distrusted, due to the proliferation of substandard automobile spare parts in the market. Unfortunately, it is difficult to identify original new spare parts. Customers would rather purchase a more expensive *tokunbo* automobile spare part than a new one whose source and quality is uncertain. With the availability of *tokunbo* spare parts, auto consumers

6 In recent times, Japanese automobiles have largely replaced the Mercedes Benz as the luxury automobiles preferred by Nigerians.

are able to maintain their vehicles and ensure that they remain on the road as status symbols; they then avoid prying and embarrassing questioning from associates who may view the inability to maintain a car as a sign of economic disempowerment.

The imported automobile second-hand sector has emerged as a huge employer of people in Nigeria, accommodating both skilled and semi-skilled labour. The primacy of *tokunbo* automobile spare parts is evidenced in the fact that sellers deceptively tag substandard and spare parts that have been locally used as '*tokunbo*' in order to convince potential customers they will make a good buy.

Finally, it is worth stressing that the *tokunbo* automobile spare parts market is dependent on the vibrant *tokunbo* vehicle market. The imported second-hand automomobile market thrives, as parts of the *tokunbo* vehicles become defective or damaged and require replacement. Except for a few very recent and not so popular brands whose *tokunbo* spare parts may not be readily available, the first preference for many consumers is a *tokunbo* spare part.

Tokunbo automobile spare parts are taken as being like the originals, and are expected to stand the test of time, even when it is clear that this is not entirely possible. When a *tokunbo* spare part that has just been bought is found to be defective, it is assumed that it is the bad one out of the whole lot, or that an *aloku* substitute has been sold to the unsuspecting buyer. A replacement may be sought, at a price, from the same seller or from another seller within the market. That *tokunbo* automobile spare parts remain sought after, despite the fact that they may be defective and unreturnable, is a direct affirmation of the supposed superiority of the imported second-hand among the consuming public. This further accentuates the practice of diffused modernity in 'glocal terms': the *tokunbo* market provides supposedly 'trusted' service parts that, with their origins in the developed world, sustain the values associated with car ownership.

Likewise, consumers generally view *tokunbo* electronic goods as some of the best gadgets around. The second-hand market allows access to gadgets that are thought of as basic necessities and as status symbols. For just about ₦50,000 (US$333), a potential buyer can obtain a colour television set, a medium sized refrigerator, a DVD player and a pressing iron. A man who has these basic gadgets, especially early in his career, is considered 'responsible', in that he spends his money on worthwhile goods and not on frivolities. Such a person is thought to have the potential to move on to greater heights. He can be proud to welcome a visitor into his house, since he is seen to be 'doing well' because '*o ti to ile re*' (which has the literal meaning: 'he has arranged his house'). In socio-cultural terms, this simply means the man has acquired the culturally perceived essential gadgets that demonstrate maturity and prepare the way for settling down and raising a family. If the possessor of such goods is a single lady, she is appreciated as a successful young woman who is acquiring some of the essentials she will transfer to her husband's house upon marriage.

At a higher level, socially perceived luxury electronic items such as touch-screen appliances, flat-screen television sets and monitors, BlackBerry phones and iPhones convey greater symbolic appreciation in the practice of modernity. Their utilization, even when they are second-hand, socially positions the owner in the class of the privileged. These gadgets integrate consumers into the globalized world modernity, even when the developed nations that are seen as representing the modern world par excellence are thousands of miles away and have progressed beyond the levels of modernity that are locally celebrated.

With the coming of the digital age, the consuming public is virtually transported into communicative cyber space in real time, interacting with family, friends, associates and strangers, and thereby erasing distance barriers – so long as the gadget is powered and the reception of internet signals is not disrupted.[7]

Tokunbo ICT allows access to online products and services. It is revolutionizing internet access and providing jobs. An appreciable volume of Nigeria's ICT and internet access equipment (especially basic cyber

7 Electric power disruptions and weak internet signals are major banes of the ICT sector in Nigeria. Power is hardly ever available – to such an extent that the government power monopoly, hitherto officially called the National Electric Power Authority (NEPA) was sarcastically named 'Never Expect Power Always' (see Olukoju 2004). The government has since re-named the power company the Power Holding Company of Nigeria (PHCN). PHCN's performance has not substantially improved.

accessories such as computers, printers, scanners, phones, wireless Ethernet, WiFi internet adapters and webcams) is sourced from the second-hand markets. However, it is imperative to reiterate that, while *tokunbo* electronics affords access to basic and advanced ICT and/or electronics technology across classes, it also swells the e-waste dump in Nigeria. Oblivious of the potential and real toxic nature of the e-waste received as second-hand electronic goods, the consuming public looks only at the benefits that these goods bring them.

Finally, *tokunbo* clothes are a unique dimension of modernity. Consumers generally believe that the quality of *tokunbo* clothes by far exceeds that of the new clothes that are readily available. Besides, *tokunbo* clothes are generally cheaper. Categorization into grades A, B and C breaks the clothes into categories that can appeal to consumers across socio-economic levels and classes. Grading tends to reflect class differences among those who buy *tokunbo* clothes. By and large, grades A and B attract middle-income earners, while grade C attracts those with less money. Grade A garments are often in such good condition they can be cleaned up and presented as new clothes in the boutiques. The general assumption in these boutiques is likely to be that the garment has not been used, and is either a 'factory return' or an item that has outlasted its season.

In actual fact, even though grades B and C are lower in quality than grade A, both are able to convey a high degree of social worth, especially if they have been produced by popular fashion labels. Even some high-income earners buy *tokunbo* clothes. The availability of popular fashion labels of high social value makes the second-hand market a popular destination for consumers, especially since the new clothes available in Nigeria are comparatively poorly made. *Tokunbo* provides access to some of the relatively recent fashions that are culturally diffused from the Western world. It thus provides the consuming public with the possibility of practising diffused modernity more or less in step with current global dominant fashion trends.

Tokunbo clothes also have a social levelling effect. Besides attracting consumers across classes, they also allow the less well-off access to wares that would otherwise be unaffordable to them and inaccessible, the exclusive preserve of the elite class. Fashion trends and labels, culturally diffused as elements of modern culture through the mass media and the internet, eventually reach the *tokunbo* market where the majority can access them. This reflects the significance of the second-hand clothing economy in 'glocal' modernity practice: it grants access to the less privileged socio-economic groups who would otherwise find the labels too expensive to buy.

Thus the wealthy do not have a monopoly over modern fashion; other less privileged members of society can now have access to it through the second-hand market. This clothing market advances the practice of modern fashion within which the person who likes to be thought of as contemporaneous and modern is physically viewed, appreciated and approved by the immediate social environment. Local fashions are, of course, relegated to the background while 'modern fashion', exemplified by Western clothing, has the ascendant position. The cost of maintaining a modern wardrobe is minimized in relative and comparative terms across classes who patronize grades A, B and C, depending on the purchasing power of the buyers. *Tokunbo* clothes give presence to the rational 'modern' person, accessing top-of-the-line fashion labels, comparable in appearance to those worn by the privileged elite who have purchased the popular labels new and at high prices.

The large spectrum of informal and formal workers in the *tokunbo* trade, including importers, crossers, security agents, wholesalers, retailers and touting agents, makes *Tokunbo* readily available locally. Once in Nigeria, the goods are openly displayed and, in form and nomenclature, they look like legal goods. Notably, by renaming smugglers 'crossers', the prevalent culture erases illegality from the act of smuggling. Crossers and members of security agencies, who network with crossers, blend into a general network of contraband *tokunbo* conveyance into the Nigerian economy.[8] Once the goods are displayed in second-hand markets, they become 'legal' commodities, 'protected' from possible legal confiscation by security agents. After contraband *tokunbo* automobiles have been purchased by consumers, they may be subject to seizure, especially by special customs agents strategically positioned on the highway. An unlucky car owner whose vehicle is impounded by the customs task force may bribe his way through, pay duties at the customs office, or forfeit the vehicle. Seized vehicles are eventually auctioned in non-transparent circumstances.

8 Informants claim security agents also work as crossers, driving in vehicles or serving as escorts to vehicles conveying contraband.

The contraband imported as second-hand is readily available in the markets and is patronized by customers across classes in the public and private sectors. It thus moves from the realm of illegality to that of legality, and its 'contraband' nature is erased via a complicated process of social restructuring. Since the goods are openly displayed in the market without any form of action from the relevant security agencies, the consuming public takes the goods to be 'legal'. They are accepted as part of the general mass of second-hand *tokunbo* goods and as a part of modern, Western culture received from Western countries.

The reconstruction of the meanings attached to the *aloku* and its consequent differentiation from imported second-hand goods (*tokunbo*) cannot be divorced from the 'glocal' reality and practice of modernity. The 'glocal' experience builds on colonial and immediate post-colonial *tokunbo* values in such a way that Nigerians contextually attach standard, durability and superiority meanings to *tokunbo* goods.

Tokunbo gives a re-use value to imported second-hand goods that goes beyond the simple meanings attached by the lower classes. The goods become symbols of high quality and are believed to have better utility value and purpose than substandard new products. The *tokunbo* market also provides relatively standard goods of almost the same quality as brand new products of the same type and provenance.

In addition, the *tokunbo* market serves as a social leveller. People who earn a low-to-middle income can still acquire goods from the second-hand market that reflect elitist values and they can make use of them in everyday social situations to the admiration and acknowledgement of others in the immediate social environment. At relatively minimal cost, they have acquired 'modernity' at the second-hand market, and are able to project positive images about their socio-economic status. Thus, they are able to attract a degree of respect and prestige that they would not perhaps be ordinarily accorded. Simply put, *tokunbo* second-hand imports are the common man's resource in the everyday, taken-for-granted practice of modernity. *Tokunbo* goods help provide some degree of social equilibrium, with greater equity in access to essential goods and a lessening of feelings of inferiority and subjugation among the less privileged classes.

Tokunbo transmits the local consumer beyond local cultural boundaries into the culture of the advanced Western nations. It symbolically reflects the Western-oriented being who appears worthy to be deemed 'modern'. With little money expended, *tokunbo* users momentarily become 'up-to-date', even when they do not in reality enjoy much modern material culture. This is because there is a huge gap between actual Western standards, continually advanced by new releases and developments, and what an ordinary Nigerian consumer buys in imported second-hand goods. The imported second-hand goods cannot really compare with new goods in quality, features and capability. Second-hand consumers simply like to believe that the imported used goods they access have comparable quality. Unfortunately they are unable to obtain the very latest releases, which are priced beyond their economic capability. Western material culture represents the physical aspects of Western modern culture through which everyday modernity is practised. Material aspects of modernity are essential to modernity practice, and so, since they are too expensive to be purchased new, the imported second-hand has to suffice. This is the stark reality of Nigeria's second-hand economy.

The wide patronage of *tokunbo* also transmits 'legality' to the process of conveying imported second-hand goods into Nigeria through a symbolic and socio-linguistic reconstruction of the context of illegal importation. Smuggling is reconstructed as 'crossing'. The processes, networks and meanings attached to 'crossing' effectively remove consciousness of the potential and real illegality of 'crossed' goods from the public domain and integrate the smuggled wares into the general gamut of second-hand imports from Western nations, with their high re-use value. Once contraband second-hand items are successfully crossed, they becomes 'legal' commodities, openly and freely patronized by consumers across all sectors of Nigerian society, from private individuals to public organizations.

In other words, in a paradox of contrasting social realities, policies and practices, *tokunbo* second-hand goods have become the mainstay of Nigeria's consumer economy, allowing access to both basic and luxury goods, across socio-economic boundaries and in both the public and private sectors. Nigeria's modern consumer culture is highly dependent on imported second-hand goods that are either legally imported or 'crossed' into the country.

This second-hand market experience is a manifestation of the country's peripheral position in the world capitalist system. Nigeria has not been left out of the globalization process, but it occupies a disadvantaged position as a peripheral and dependent partner. Lacking productive capability, Nigeria looks up to the developed nations for the actualization of its modernity, and in its quest to catch up and close the development gap. Official maladministration, corruption and disastrous economic policies by successive governments have grossly eroded the nation's productive capability over the years, leading to economic dependency, and by extension cultural dependency. Since the country is so weakened, Nigeria's economic and cultural dependency is sustained by second-hand modernity supported by obsolete and used imports.

It is a paradoxical symbiotic system that at the same time supplies the consumer needs of Nigerians and evacuates waste from the developed world at minimal cost. In Nigeria, the consuming public accepts used goods as viable, rational alternatives for the daily representation of modernity in social and economic relations. The consuming public appears 'modern' and 'Western', but its members are really dependent consumers of imported second-hand goods. Symbolically these are described as *tokunbo* and are locally accepted as 'standard' and 'good quality'. As peripheral dependents, members of Nigeria's consuming public patiently and eagerly await the import of used goods to provide the access to modern goods they so much desire. Without these used goods, the average Nigerian would be denied basic comforts and the added luxuries that in fact make up modernity. Without them life would symbolically seem 'brutish' in the perceptions of the interacting public.

It is worth noting that, at present, the Nigerian *tokunbo* culture systematically replaces the culture of acquiring new products. *Tokunbo* imports are taking up the meaning of 'the trusted new', while new goods that are readily available (especially automobile spare parts, electronic items and clothes) are deemed possible fakes. This is because the majority of the local population are too pauperized to afford new products of the highest standard and because it is difficult to differentiate between originals and fakes in a market penetrated by substandard goods coming with impunity over Nigeria's extremely porous borders in an almost perpetual flow.

Hence, discarded goods in the developed world become consumers' favourites in Nigeria. Nevertheless second-hand imports cannot be totally relied on, as a good chunk of the used items are irreparable discards, lacking any reasonable re-use value. Nigeria's dismal economy and largely pauperized consumers thankfully receive defective second-hand goods with the hope of repairing and putting them to good use. Such 'adverse selection', as it is called (Waldman 2004, 2003; Hendel and Lizzeri 1999), does not discourage the Nigerian second-hand buyer. The poor consumer simply bears the brunt of repair or replacement with another defective second-hand item. There is no system of protection in this market. The Standard Organization of Nigeria, the official standards regulatory agency, is making some efforts to discourage the sale of substandard new goods; but, along with other related government establishments, it seems uninterested in taking proactive measures to protect the rights of Nigerian consumers who buy second-hand imports.

Of course, as Nigerians access modernity through the *tokunbo* channel, their country continues to serve as one of the major recipients of waste that the landfills in developed countries cannot accommodate. Both the senders and the recipients are seemingly happy with this arrangement: the developed nations are happy that their 'benevolent' exports take care of landfill shortages and potential environmental challenges, while the nationals of developing nations gladly receive used goods as alternatives that satisfy basic needs and, through ostentation, convey symbolic meanings of modernity. The way in which these throw-aways from the developed world assume meanings of 'quality', 'standard' and 'value' across class boundaries in Nigeria is a unique 'glocal' consequence of second-hand modernity.

CHAPTER 12

Summary and Conclusions

This book has shown that the *tokunbo* phenomenon has a direct relationship with Nigeria's experience of pre-colonial, colonial and post-colonial contacts with the Western world. The pre-colonial contacts of the Yoruba with this Western world between the sixteenth and seventeenth centuries signalled a new experience for Africans with significant impact on their society. European merchants represented the 'advanced people' from across the seas, with material goods of high value for exchange. They crossed the wide seas from a different continent, a feat the local population, with its limited technology, found incredible. The Atlantic Ocean (*okun*) was held in awe, and the ability to cross it created a sense of wonder around Europeans and the merchandise they had to offer for exchange.

The social construction of the 'superiority' of European society, culture and merchandise, which was hitherto voluntary and based on exchange of goods, took more formal and fundamental dimensions with colonization. Colonization had the primary goal of ensuring free access for Europeans to trade in Africa. To achieve this, the territory had to be subjected to the control of European countries, who agreed to the terms of partition at the Berlin Conference of 1884–1885 (Asiwaju 2003–2004; Asiwaju and Adeniyi 1989; Asiwaju 1985, 1976, 1975; Shepperson 1985). According to Stone (1988: 57): 'The Berlin Conference was convened because collaborative arrangements, on which European states had hitherto relied, were beginning to break down ... Continued commercial access to Africa was the common objective, not control of its territory. What has been described as "the old system of free trade imperialism in West Africa" was threatened.'

The primary goal of the Berlin Conference, then, was to ensure that Europeans controlled African trade, but while colonization secured African trade routes, it also brought about the re-orientation of African consumption patterns, tastes and attributions of value towards European goods. Colonization achieved this through direct and indirect control of the indigenous social system, with a primary and ultimate aim of inculcating Western values in the local population (Kusiak 2010; Braun 2002; Olutayo 1991). This was the sequel to the general perception amongst the European powers that the local African populations were 'uncivilized', 'savage' and in need of Western modernization.

'Modernizing' the native also enhanced trade prospects. This was because there is a direct relationship between the immaterial aspects of a culture (for example norms, values, expectations and roles among other indices) and cultural reification through the material aspects of that culture (that is, material goods). Material culture presents in physical form aspects of the immaterial culture. Without its intercession the immaterial culture may only be verified and actualized through continuous and prolonged interaction until norms have been internalized.

Material culture transmits immaterial culture in real time and physically. It can easily be appreciated through the senses of sight, hearing, touch, taste and smell, as against the norms, values and social expectations of immaterial culture, which require a longer time to internalize, appreciate and interpret appropriately. As social beings appreciate, accept, acquire and utilize diffused material culture, the process of internalization of immaterial culture is advanced, because the visible physical materials attest to the viability of immaterial culture.

In like manner, the internalization of immaterial aspects of culture advances the utilization and/or consumption of material aspects. Material culture brings into the open the immaterial culture that has been diffused and internalized. Material culture is a symbol that gives meaning to a social being within the context of his/her existence and the surrounding dominant societal values. It overtly reflects the constructed 'self-concept'. It gives physical and reified meaning to the 'self' and/or the social perception of the individual, such that the 'self' and/or personality of an individual is primarily adjudged from his/her physical appearance presented by the practised or utilized material culture.

Material culture thus allows physical identification along stratified boundaries. Seemingly innocuous material things, such as clothes, household goods and automobiles, are exemplary aspects of material culture that are embedded with symbolic meanings. The contextual interpretations of these symbolic meanings reflect translations beyond the ordinary. The interpretations situate individuals within contextual boundaries and classes on the basis of the material cultural artefacts they make use of and the social meanings that have been attached to them by those in the immediate social environment. Simply put, the symbolism of the material culture influences social perception about a person's class position and whether he/she can be considered 'modern' or otherwise.

In the colonial period, the political, administrative and social structures were directed at 'modernizing' the native. This entailed the inculcation of 'modern', Western values. Though the British imperial system of indirect rule seemingly involved native authorities in local administration (Watts 2004; Vaughan 2003; Majid 1968), it was a system through which the British colonial officials effectively transferred 'modern' values to the natives. The native authorities served as intermediate political authorities between the British officials and the local populations. Colonial government policies were implemented through native authorities, who were obliged to ensure compliance among the colony's subjects on pain of sanctions.

The British education system had a formative role too. It produced an educated elite which became the exemplar of the 'modernity' people sought to emulate. Religious institutions – in this case the ones run by Christian missionaries – also gave credence to the ascendancy of modernity through their evangelism and their mission schools.

Modern values, inculcated by political, educational and religious institutions, were diffused into the family unit where the primary work of socialization takes place. The child who was socialized into 'modernity' acquired the potential capability of moving upwards in society. Upward societal mobility could follow for the entire family, by virtue of the indigenous cultural values which favour kin mutual dependence, mutual assistance and social survival. Since internalization of modernity enhances social classification, access to resources and survival, 'modern culture' assumed a dominant position within the indigenous society. At the level of material culture, the consumption of European and/or Western imports overtly came to 'certify' the 'modern' social being. This explains the re-orientation of the economy to the production, importation and consumption of European (and later American) goods among the indigenous population, even as colonial administrators viewed native consumption of European goods as an indication of growth and wealth creation.

As part of the overt expression of modernity, the indigenous society and culture coined the name 'Tokunbo' as the nomenclature for children conceived or delivered abroad (especially in Europe or North America). This naming practice was predicated on aspects of Yoruba culture, which favoured giving meaningful names to new-born babies. The Yoruba-speaking people of South-Western Nigeria held the belief that conception and delivery were divine. The circumstances of a birth could reveal a child's destiny and position within society and the home. Twins newly born were called *Taye* and *Kehinde*. *Taye* was the first to be delivered but this twin was regarded as junior to *Kehinde* ('the last to come') who had been sent to *to aye wo* ('go ahead to observe or "taste" the world').

Likewise, the Yoruba gave names that depicted social status and honour. Such names would have prefixes such as *ola* ('honour') and *ade* (the 'crown' of royalty), and there were many other names signifying similar social constructs. Names could also indicate religious inclinations. Such names would have religious and/or deity prefixes. Examples include: *Fadayo* ('the Ifa deity has become joy'); *Fadipe* ('the Ifa deity has paid the sacrificial price'); *Ogunshina* ('Ogun, the god of iron, has opened the way'); and *Oluwaseun* ('thanks be to God'). Simply put, Yoruba naming depicted the circumstances and context of a person's birth. It gave others an insight into the name-bearer's social history and personality. Both given names and surnames revealed something of the circumstances of a person's birth, the genealogical connections, religious affiliation, traditional stratified hierarchy and the family's hopes for the future success of the bearer (Akinyemi 2005; Akinnaso 1980; Ekundayo 1977).

'Tokunbo' as a human name needs to be appreciated in this context. 'Tokunbo' indicates that the bearer of the name is foreign born. Usually, the assumption is that a person named 'Tokunbo' must have been conceived or delivered in Europe or North America. The social conception of the developed world as prime harbinger of modernity and development is momentarily transferred to the bearer of the 'Tokunbo' name and, by extension, to his/her family. If the parents could conceive the child abroad, then the child must belong to the elite class. The elite class enjoys the social status of the privileged that have internalized modern and/or Western culture. As people of modern orientation, 'Tokunbo' name-bearers are socially constructed within the context of being up-to-date and contemporary and they are expected to express Western values in everyday social relations.

This represents a unique form of name symbolism. In this wise, it is important to focus on the meanings attached to names. These meanings impact on the social context of the name-bearer and the ensuing social values and culture. They determine human classifications and have a direct impact on the social construction of the 'self'. Norms, values and expected social behaviour accompany name symbolism.

Name symbolism entails contextual culture(s) relating to names and the meanings attached to them. Such meanings condition the actions and reactions a name may engender. Depending on the meanings attached, names might engender reactions of awe, stigma or social classification; alternatively they might serve simply for personal identification. For example, while members of royalty would bear names invoking their aristocratic connections, slaves on the plantations bore stigmatizing names that indicated their loss of rights and their sinking to the sub-human, with the status of 'things' or 'chattels'. In modern times, names also serve as human signifiers for personal identification, hence differentiating between actors A and B.

Over time, through the processes and stages of socialization, names symbolically impact on the social construction of self. They give identity to their bearers who are individualized through the names they have been given and are socially perceived through the lens of the social constructs generated through interactions within the social system in which they operate and exist.

In this context, it is important to note that giving a child conceived and/or delivered outside Nigeria the name 'Tokunbo' was a rational act, in that it created an aura of elitist values around the child right from birth. The child's family was also perceived as elite by extension. The child was treated as a privileged being by compeers and other actors within his/her immediate social environment. The special attention and privileges a *Tokunbo* bearer attracted was as a result of the social perception in Nigeria that the Western world was the centre of 'modernity' and development. Local society projected the social perception and values attached to the Western world – an elitist social space – onto the person named 'Tokunbo'.

As from the 1990s however, the term *tokunbo* has been transferred to imported second-hand goods, which is what it now signifies. As a personal name, 'Tokunbo' no longer attracts special social prestige bordering on elitism, as it used to earlier. In fact, it may gradually become extinct as a human name. Nevertheless, the tag *tokunbo* transferred to imported second-hand goods does retain some of the connotations the name used to have. The research for this book revealed that the *tokunbo* tag conjures up notions of good quality and high value for these items.

Imported second-hand goods gradually gained popularity across class boundaries in Nigeria in the 1990s, following the deplorable and appalling impact of the massive economic downturn of the previous decade. Western goods had by that time gained huge patronage within the local population. Now with low purchasing power, Nigerians found most such goods beyond reach. Inflation rates between 1986 and 1996 were mostly in double digits, reaching a peak of 72.8 per cent in 1995. Inferior Asian goods (especially electronic appliances, clothes and automobile spare parts) replaced high quality Western goods in the stores. Asian products proved, however, to be consumers' nightmares because they ceased to function after a short period of use. Consequently, the local social environment and consuming public opted for imported second-hand alternatives. Depending on the goods available for sale, the buyers came from all classes.

The adoption of imported second-hand products across class boundaries followed a sequential order. To begin with, members of the middle class who could no longer afford brand new vehicles opted for imported second-hand cars. In spite of the obvious fact that these vehicles were used, they were celebrated as 'new' automobiles (*oko titun*). The success of imported second-hand automobiles among the middle classes set the stage for the adoption of imported used automobiles by the upper classes in a quest for models like Mercedes Benz and BMW that would be perceived as luxurious and prestigious. Indeed, since the middle-class users of imported used automobiles, also occupied professional positions in the public and private sectors and served as the prime policy advisers, designers and implementers, it is not surprising that the Nigerian public and private sectors also opted for imported second-hand automobiles. Over time, the Nigerian roads became predominantly filled with such vehicles – and they still are.

The success of imported second-hand automobiles also created a market for automobile spare parts. Although the imported used vehicles delighted their buyers, they also posed major maintenance challenges, almost from the time of purchase. New, readily available spare parts were largely inferior in quality, in most people's estimation. Consumers still refer to them as '*Taiwan*', an indication of their Asian origin. By and large, they lack consumer credibility.

The importation of second-hand automobile spare parts has offered car-owners a viable alternative to the good quality, but expensive, new ones. In the 1990s, in South-Western Nigeria (and particularly Ibadan), Alhaji Mufu Lanihun pioneered the large-scale import of used automobile spare parts. Within a short while, these parts came to replace new spares as the consumers' preference.

In like manner, consumers have adopted imported electronic goods as alternatives to out-of-reach new electronic devices of Western origin. Although Chinese electronic goods (especially mobile phones) attract a relatively high degree of patronage, due to their low cost and attractive features, they are derided as '*Chinco*'. *Chinco* products are generally perceived as being of low quality and unequal in standard to those made by popular Western labels.

In the quest to practise modernity and reconnect with Western brands socially perceived as items of high standard, the consuming public in Nigeria has been greatly attracted to second-hand electronic goods coming from the West. As material aspects of culture, second-hand electronic items level the gap socially and psychologically between those who can afford new Western electronic gadgets and those who can only opt for alternatives. For example, irrespective of the actual context and condition of purchase – and irrespective too of whether they are new or imported second-hand – smart phones and LCD television sets convey and confer similar degrees of social appreciation and respect on their users. The owners are as much appreciated as owners of new models. Those close to them admire their achievement in obtaining the bargains, and those who know less about their actual socio-economic level or class status, and are unaware that the items are second-hand, imagine they belong to the elite.

Though basically similar to the practices described above, the trade in imported second-hand clothes differs somewhat, in that the purchase of such used garments has been a regular feature of Nigeria's economy since the colonial period. The trade was largely conducted for the benefit of the poor and low-income earners. Among the Yoruba of South-Western Nigeria, imported used clothes were scornfully referred to as *bosikoro* ('hide in a secluded place'). In the South-Eastern region, the popular term for them was *Okrika* (explained later), while the pidgin English term was *bend-down* ('bend down'). Both terms *bosikoro* and *bend-down* carry a stigma. Imported second-hand clothes were largely thought of as the scorned preserve of the economically deprived. A buyer would carefully select his/her choice from the lot, while being careful not to be spotted at the used clothes outlets by any associates. Poor consumers not only tried as hard as they could not to be seen purchasing second-hand clothes, they tended to hide the fact that such clothes were second-hand after they have been purchased.

The term *bend-down* simply refers to the manner in which imported used clothes were spread out on the bare floor while buyers bent down or squatted to pick their choices. This was a different scene from the stores and boutiques where the clothes were hung up on the walls.

An informant who claimed that his family had traded in imported second-hand clothes for more than six decades said that the real Igbo term for second-hand clothes is *okaraka*, which means 'torn'.[1] They are called *okaraka* because each bale of garments contains many torn clothes. Over time, the term has been changed from *okaraka* to *Okrika*. The change may have been due to cross-cultural diffusion, especially between Igbo traders and traders from other parts of Nigeria who might have unconsciously re-termed the old word '*Okrika*'. This change could have occurred in the

1 The informant had to transfer his operational base to the Benin Republic around the year 2000, due to unfavourable policies against imported second-hand clothes in Nigeria, which threatened the survival of his business. His goods are transported to Nigeria through a special network of retail buyers who work with 'crossers'.

process of transaction, because non-Igbo traders and customers may have been rather more linguistically familiar with Okrika, a settlement that had contact with Europeans (especially Portuguese traders and Christian missionaries) from as early as the fifteenth century. Okrika was a commercial port known especially for the export of palm products after the abolition of the slave trade by the British. It remained a popular commercial town till the first three decades of the twentieth century (Derefaka and Anozie 2002; Gleason and Ibubuya 1991; Williamson 1962).

Today, imported second-hand clothes are no longer the exclusive preserve of the poor. They are also patronized by middle-class professionals. The findings of this research revealed that consumers prefer second-hand clothes because of their perceived quality vis-à-vis inferior garments from China, which easily fade and/or are damaged after a short period of use. The social perception of imported second-hand clothes has consequently been reconstructed from the scornfully regarded *bosikoro*, *okrika* or *bend-down* to the highly regarded *tokunbo*. Second-hand clothes are openly merchandized in major markets, with people of diverse walks of life openly doing business, picking, bargaining and paying for their choices. In fact, clothing accessories such as female underwear and handbags are commonly recommended and preferred, as being of better quality than new items. Unscrupulous traders hence display low-quality new bags and claim they are *tokunbo* while many *tokunbo* clothes are displayed in boutiques as 'new'.

This takes us to the social reconstruction of imported second-hand goods as *tokunbo*. These goods provide a door giving even ordinary people access to Western material culture so that they can practise modernity. The *tokunbo* tag confers values on imported second-hand goods which raise them above the ordinary. Economic reasons may explain the public's initial opting for the imported second-hand; but they do not adequately explain the socio-cultural dimension, which has in turn advanced the second-hand economy in South-Western Nigeria. The local population attach meanings of superiority to second-hand goods. The meanings attached have a direct relationship to the negative experience Nigerians have had with substandard imports from Asia (particularly China) and the high cost of high-quality new goods from Western countries.

Western goods represent the up-to-date material culture consumers desire in modernity practice, but new Western products are largely out of the range most can afford. Substandard alternatives, on the other hand, are seldom durable and they also reflect the corrupt dimensions of modern material culture, arriving in the country illegally over Nigeria's porous borders. Though the substandard alternatives may be cheaper than *tokunbo* goods, they do not convey the same messages of modern practice and of being of a better class, and, above all, give no access to 'modern' (that is, Western) culture. Second-hand imports from Western nations offer the popular brand names consumers desire. Besides, they are more durable than the Asian (Chinese) alternatives and serve better the utility and cultural purposes for which they are acquired.

Since second-hand imports can serve the same symbolic purposes as unaffordable new products the local social system has abandoned the old disdainful term *aloku* to describe them. Through prevalent social interactions, the local population has, over time, devised a dichotomy between domestically used goods and imported ones. Goods domestically used have retained the tag *aloku*, while the more socially valued term *tokunbo* has been transferred from human beings to imported second-hand artefacts.

It is noteworthy that new (unused) imports are not regarded as *tokunbo* even though they also come from across the seas. The meanings attached to *tokunbo* thus contain an extra dimension. *Tokunbo* conveys meanings of originality, high standards and superiority, reifying the qualities associated with Western nations (as against the poor quality associated with China). *Tokunbo* also indicates that the imports have been used and differ in this way from new products. By and large, however, the main function of the *tokunbo* tag is to sustain a notion of supposed high quality and transform the goods into viable surrogates for expensive new goods.

The meanings attached to *tokunbo* suggest high degrees of modernity and an association with Western civilization. Just as a human being named 'Tokunbo' is socially judged to be of the privileged class, with a degree of internalization of Western culture, so *tokunbo* imputes meanings of good standard on imported second-hand products. *Tokunbo* is predicated on the appreciation of Western culture by the Yoruba of South-Western Nigeria. It is associated with notions such as *Oyinbo ti so aye d'ero* ('the white man has made life easy'). This notion is usually employed to describe modern labour-saving devices and technologies that have transformed tasks that once involved a lot of effort. Thus sharing in 'modernity', as propagated by Western culture and its dynamics, represents the epitome of civilization, even if it means utilizing goods already used in Western nations. Such goods are socio-culturally transformed from their 'used' context to be considered comparable with 'new' products.

Paradoxically, however, *tokunbo* goods are not in any way comparable to standard new imports. Personal observation and the respondents' attestations indicate that *tokunbo* goods are usually in certain states of degradation. More often than not, consumers have to repair purchased *tokunbo* goods before they use them. For instance, they often have to repair or change some parts of *tokunbo* automobiles almost immediately or shortly after purchase. Imported used automobile spare parts also fail, while about 75 per cent of used electronic items imported into Nigeria are unusable, having already reached the ends of their life cycles. Even imported second-hand electronic items found usable may last only a short while before they have to be discarded. Every bale of imported used clothing also contains a huge number of damaged or faded garments. This explains the grading of *tokunbo* goods into A, B and C on the basis of their perceived quality. In actual fact, *tokunbo* goods do not have the quality attributed to them.

Nevertheless, *tokunbo* goods are better than substandard new products. Besides the term *tokunbo* superimposes a social notion that they have 'sufficient comparable standard' to stand next to new products of Western origin. *Tokunbo* goods are thus seen as the viable and rational alternatives to expensive new products. In the hearts and minds of the consuming public, the term *tokunbo* symbolically translates imported second-hand goods into the category of the 'new'. Hence *tokunbo* symbolism socially rationalizes second-hand patronage and expands the reach of the second-hand economy in South-Western Nigeria.

The expansion of the second-hand economy has both legal and illegal dimensions. The legal dimension includes all non-prohibited second-hand imports that come into Nigeria by legitimate means. The illegal dimension involves an intricate, labyrinthine social network of actors who not only bring in prohibited second-hand items, but see to their consequent symbolic transformation into goods with socially acceptable dimensions, capable of rationally satisfying socially defined wants within the economy. Included in the import prohibition list are used automobiles older than fifteen years (the age was increased from ten to fifteen years in 2011), used textiles and certain categories of used electronic appliances including refrigerators, deep freezers, air-conditioners and compressors.

Prohibited items are sometimes smuggled into Nigeria through the nation's seaports with the active connivance of unscrupulous clearing agents and corrupt customs officials. Most prohibited imports, however, come in through Nigeria's border with the Republic of Benin. This neighbouring country serves as a major transit point for importing both unprohibited and prohibited second-hand goods into Nigeria. A special class of smugglers called 'crossers' operates on the Benin side of the border: they are mostly Nigerians.

The logic of expressing smuggling as 'crossing' is associated with the social reconstruction of meanings attached to smuggling. Prohibited items still attract popular patronage in Nigeria and are openly displayed in markets. Both small-scale and large-scale importers of prohibited items view their task as essential for bringing consumers the goods they want, irrespective of the illegality behind the trade. Since smuggling connotes illegality, the conveying network (importers, smugglers, sellers, corrupt customs and security agents) and the interacting public who constitute the customer base have transmuted 'smuggling' and its attached meanings to 'crossing', giving the activity the legitimacy bestowed by prevalent social use and shared values. Socio-psychologically, the term 'crossing' makes the smuggling unobjectionable, particularly among primary importers and 'crossers', and it normalizes prohibited and contraband goods in the second-hand market.

The social normalization of prohibited and contraband goods is further strengthened for the general public by the claims of both importers and crossers that customs officials have been paid 'duties' before the items were imported. In actual fact, the 'duties' paid were bribes made to corrupt customs officials in order to fast-track illegal imports and avoid the confiscation of prohibited goods. This explains why there is such an elaborate network between crossers and customs officials. It is not everyone that can 'cross' goods. The customs and security officials who are involved in these deals know the identities of the crossers'. Once the deals have been sealed, the prohibited items are conveyed into Nigeria.

These prohibited items are displayed in popular markets and are purchased and used by consumers without any molestation from anti-smuggling security agents. The only exception, in recent times, is the case of imported used automobiles. Anti-smuggling customs units do not raid auto dealers and impound vehicles lacking valid customs papers; rather they subject the purchasers of imported second-hand cars to sanctions, which range from fines to having their vehicles confiscated and auctioned to privileged individuals who have connections with the customs service. Some victims manage to bribe their way through, only to have their vehicles impounded by another team of the special customs task force. These cases notwithstanding, most prohibited imports, once bought at the second-hand markets, can be enjoyed with minimal or no sanctions from security agents.

The scenario summarized above describes the 'glocal' realities of the second-hand economy as Nigeria increasingly integrates into the globalizing world. Its integration remains at a peripheral level, however. Nigeria is a nation that specializes in the export of primary products (raw materials) to the developed world and has little productive capacity for manufactured goods. In addition, the economic realities of trade in contemporary times ensures that there is a massive export of used goods to Nigeria and other Third World nations.

The export of cheap used goods to Nigeria should be understood within the context of the challenges the developed world faces with waste management, the economic downturn in Nigeria and the unrelenting thirst Nigerians have for Western goods in their quest for modernity practice through Western material culture. On the one hand, with increasingly declining landfills, developed nations are faced with the challenge of the proliferating waste that is a consequence of progressive industrialization. On the other hand, Nigeria is in a debilitating economic situation, caused by corruption and gross mismanagement by successive leaders, leading to a pauperized population. Despite its poverty, this population harbours a culture that favours modernity practice as described and defined by Western civilization. Consumption of Western material goods is seen as an overt reification of modernity.

Modernity practice embodies notions of being up-to-date, of comfort and of the 'good life'. Consumers' striving to attain modernity through the utilization of Western goods is satisfied at the second-hand imports market, where alternatives originating from the developed Western nations are available. Thus, momentarily, the developed world's waste problems are solved by the Third World's demand for used imports. Particularly in Nigeria, this demand arises from economic weakness caused by inflation and economic disempowerment coupled with consumers' insatiable taste for Western material culture.

Consequently, as the second-hand economy grows in Nigeria (especially the South-West), the country continues to be a dumping ground for goods described as 'waste' in wealthy nations, but which have sufficient re-use potential for the economically disadvantaged. These poor consumers accept second-hand imports as alternatives in an overt practice of a modernity achieved through consumption of Western material culture.

To conclude: by transmuting the concept of second-hand imports from *aloku* to *tokunbo*, the social and cultural economy of South-Western Nigeria has symbolically rationalized the practice of importing and using these used items and has created a conducive atmosphere for the continued appreciative consumption of what was hitherto disdained. The dynamics of the *tokunbo* phenomenon symbolically recreate imported second-hand goods so that they seem like 'new' goods, and it also encourages legal and illegal inflows into the local economy of used goods disposed of as waste in the developed world.

The differing meanings attached to the 'used' by the cultures of the developed world and of Nigeria keep the second-hand trade going. The developed world sends out waste while Nigerian consumers gladly receive them as *tokunbo*. Ultimately, Nigeria, along with other Third World nations, pays the price of receiving an evacuation of waste from the developed nations. As the developed world ships its waste to an appreciative consuming population, Nigeria is progressively becoming a perilous dumping ground, and Nigerians are being exposed to toxicity and health hazards even as they celebrate reception of the *tokunbo*.

Bibliography

Abarry, A. (1997). 'The Naming Drama of the *Ga* People', *Journal of Black Studies* 27, 365–377.

Abraham, M. (2008). 'Globalization and the Call Center Industry', *International Sociology*, 23(2), 197–210.

Aceto, M. (2002). 'Ethnic Personal Names and Multiple Identities in Anglophone Caribbean Speech Communities in Latin America', *Language in Society*, 31(4), 577–608.

Achterberg, P. J., Heilbron, D. Houtman and S. Aupers (2011). 'A Cultural Globalization of Popular Music? American, Dutch, French, and German Popular Music Charts (1965 to 2006)', *American Behavioral Scientist*, 55(5), 589–608.

Adejunmobi, S. A. (1978). 'Higher Education and National Development in Nigeria', *Improving College and University Teaching*, 26(1), 39–43.

Adeloye, L. (2011). 'SON's Battle with Substandard Goods Enters Phase Two', *Punch* <http://odili.net/news/source/2011/sep/9/811.html>, accessed 2 November 2011.

Adeoye, S. (2009). 'Marking up Casualty Rates', *Tell*, 50, 40–42.

Afigbo, A. E. (2009). 'Africa and the Abolition of the Slave Trade', *The William and Mary Quarterly*, LXVI(4), 705–716.

Ahunwan, B. (2002). 'Corporate Governance in Nigeria', *Journal of Business Ethics*, 37(3): 269–287.

Ajayi, A. B., and O. O. Dosunmu (2002). 'Environmental hazards of importing used vehicles into Nigeria', *Proceedings of International Symposium on Environmental Pollution Control and Waste Management*, 7–10 January 2002, Tunis (EPCOWM'2002): 521–532.

Ake, C. (1982). *A Political Economy of Africa*. New York: Longman Publishing Group.

Akinnaso, F. N. (1980). 'The Sociolinguistic Basis of Yoruba Personal Names', *Anthropological Linguistics*, 22(7), 275–304.

Akinwale, A. A. (2009). *Intrapreneural Behaviour of Vocational Trainees in Furniture and Tailoring Workshops in Lagos State, Nigeria*. PhD Thesis, Department of Sociology, University of Ibadan, Ibadan, Nigeria.

Akinyemi, A. (2005). 'Integrating Culture and Second Language Teaching through Yorùbá Personal Names', *The Modern Language Journal*, 89(1), 115–126.

Akpan-Obong, P. (2010) 'Unintended Outcomes in Information and Communication Technology Adoption: A Micro-level Analysis of Usage in Context', *Journal of Asian and African Studies*, 45(2), 181–195.

Alber, E. (2002). 'Motorization and Colonial Rule: Two Scandals in Dahomey, 1916', *Journal of African Cultural Studies*, 15(1), 79–92.

Al-Krenawi, A and J. R. Graham (2000). 'Islamic Theology and Prayer: Relevance for Social Work Practice', *International Social Work*, 43(3), 289–304.

Allen, C. (1992). 'Restructuring an Authoritarian State: Democratic Renewal in Benin', *Review of African Political Economy*, 54, 42–58.

Almack, K. (2005). 'What's in a Name? The Significance of Surnames Given to Children Born with Lesbian-Parent Families', *Sexualities*, 8(2), 239–254.

Anari, A, J., Kolari and J. Mason (2005). 'Bank Asset Liquidation and the Propagation of the U.S. Great Depression', *Journal of Money, Credit and Banking*, 37, 753–773.

Anderson, S. P., and V. A. Ginsburgh (1994). 'Price Discrimination via Second-hand Markets', *European Economic Review*, 38, 23–44.

Appadurai, A. (ed.) (1986). *The Social Life of Things: Commodities in Cultural Perspective*. Cambridge: Cambridge University Press.

Asiwaju, A. I. (1975). 'Formal Education in Western Yorubaland, 1889–1960: A Comparison of the French and British Colonial Systems', *Comparative Education Review*, 19(3), 434–450.

—— (1976). *Western Yorubaland under European Rule 1889–1945: A Comparative Analysis of French and British Colonialism*. London: Longman.

—— (2003–2004). 'African History in Comparative Perspective', *Afrika Zamani*, 11 & 12: 1–17.

—— (ed.) (1985). *Partitioned Africans: Ethnic Relations across Africa's International Boundaries 1884–1984*. London: C. Hurst & Co.

Asiwaju, A. I., and P. O. Adeniyi (eds) (1989). *Borderlands in Africa: A Multidisciplinary and Comparative Focus on Nigeria and West Africa*. Lagos: University of Lagos Press.

Aspers, P. (2008). 'Knowledge and Valuation in Markets', *Theory and Society*, 38, 111–131.

Atanda, J. A. (1980). *An Introduction to Yoruba History*. Ibadan: Ibadan University Press.

Ayinla, M. (2011). *Against all odds, Tokunbo Tyres Thrive*. <http://nationalmirroronline.net/community-mirror/14598.html>, accessed 27 October 2011.

Baban, F., and F. Keyman (2008). 'Turkey and Postnational Europe: Challenges for the Cosmopolitan Political Community', *European Journal of Social Theory*, 11(1), 107–124.

Baden, S., and C. Barber (2005). *The Impact of Second-hand Clothing Trade on Developing Countries*. OXFAM September 2005.

Ball, S. J., A. G. Dworkin and M. Vryonides (2010). 'Globalization and Education: Introduction', *Current Sociology*, 58(4), 523–529.

Bangura, B. (1987). 'The Recession and Workers' Struggles in the Vehicle Assembly Plants: Steyr-Nigeria', *Review of African Political Economy*, 39, 4–22.

Baran, P. (1952). *Political Economy of Growth*. Monthly Press Review.

Bauman, Z. (1998). 'On Glocalization: or Globalization for some, Localization for some others', *Thesis Eleven*, 54(1), 37–49.

Becker, R., and G. Mehlkop (2006). 'Social Class and Delinquency: An Empirical Utilization of Rational Choice Theory with Cross-Sectional Data of the 1990 and 2000 German General Population Surveys (ALLBUS)', *Rationality and Society*, 18(2), 193–235.

Beckford, G. L. (1989). 'Plantation Capitalism, Underdevelopment, and Transformation: With Special Reference to the Caribbean'. In M. T. Martin and T. R. Kandal (eds), *Studies of Development and Change in the Modern World*, pp. 150–165. New York: Oxford University Press.

Ben-Amos, P. (1973). 'Symbolism in Olokun Mud', *African Arts*, 6(4), 28–31, 95.

Benders, J., and K. Van Veen (2001). 'What's in a Fashion? Interpretative Viability and Management Fashions', *Organization*, 8(1), 33–53.

Benson, S. (2006). 'Injurious Naming: Naming, Disavowal and Recuperation in the Context of Slavery and Emancipation'. In G. Vom Bruck and B. Bodenhorn (eds), *An Anthropology of Names and Naming*, 178–194. Cambridge: Cambridge University Press.

Berlin, I. (1996). 'From Creole to African: Atlantic Creoles and the Origin of African American Society in Mainland North America', *The William and Mary Quarterly*, 53(2), 251–88.

Besnier, N. (2004). 'Consumption and Cosmopolitanism: Practising Modernity at the Second-hand Marketplace in Nukuálofa, Tonga', *Anthropological Quarterly*, 77(1), 7–45.

Best, H. (2009). 'Organic Farming as a Rational Choice: Empirical Investigations in Environmental Decision Making', *Rationality and Society*, 21(2), 197–224.

Beuving, J. J. (2004). 'Cotonou's Klondike: African Traders and Second-hand Car Markets in Benin', *Journal of Modern African Studies*, 42(4), 511–537.

——(2006). 'Lebanese Traders in Cotonou: A Socio-cultural Analysis of Economic Mobility and Capital Accumulation', *Africa*, 76(3), 324–351.

Biehl, A. R. (2001). 'Durable Goods Monopoly with Stochastic Values', *RAND Journal of Economics* 32(3), 565–577.

Boli, J., and M. A. Elliot (2008). 'Facade Diversity: The Individualization of Cultural Difference', *International Sociology*, 23(4), 540–560.

Bondarenko, D. M. (2003). 'Advent of the Second (Oba) Dynasty: Another Assessment of a Benin History Key Point', *History in Africa* 30, 63–85.

——, and P. M. Roese (2004). 'Between the Ogiso and Oba Dynasties: An Interpretation of Interregnum in the Benin Kingdom', *History in Africa* 31, 103–115.

Braun, B. (2002). 'Colonialism's afterlife: vision and visuality on the Northwest Coast', *Cultural Geographies*, 9(2), 202–247.

Buchert, M., A. Hermann, W. Jenseit, H. Stahl, B. Osyguß and C. Hageluken (2007). *Optimization of Precious Metals Recycling: Analysis of Exports of Used Vehicles and Used Electronic Devices at Hamburg Port.* Darmstadt, 28th February 2007 Oko-Institut e.V.

Buskens, V., and J. Weesie (2000). 'An Experiment on the Effect of Embeddedness in Trust Situations: Buying a Used Car', *Rationality and Society*, 12(2), 227–253.

Byerlee, D. (1987). 'The Political Economy of Third World Food Imports: The Case of Wheat', *Economic Development and Cultural Change* 35(2), 307–328.

Casey, C. (2004). 'Bureaucracy Re-Enchanted? Spirit, Experts and Authority in Organizations', *Organization*, 11(1): 59–79.

Central Bank of Nigeria (2002). *Statistical Bulletin.* Abuja: Central Bank of Nigeria.

Charmaz, K. (2006). 'The Power of Names', *Journal of Contemporary Ethnography*, 35(4), 396–399.

Choi, N. (2006). 'Symbolism of Hairstyle in Korea and Japan', *Asian Folklore Studies* 65(1), 69–86.

Chris Carey's Collections (2010). *Pricelist.* <http://chriscareyscollections.co.uk/pricelist.html>, accessed 14 September 2010.

Chugh, S., and P. Hancorck (2009). 'Network of Aestheticization: The Architecture, Artefacts and Embodiment of Hairdressing Salons', *Work, Employment and Society* 23(3), 460–476.

Coleman, J. S. (1971). *Nigeria: Background to Nationalism.* Berkeley: University of California Press.

Copeland, R. W. (2010). 'The Nomenclature of Enslaved Africans as Real Property or Chattels Personal: Legal Fiction, Judicial Interpretation, Legislative Designation, or Was a Slave a Slave by Any Other Name', *Journal of Black Studies* 40(5), 946–959.

Courpasson, D., and S. Clegg (2006). 'Dissolving the Iron Cages? Tocqueville, Michels, Bureaucracy and the Perpetuation of Elite Power', *Organization* 13(3), 319–343.

Crewe, L. (2000). 'Geographies of Retailing and Consumption', *Progress in Human Geography*, 24(2), 275–290.

Crowder, M. (1968). *West Africa under Colonial Rule.* London: Hutchinson & Co.

Crumbley, D. H. (1992). 'Impurity and Power: Women in Aladura Churches', *Africa: Journal of the International African Institute*, 62(4), 505–522.

Czaga, P., and B. Fliess (2005). 'Used Goods Trade: A Growth Opportunity', *OECD Observer* No. 246/247 December 2004-January 2005. <http://www.oecdobserver.org/news/fullstory.php/aid/1505/used_goods_trade.html>, accessed 6 July 2010.

Dandeker, C., S. Wessely, A. Iversen and J. Ross (2006). 'What's in a Name? Defining and Caring for "Veteran": The United Kingdom in International Perspective', *Armed Forces & Society*, 32(2), 161–177.

Darwar, N., and P. Parker (1994). 'Marketing Universals: Consumers' Use of Brand Name, Price, Physical Appearance and Retailer Reputation as Signals of Product Quality', *The Journal of Marketing*, 58(2), 81–85.

Davis, J. H., and J. A. Ruhe (2003). 'Perceptions of Country Corruption: Antecedents and Outcomes Perceptions of Country Corruption: Antecedents and Outcomes', *Journal of Business Ethics*, 43(4), 275–288.

Denzin, N. K. (1990). 'Reading Rational Choice Theory', *Rationality and Society*, 2(2), 172–189.

Derefaka, A. A., and F. N. Anozie (2002). 'Economic and Cultural Prehistory of the Niger Delta', *African Arts*, 35(1), 78–83, 96.

Dhebar, A. (1994). 'Durable-Goods Monopolist, Rational Consumers and Improving Products', *Marketing Science*, 13(1), 100–120.

Diakparomre, A. M. (2010). 'Symbolism in Urhobo Mask Performances', *Journal of Asian and African Studies*, 45(5), 467–484.

Dinneya, G. E., and A. Tsegaye (2004). 'Constructing a Cardinal Measure of Democratic Development in a Transition Polity: The Nigerian Example', *Canadian Journal of Political Science / Revue Canadienne de Science Politique*, 37(2), 347–373.

Dixon, P. J. (1991). '"Uneasy Lies the Head": Politics, Economics, and the Continuity of Belief among Yoruba of Nigeria', *Comparative Studies in Society and History*, 33(1), 56–85.

Domingues, J. (2002). 'Modernity, Complexity and Mixed Articulation', *Social Science Information*, 22(2), 223–247.

——(2009). 'Modernity and Modernization Moves: Latin America in Comparative Perspective', *Theory, Culture and Society*, 26(7&8), 208–227.

Drewal, H. J. (1998). 'Yoruba Beadwork in Africa', *African Arts*, 31(1), 18–27, 94.

——J. Pemberton, III and R. Abiodun (1989). 'Yoruba: Nine Centuries of African Art and Thought, *African Arts*, 23(1), 68–77, 104.

Easterly, W. (2001). 'The Middle Class Consensus and Economic Development', *Journal of Economic Growth*, 6(4), 317–335.

Echenim, S. (2011). 'Lagos Leads New Partnership on Waste Awareness', *The Punch*, 28 February 2011.

Eding, C., and C. Stern (2003). 'Scandinavian Rational Choice Sociology', *Acta Sociologica*, 46(1), 5–16.

Egwaikhide, F. O. (2000) *Determinants of Imports in Nigeria: A Dynamic Specification*. <http://valuefronteiraonline.com/public_upload/file/Determinants%20of%20Imports%20in%20Nigeria%20-A%20Dynamic%20Specification.pdf>, accessed 12 April 2011.

Eisenstadt, S. N. (2001). 'The Civilizational Dimension of Modernity: Modernity as a Distinct Civilization', *International Sociology*, 16(3), 320–340.

—— (2010). 'Modernity and Modernisation' *Sociopedia.isa* <http://www.sagepub.net/isa/admin/viewPDF.aspx?&art=Modernity.pdf>, accessed 15 June 2010.

Ejiogu, E. C. (2007). 'Historical Statistics as Text: Unusual Indicators of How Ordinary British Folk Reaped from the World-Economy, 1800–1960', *Journal of Asian and African Studies*, 42(1), 73–115.

Ekundayo, S. A. (1977). 'Restrictions on Personal Name Sentences in the Yoruba Noun Phrase', *Anthropological Linguistics*, 19(2), 55–77.

Elster, J. (2009). 'Interpretation and Rational Choice', *Rationality and Society*, 21(1), 5–33.

Elvik, R. (1993) 'The Effects on Accidents of Compulsory Use of Daytime Running Lights For Cars In Norway', *Accident Analysis & Prevention*, 25(4), 383–398.

Emmison, M. (2003). 'Social Class and Cultural Mobility: Reconfiguring the Cultural Omnivore Thesis', *Journal of Sociology*, 39(3), 211–230.

Entwistle, J. (2006). 'The Cultural Economy of Fashion Buying', *Current Sociology*, 54(5), 704–724.

Esser, H. (1993a). 'The Rationality of Everyday Behaviour: A Rational Choice Reconstruction of the Theory of Action by Alfred Schutz', *Rationality and Society*, 5(1): 7–31.

—— (1993b) 'How "Rational" is the Choice of "Rational Choice"?: A response to Randall Collins, Christopher Predergast and Ija Sruba', *Rationality and Society*, 5(3), 408–414.

Esteban, S., and M. Shum (2007). 'Durable-goods Oligopoly with Secondary Markets: The Case of Automobiles', *RAND Journal of Economics*, 58(2), 332–354.

Eweje, G. (2006). 'Environmental Costs and Responsibilities Resulting from Oil Exploitation in Developing Countries: The Case of the Niger Delta of Nigeria', *Journal of Business Ethics*, 69(1), 27–56.

Ezeala-Harrison, F. (1993). 'Structural Re-Adjustment in Nigeria: Diagnosis of a Severe Dutch Disease Syndrome', *American Journal of Economics and Sociology*, 52(2), 193–208.

Fandrich, I. J. (2007). 'Yoruba Influences on Haitian Vodou and New Orleans Voodoo' 37(5), 775–791.

Farmer, C. M., and A. F. Williams (2002). 'Effects of Daytime Running Lights on Multiple-Vehicle Daylight Crashes in The United States', *Accident Analysis & Prevention*, 34(2), 197–203.

Farmer, M. K. (1992). 'On the need to make a Better Job of Justifying Rational Choice Theory', *Rationality and Society*, 4(4), 411–420.

Fasiku, G. (2006). 'Yoruba Proverbs, Names and National Consciousness', *The Journal of Pan African Studies*, 1(4), 50–63.

Federal Republic of Nigeria (2006a). *National Bureau of Statistics: The Nigerian Statistical Fact Sheets on Economic & Social Development.* Abuja: Federal Republic of Nigeria.

——(2006b). *Abstract of Statistics.* National Bureau of Statistics Chapter 13. <http://www.nigerianstat.gov.ng/annual_report.htm>, accessed on 12 January 2009.

Field, S. et al. (2007). *Who Benefits From the Second-Hand Clothing Trade?: The Case of Kenya*: Full Research Report ESRC End of Award Report, RES-000-22-0617. Swindon: ESRC <http://www.esrc.ac.uk/my-esrc/grants/res-000-22-0617/outputs/Read/1c80f84b-b2e1-4c20-ae33-e5fe96d90f8c>, accessed 26 April 2011.

Finch, J. (2008). 'Naming Names: Kinship, Individuality and Personal Names', *Sociology*, 42(4), 709–725.

Fincham, R., and R. Roslender (2004). 'Rethinking the Dissemination of Management Fashion: Accounting for Intellectual Capital in UK Case Firms', *Management Learning*, 35(3), 321–336.

Fletcher, G. (2001). 'Book Review: Consumption and Material Culture in Contemporary Japan', *Journal of Sociology*, 37(4): 411–412.

Flynn, D. K. (1997). 'We are the Border: Identity Exchange and the State along the Benin-Nigeria Border', *American Ethnologist*, 24(2): 311–330.

Foster, H. J. (1976). 'Partners or Captives in Commerce?: The Role of Africans in the Slave Trade', *Journal of Black Studies*, 6(4), 421–434.

Fourcade, M. (2007). 'Theories of Market and Theories of Society', *American Behavioral Scientist*, 50(8), 1015–1034.

Frank, A. G. (1967). *Capitalism and Underdevelopment in Latin America: Historical Studies of Chile and Brazil.* Monthly Press Review.

Furusa, M. (2009). 'Spelling Our Proper Name: Reconceptualizing the Order of Africana/Black Studies', *Journal of Black Studies*, 40(1), 24–40.

Gagne, L. (2007). 'Non-rational Compliance with Social Norms: Sincere and Hypocritical', *Social Science Information*, 40(3), 445–469.

Gartman, D. (2004). 'Three Ages of the Automobile: The Cultural Logics of The Car', *Theory, Culture & Society*, 21(4/5), 169–195.

Giulianotti, R. (1995). 'Soccer and the Politics of Carnival: An Ethnographic Study of Scottish Fans in Sweden', *International Review for the Sociology of Sport*, 30(2), 191–220.

——(2002). 'Soccer Goes Glocal', *Foreign Policy*, 131, 82–83.

——(2006). 'Glocalization, Globalization and Migration: The Case of Scottish Football Supporters in North America', *International Sociology*, 21(2), 171–198.

——(2007). 'Recovering the Social: Globalization, Soccer and Transnationalism', *Global Networks*, 7(2), 166–186.

——with R. Robertson (2004). 'The Globalization of Soccer: A Study in the Glocalization of the "Serious Life"', *British Journal of Sociology*, 55(4), 545–568.

Gleason, J., and A. Ibubuya (1991). 'My Year Reached, We Heard Ourselves Singing: Dawn Songs of Girls Becoming Women'. In Ogbogbo, Okrika, Rivers State, Nigeria, *Research in African Literatures*, 22(3), 135–148.

Global Finance (2011). *Nigeria Country Report*, <http://www.gfmag.com/gdp-data-country-reports/207-nigeria-gdp-country-report.html#axzz1ytgpDIio>, accessed on 26 June 2012.

Gray, R. (1982). 'Christianity, Colonialism, and Communications in Sub-Saharan Africa', *Journal of Black Studies*, 13(1), 59–72.

Greenpeace (2005). *TOXIC TECH: Looming e-waste problems for Thailand and Philippines*, <http://www.greenpeace.org/seasia/ph/News/news-stories/toxic_threat_in_th_rp/>, accessed 29 March 2010.

——(2009a). *Where does E-Waste End Up?* <http://www.greenpeace.org/international/en/campaigns/toxics/electronics/the-e-waste-problem/where-does-e-waste-end-up/>, accessed 20 November 2010.

——(2009b) *Undercover operation exposes illegal dumping of e-waste in Nigeria*, <http://www.greenpeace.org/international/en/news/features/e-waste-nigeria180209/>, accessed 28 April 2011.

Greenwood, J., and G. Uysal (2005). 'New Goods and the Transition to a New Economy', *Journal of Economic Growth*, 10(2), 99–134.

Guite, H. (1962). 'European Education in West Africa', *University Review*, 2(10), 25–29.

Gutkind, P. and I. M. Wallerstein (1985). *The Political Economy of Contemporary Africa*. Thousand Oaks: Sage Publications.

Hall, T. D. (2004). 'The Modern/Colonial/Capitalist World-System in the Twentieth Century: Global Processes, Antisystemic Movements, and the Geopolitics of Knowledge', *Contemporary Sociology: A Journal of Reviews*, 33(2), 221–222.

Hampton, K. N. (2010). 'Internet Use and the Concentration of Disadvantage: Glocalization and the Urban Underclass', *American Behavioral Scientist* 53(8): 1111–1132.

Handler, J. S., and J. Jacoby (1996). 'Slave Names and Naming in Barbados, 1650–1830', *The William and Mary Quarterly*, 53(4), 685–728.

Hansen, K. T. (2004). 'Helping or Hindering?: Controversies around the International Second-Hand Clothing Trade', *Anthropology Today*, 20(4), 3–9.
Hansen, P. (2004). 'In the Name of Europe', *Race & Class*, 45(3), 49–62.
Hargreaves, J. D. (1985). 'The Making of the Boundaries: Focus on West Africa'. In Asiwaju, A. I. (ed.), *Partitioned Africans: Ethnic Relations across Africa's International Boundaries 1884–1984*, pp. 19–28. London: C. Hurst & Co.
Hatas, E. (2002). 'Symbolism and Social Phenomena: Toward the Integration of Past and Current Theoretical Approaches', *European Journal of Social Theory*, 5(3), 351–366.
Hawley, J. M. (2006). 'Digging for Diamonds: A Conceptual Framework for Understanding Reclaimed Textile Products', *Clothing and Textiles Research Journal*, 24(3), 262–275.
Hechter, M. (1994). 'The Role of Values in Rational Choice Theory', *Rationality and Society* 6(3), 318–333.
Hendel, I., and A. Lizzeri (1999). 'Adverse Selection in Durable Goods Markets', *The American Economic Review*, 89(5), 1097–1015.
Hernández-Coss, R., and C. E. Bun (2007). *The UK-Nigeria Remittance Corridor: Challenges of Embracing Formal Transfer Systems in a Dual Financial Environment*. World Bank Working Paper 92, Washington, DC: The World Bank.
Hill, G. (1997). 'History, Necessity, and Rational Choice Theory', *Rationality and Society*, 9(2), 189–213.
Hill, R. (2001). 'Surviving in a Material World: Evidence from Ethnographic Consumer Research on People in Poverty', *Journal of Contemporary Ethnography*, 30(4), 364–391.
—— (2002). 'Consumer Culture and the Culture of Poverty: Implications for Marketing Theory and Practice', *Marketing Theory*, 2(3), 273–293.
Hopkins, A. G. (1980). 'Property Rights and Empire Building: Britain's Annexation of Lagos, 1861', *The Journal of Economic History*, 40(4), 777–798.
Hotta, Y., M. Elder, H. Mori and M. Tanaka (2008). 'Policy Considerations for Establishing an Environmentally Sound Material Flow in East Asia', *The Journal of Environment and Development*, 17(1), 26–50.
Huang, S., Y. Yang and K. Anderson (2001). 'A Theory of Finitely Durable Goods Monopoly with Used-Goods Markets and Transaction Cost', *Management Science*, 47(1), 1515–1532.
Hudson, L. B. (1984). 'Modern Material Culture Studies: Anthropology as Archaeology', *American Behavioral Scientist*, 28(1), 31–39.
Hudson, R. (2000). 'One Europe or Many? Reflections on Becoming European', *Transactions of the Institute of British Geographers*, 25(4), 409–426.

Hung, K. H., S. Y. Li and R. Belk (2007). 'Glocal Understandings: Female Readers' Perceptions of the New Woman in Chinese Advertising', *Journal of International Business Studies*, 38(6), 1034–1051.

Ikporukpo, C. (2002). 'The Tokunbo Phenomenon and the Transformation of the Motor Mechanic Trade in Ibadan'. In Guyer, J. I., Denzer, L. and Agbaje, A. (eds), *Money Struggles and City Life: Devaluation in Ibadan and other Urban Centres in Southern Nigeria, 1986–1996*, 133–146. Portsmouth, NH: Heinemann.

Inglehart, R., and W. E. Baker (2000). 'Modernization, Cultural Change, and the Persistence of Traditional Values', *American Sociological Review*, 65(1), 19–51.

Ismail, O. (2009). 'The Dialectic of "Junctions" and "Bases": Youth, "Securo-Commerce" and the Crises of Order in Downtown Lagos', *Security Dialogue*, 40(4–5), 463–487.

Jaeger, C. C. (1993). 'The Cultural Evolution of Rational Choice', *International Sociology*, 8(4), 497–503.

James, J. (2001). 'Information Technology, Cumulative Causation and Patterns of Globalization in the Third World', *Review of International Political Economy*, 8(1), 147–162.

Jansson, A. (2002). 'The Mediatization of Consumption: Towards an Analytical Framework of Image Culture', *Journal of Consumer Culture*, 2(1), 3–31.

Joas, H. (1999). 'The Modernity of War: Modernization Theory and the Problem of Violence', *International Sociology*, 14(4), 457–472.

Johnson, S. (1921). *History of the Yorubas.* Lagos: C. S. S. Bookshops.

Joseph, R (1978). 'Affluence and Underdevelopment: The Nigerian Experience', *The Journal of Modern African Studies*, 16(2), 221–239.

—— (1991). *Democracy and Prebendal Politics in Nigeria: The Rise and Fall of the Second Republic.* Ibadan: Spectrum Books.

Kaufman, P. (2005). 'Middle Class Social Reproduction: The Activation and Negotiation of Structural Advantages', *Sociological Forum*, 20(2), 245–270.

Kaya, I. (2004). 'Modernity, Openness, Interpretation: A Perspective on Multiple Modernities', *Social Science and Information*, 43(1), 35–57.

Keyder, C. (2006). 'Moving in from the Margins? Turkey in Europe', *Diogenes*, 53(2), 72–81.

Khabib, S. M. (1995). 'Personal Names and Name Change', *Journal of Black Studies*, 25(3), 349–353.

Kieh, G. K., and P. O. Agbese (1993). 'From Politics Back to the Barracks in Nigeria: A Theoretical Exploration', *Journal of Peace Research* 30(4), 409–426.

Klink, R. R. (2000). 'Creating Brand Names with Meaning: The Use of Sound Symbolism', *Marketing Letters*, 11(1), 5–20.

—— (2003). 'Creating Meaningful Brands: The Relationship between Brand Name and Brand Mark', *Marketing Letters*, 14(3), 143–157.

—— (2009). 'Gender Differences in New Brand Name Response', *Marketing Letters*, 20(3), 313–326.

Kochuyt, T. (2009). 'God, Gifts and Poor People: On Charity in Islam', *Social Compass*, 56(1), 98–116.

Kolapo, F. J. (2000). 'CMS Missionaries of African Origin and Extra-Religious Encounters at the Niger-Benue Confluence, 1858–1880', *African Studies Review*, 43(2), 87–115.

Kraus, J. (2002). 'Capital, Power and Business Associations in the African Political Economy: A Tale of Two Countries, Ghana and Nigeria', *The Journal of Modern African Studies*, 40(3), 395–436.

Krossa, A. S. (2009). 'Conceptualizing European Society on Non-Normative Grounds: Logics of Sociation, Glocalization and Conflict', *European Journal of Social Theory*, 12(2), 249–264.

Kumar, P. (2002). 'Price and Quality Discrimination in Durable Goods Monopoly with Resale Trading', *International Journal of Industrial Organization*, 20, 1313–1339.

Kusiak, P. (2010). 'Instrumentalized Rationality, Cross-cultural Mediators, and Civil Epistemologies of late Colonialism', *Social Studies of Science* 40(6): 871–902.

Lahlou, S. (2008). 'Identity, Social Status, Privacy and Face-keeping in Digital Society', *Social Science Information*, 47(3), 299–330.

Lahno, B. (2007). 'Rational choice and Rule-Following Behaviour', *Rationality and Society* 19(4), 425–450.

Lange, M., J. Mahoney and M. von Hau (2006). 'Colonialism and Development: A Comparative Analysis of Spanish and British Colonies', *The American Journal of Sociology*, 111(5), 1412–1462.

Larmie, M. (2008). *A Sociological Study of Beach Churches in Lagos State, Nigeria (A Study of Bar Beach and Kuramo Beach).* A B.Sc. Project in the Department of Sociology, University of Lagos, Akoka, Lagos, Nigeria.

Larney, M., and A. M. van Arrdt (2010). 'Case Study: Apparel Industry Waste Management: A Focus on Recycling in South Africa', *Waste Management and Research* 28, 36–43.

Larsen, J. A., H. T. Allan, K. Bryan and P. Smith (2005). 'Overseas Nurses' Motivations for Working in the UK: Globalization and Life Politics', *Work, Employment & Society*, 19(2), 349–368.

Law, R. C. C. (1973). 'The Heritage of Oduduwa: Traditional History and Political Propaganda among the Yoruba', *The Journal of African History*, 14(2), 207–222.

Lazarev, V., and P. R. Gregory (2002). 'The Wheels of a Command Economy: Allocating Soviet Vehicles', *The Economic History Review*, 55(2), 324–348.

Lee, C., F. Nielsen and A. Alderson (2007). 'Income Inequality, Global Economy and the State Income', *Social Forces*, 86(1), 77–111.

Lee, Y. H., and S. H. Ang (2003). 'Interference of Picture and Brand Name in a Multiple Linkage Ad Context', *Marketing Letters*, 14(4): 273–288.

Lehmann, W. (2009). 'Becoming Middle Class: How Working-class University Students Draw and Transgress Moral Class Boundaries', *Sociology*, 43(4), 631–647.

Lemire, B. (1988). 'Consumerism in Preindustrial and early Industrial England: The Trade in Second-hand Clothes', *The Journal of British Studies*, 27(1), 1–24.

Levitt, P. (1998). 'Social Remittances: Migration Driven Local-Level Forms of Cultural Diffussion', *International Migration Review*, 32(4), 926–948.

Licandro, O., L. A. Puch and A. Sampayo (2008). 'A Vantage Mode of Trade in Second-hand Markets and Lifetime of Durable Goods', *Mathematical Population Studies*, 15(4), 249–266.

Lieberson, S., and K. S. Mikelson (1995). 'Distinctive African American Names: An Experimental, Historical and Linguistics Analysis of Innovation', American *Sociological Review*, 60(6), 928–946.

Lilley, K. D. (2004). 'Cities of God? Mediaeval Urban forms and their Christian Symbolism', *Transactions of the Institute of British Geographers*, 29(3), 296–313.

Lindenberg, S., and B. S. Frey (1993). 'Alternatives, Frames, and Relative Prices: A Broader View of Rational Choice Theory', *Acta Sociologica*, 36(9), 191–205.

Lindenfeld, D. (2005). 'Indigenous Encounters with Christian Missionaries in China and West Africa, 1800–1920: A Comparative Study', *Journal of World History*, 16(3), 327–369.

Linehan, D. (2003). 'Regional Survey and the Economic Geographies of Britain 1930–1939', *Transactions of the Institute of British Geographers*, 28(1), 96–122.

Logan, I. B., and K. Mengisteab (1993). 'IMF-World Bank Adjustment and Structural Transformation in Sub-Saharan Africa', *Economic Geography*, 69(1), 1–24.

Lord, E. (2002). 'Given Names and Inheritance'. In D. Postles (ed.), *Naming Society and Regional Identity*, 169–192. Oxford: Leopard's Head Press.

Lovett, F. (2006). 'Rational Choice Theory and Explanation', *Rationality and Society*, 18(2), 237–272.

Luthar, B. (2006). 'Remembering Socialism: On Desire, Consumption And Surveillance', *Journal of Consumer Culture*, 6(2), 229–259.

Magid, A. (1968). 'British Rule and Indigenous Organization in Nigeria: A Case-Study in Normative-Institutional Change', *The Journal of African History*, 9(2), 299–313.

Mangieri, T. (2006). *African Cloth, Export Production, and Second-hand Clothing*, <http://www.cggc.duke.edu/pdfs/workshop/Kenya%20cloth%20&%20clothing.pdf>, accessed 26 April 2006.

Martin, B. L. (1991). 'From Negro to Black to African American: The Power of Names and Naming', *The Political Science Quarterly*, 106(1), 83–107.

Martinelli, A. (2003a). 'Markets, Governments, Communities and Global Governance', *International Sociology*, 18(2), 291–323.

—— (2003b). 'Global Order or Divided World: Introduction', *Current Sociology*, 51(2), 95–100.

Mary, A. (2005). '*Metissage* and *Bricolage* in the Making of African Christian Identities', *Social Compass*, 52(3), 281–294.

Mason, M. (2009). 'Keeping up Appearances: The International Politics of Slave Trade Abolition in the Nineteenth-Century Atlantic World', *The William and Mary Quarterly*, LXVI(4), 809–832.

Mberu, B. C. (2007). 'Household Structure and Living Conditions in Nigeria', *Journal of Marriage and Family*, 69(2), 513–527.

McCabe, D. (2002). 'Histories of Errancy: Oral Yoruba *Abiku* Texts and Soyinka's *Abiku*', *Research in African Literatures*, 33(1), 45–74.

McGovern, P. (2003). 'Rational Choice Theory, the New Economic Sociology and Functionalism', *Work, Employment and Society*, 17(4), 747–756.

McIntyre, W. D. (1963). 'Commander Glover and the Colony of Lagos, 1861–73', *The Journal of African History*, 4(1), 57–79.

McMichael, P. (2008). *Development and Social Change: A Global Perspective.* Los Angeles: Pine Forge Press.

McVeigh, K. (2009). *Charities Fight Over Second-hand Clothes Market: Charities With Shops Complain About Other Charities Linking Up With Commercial Textile Merchants*, <http://www.guardian.co.uk/money/2009/nov/15/charities-clothes-market>, accessed 26 April 2011.

Meagher, K. (1997). 'Shifting the Imbalance: The Impact of Structural Adjustment on Rural-Urban Population Movements in Northern Nigeria', *Journal of Asian and African Studies*, 32(1–2), 81–92.

Mehlkop, G. and P. Graeff (2010). 'Modelling a Rational Choice Theory of Criminal Action: Subjective Expected Utilities, Norms, and Interpretations', *Rationality and Society* 22(2), 189–222.

Mellor, P. A. (2000). 'Rational Choice and Sacred Contagion?: "Rationality", "Non-Rationality" and Religion', *Social Compass*, 47(2), 273–292.

Mercer, C. (2004). 'Engineering Civil Society: ICT in Tanzania', *Review of African Political Economy*, 31(99), 49–64.

Meyer, B. (2004). 'Christianity in Africa: From African Independent to Pentecostal-Charismatic Churches', *Annual Review of Anthropology*, 33, 447–474.

Mills, M. B. (2005). 'Engendering Discourses of Displacement: Contesting Mobility and Marginality in Rural Thailand', *Ethnography*, 6(3), 385–419.

Money, A. (2007). 'Material Culture and the Living Room: The Appropriation and Use of Goods in Everyday Life', *Journal of Consumer Culture*, 7(3), 355–377.

Munkirs, J. R., D. R. Braunfeld, S. A. Carter, B. Kuester, C. Myart (1993). 'The Automobile Industry, Political Economy, and a New World Order', *Journal of Economic Issues*, 27(2), 627–638.

Mysterud, I. (2004). 'One Name for the Evolutionary Baby? A Preliminary Guide for Everyone Confused by the Chaos of Names', *Social Science Information*, 43(1), 95–114.

National Bureau of Statistics (2012) *Foreign Trade Statistics (First Quarter 2012)*, No. 502 <http://resourcedat.com/wp-content/uploads/2012/06/Foreign-Trade-Q1-2012.pdf>, accessed 6 June 2012.

Nestorović, C., and M. Vale (1991). 'The Automobile Industry in the East: National and International Strategies', *Eastern European Economics*, 29(4), 34–85.

Nevadomsky, J., and N. Rosen (1988). 'The Initiation of a Priestess: Performance and Imagery in *Olokun* Ritual' *TDR*, 32(2), 186–207.

Newcomb, J. (2000). 'Depression Auto Styling', *Winterthur Portfolio*, 35(1), 81–100.

Nigeria Customs Service (2011). *Import Prohibition List*, <http://www.customs.gov.ng/ProhibitionList/import.php>, accessed 8 April 2011.

Nigerian Tribune (2011). *Tyres' Expiry Dates: What Significance for the Nigerian Driver?* <http://tribune.com.ng/index.php/features/14448-tyres-expiry-dates-what-significance-for-the-nigerian-driver>, accessed October 08 2011.

Niger-Thomas, M. (2001). 'Women and the Art of Smuggling', *African Studies Review*, 44(2), 43–70.

Obadare, E. (2006). 'Playing Politics with the Mobile Phone in Nigeria: Civil Society, Big Business & the State', *Review of African Political Economy*, 33(107), 93–111.

Obinna, C. (2011). *SON DG Warns Importers over Substandard Goods Vanguard*, <http://www.vanguardngr.com/2011/09/son-dg-warns-importers-over-substandard-goods/>, accessed 2 November 2011.

Odulana, J. A., and J. A. Olomajeye (1999). 'The Impact of Government's Alleviation of Poverty Program on the Urban Poor in Nigeria', *Journal of Black Studies* 29(5), 695–705.

Ogundiran, A. (2002). 'Of Small Things Remembered: Beads, Cowries, and Cultural Translations of the Atlantic Experience in Yorubaland', *The International Journal of African Historical Studies*, 35(2/3), 427–457.

Ogundiran, A. O. (2001). 'Ceramic Spheres and Regional Networks in the Yoruba-Edo Region, Nigeria, 13th–19th Centuries AC', *Journal of Field Archaeology*, 28(1/2), 27–43.

——(2002). 'Filling a Gap in the Ife-Benin Interaction Field (Thirteenth–Sixteenth Centuries AD): Excavations in Iloyi Settlement, Ijesaland', *The African Archaeological Review*, 19(1), 27–60.
Ogunleye, T. M. (2006). '*Aroko, Mmomomme Twe, Nsibidi, Ogede and Tusona*: Africanism in Florida's Self-Emancipated Africans' Resistance to Enslavement and War Stratagem', *Journal of Black Studies*, 36(3), 396–414.
Okechuku, C., and V. Onyemah (1999). 'Nigerian Consumer Attitudes toward Foreign and Domestic Products', *Journal of International Business Studies* 30(3), 611–622.
Okonkwo, C. N. (2004). 'A Critical Divination: Reading Sula as *Ogbanje-Abiku*' *African American Review*, 38(4), 651–668.
Okpu, U. (1985). 'Inter-Party Political Relations in Nigeria 1979–1983', *Africa Spectrum*, 20(2), 191–209.
Olukoju, A. (2004). '"Never Expect Power Always": Electricity Consumers' Response to Monopoly, Corruption and Inefficient Services in Nigeria', *African Affairs* 103(410): 51–71.
Olutayo, A. O. (1991). *The Development of Underdevelopment: Rural Economy of Colonial South-Western Nigeria.* PhD thesis in Sociology, the Faculty of the Social Sciences, University of Ibadan, Ibadan.
——(1994). 'Systemic Source of Working Children in Africa: The Case of Nigeria', *Childhood Journal*, 4, 207–211.
——(1999). 'The Igbo Entrepreneur in the Political Economy of Nigeria', *African Study Monographs*, 20(3), 147–174.
———, and Omobowale, A. O. (2006). 'The Youth and the Family in Transition in Nigeria', *Review of Sociology of the Hungarian Sociological Association*, 11, 1–11.
——(2007). 'Capitalism, Globalization and the Underdevelopment Process in Africa: History in Perpetuity', *Africa Development*, XXXII(2), 97–112.
Omeje, K. (2006). 'Petrobusiness and Security Threats in the Niger Delta, Nigeria', *Current Sociology*, 54(3), 477–499.
Omobowale, A. O. (2006). *Political Clientelism and Rural Development in Selected Communities in Ibadan, Nigeria.* An unpublished PhD thesis, Department of Sociology, University of Ibadan.
——(2008). 'The *Tokunbo*: A Sociological Examination of the Imported Second-hand Automobiles Market in Nigeria'. In Tunc, T. E. and Babic, A. A. (eds), *The Globetrotting Shopaholic: Consumer Spaces, Products, and their Cultural Places*, 183–191. Newcastle upon Tyne: Cambridge Scholars Publishing.
——(2009a). 'Oil and Nigeria's Niger-Delta'. In Olutayo, O. A., Ogundiya, I. S. and Amzat, J. (eds), *State and Civil Society Relations in Nigeria*, 391–404. Ibadan: Hope Publications.

——(2009b) 'Nigeria, Protest and Revolution, 20th Century'. In I. Ness (ed.), *International Encyclopedia of Revolution and Protest*, 2482–2484. Oxford: Willey-Blackwell Publishing.

——, H. O. J. Akinade and M. O. Omobowale (2011). 'Ember-Months and Disaster Beliefs in Nigeria', *International Journal of Social Sciences and Humanities Review*, 2(2), 32–40.

——, and A. O. Olutayo (2009). '*Afin*: The Sanctity of the "White Skin" in Yoruba Belief System', *Journal of Environment and Culture*, 6(1&2), 111–122.

——, M. O. Omobowale and O. O. Ajani (2010). 'Emigration and the Social Value of Remittances in Nigeria'. In E. Yewah and D. R. Togunde (eds), *Across the Atlantic: Immigrants in the United States*, 127–136. Illinois: Common Ground Publishers.

Onimode, B. (1978). 'Imperialism and Multinational Corporations: A Case Study of Nigeria', *Journal of Black Studies*, 9(2), 207–232.

Orbach, B. Y. (2004). 'The Durapolist Puzzle: Monopoly Power in Durable-Goods Markets', *Yale Journal of Regulation* 21(1), 67–118.

Orie, O. O. (2002). 'Yoruba Names and Gender Marking', *Anthropological Linguistics*, 44(2), 115–142.

Oronsaye, S. (2011). *Nigeria gets N1.5tr in Remittances*, <http://234next.com/csp/cms/sites/Next/Money/Finance/5641033-147/nigeria_gets_n1.5tr_in_remittances_.csp>, accessed 2 May 2011.

Osibanjo, O., and I. C. Nnorom (2007) 'The Challenge of Electronic Waste (e-Waste) Management in Developing Countries', *Waste Management and Research* 25, 489–501.

——, and K. C. Ogbonna (2008). 'Modelling Waste Generation by the Telecom Sector in Nigeria: The Grey Side of the Impressive Outing', *Waste Management and Research*, 26, 317–326.

Otite, O. (1977) 'Symbolism and Sentiments in Nigerian Politics', *The Nigerian Journal of Sociology and Anthropology*, 3(1), 33–54.

Oyetade, S. O. (1995). 'A Sociolinguistic Analysis of Address Forms in Yoruba', *Language in Society*, 24(4), 515–535.

Pang, L. (2008). 'China who Makes and Fakes: A Semiotics of the Counterfeit', *Theory, Culture and Society*, 25(6), 117–140.

Parkins, I. (2010). 'Fashion as Methodology: Rewriting the Time of Women's Modernity', *Times and Society*, 19(1), 98–119.

Peck, I., and N. Pinto (2003). *Distribution of Second-hand Clothes in Angola Implemented by Practical Solidarity.* SIDA Evaluation 03/28 Stockholm: SIDA May 2003.

Pedriana, N. (2005). 'Rational Choice, Structural Context, and Increasing Returns: A Strategy for Analytic Narrative in Historical Sociology', *Sociological Methods and Research*, 3(3), 349–382.

Peel, J. D. Y. (1978). 'Olaju: A Yoruba Concept of Development', *Journal of Development Studies* 14, 135–165.
——(1979). 'Kings, Titles, and Quarters: A Conjectural History of Ilesha I: The Traditions Reviewed', *History in Africa* 6, 109–153.
——(1980a). 'Inequality and Action: The Forms of Ijesha Social Conflict', *Canadian Journal of African Studies / Revue Canadienne des Études Africaines*, 14(3), 473–502.
——(1980b). 'Kings, Titles & Quarters: A Conjectural History of Ilesha Part II: Institutional Growth', *History in Africa* 7, 225–257.
——(1984). 'Making History: The Past in the Ijesha Present', *Man*, New Series, 19(1), 111–132.
——(1990). 'The Pastor and the *Babalawo*: The Interaction of Religions in Nineteenth Century Yorubaland', *Africa* 60(3), 338–369.
Pelletiere, D., and K. A. Reinert (2004). 'Used Automobile Protection and Trade: Gravity and Ordered Probit Analysis', *Empirical Economics* 29, 737–751.
——(2006). 'World Trade in Used Automobiles: A Gravity Analysis of Japanese and US Exports', *Asian Economic Journal*, 20(2), 161–172.
——(2010). 'World Exports of New and Used Automobiles: A Gravity Model Comparison among the European Union, Japan and United States', *International Economic Journal* 24(1), 103–110.
Peterson, D. E. (2001). 'A Perspective on Indexing Slaves' Names', *The American Archivist*, 64(1), 132–142.
Pieterse, J. N. (1996). 'The Development of Development Theory: Towards Critical Globalism', *Review of International Political Economy* 3(4), 541–564.
Polanska, D. V. (2010). 'Gated Communities and the Construction of Social Class Markers in Postsocialist Societies: The Case of Poland', *Space and Culture*, 13(4), 421–435.
Porter, R. H., and P. Sattler (1999). *Patterns of Trade in the Market for Used Durables: Theory and Evidence.* The Center for the Study of Industrial Organization, Northwestern University, Working Paper #0002, May 1999.
Probst, P. (1989). 'The Letter and the Spirit: Literacy and Religious Authority in the History of the Aladura Movement in Western Nigeria', *Africa: Journal of the International African Institute*, 59(4), 478–495.
Rambo, E. H. (1999). 'Symbolic Interests and Meaningful Purposes: conceiving Rational Choice as Cultural Theory', *Rationality and Society*, 11(3), 317–342.
Rau, H. (2002). 'Unification: Time Divided – Time United?: Temporal Aspects of German Unification', *Time & Society*, 11(2/3), 271–294.
Ray, B. C. (1993). 'Aladura Christianity: A Yoruba Religion', *Journal of Religion in Africa*, 23(3), 266–291.

Reid-Merritt, P. (2009). 'Defining Ourselves: One Name, One Discipline?', *Journal of Black Studies*, 40(1), 6–7.
Reynolds, R. R. (2002). 'An African Brain Drain: Igbo Decisions to Immigrate to the US', *Review of African Political Economy*, 29(92), 273–284.
Ritzer, G. (2003). 'Rethinking Globalization: Glocalization/Grobalization and Something/Nothing', *Sociological Theory* 21(3), 193–209.
—— (2008). *Sociological Theory*. New York: McGraw Hill.
——, and D. Goodman (2003). *Sociological Theory*. New York: McGraw Hill.
Roche, M. (2003). 'Mega-Events, Time and Modernity: On Time Structures in Global Society', *Time & Society* 12(1), 99–126.
Rodney, W. (1973). *How Europe Underdeveloped Africa*. London: Bogle-L'Ouverture Publications and Dar-Es-Salaam: Tanzanian Publishing House.
Rothstein, B., and D. Eek (2009). 'Political Corruption and Social Trust: An Experimental Approach', *Rationality and Society*, 21(1), 81–112.
Roudometof, V. (2005). 'Transnationalism, Cosmopolitanism and Glocalization', *Current Sociology* 53(1), 113–135.
Rule, J. B. (1992). 'Rational Choice and the Limits of Theoretical Generality', *Rationality and Society*, 4(4), 451–469.
Rust, J. (1986). 'When is it Optimal to Kill off the Market for Used Goods', *Econometrica*, 54(1), 65–86.
Sako, S. (2002). 'Brain Drain and Africa's Development: A Reflection', *African Issues* 30(1), 25–30.
Sato, Y. (2010). 'Rational Choice Theory', *Sociopedia.isa* 2010 ISA.
Scarbrough, H. (2002/2003). 'The Role of Intermediary Groups in Shaping Management Fashion: The Case of Knowledge Management', *International Studies of Management & Organization*, 32(4), 87–103.
Scheld, S. (2007). 'Youth Cosmopolitanism: Clothing, the City and Globalization in Dakar, Senegal', *City and Society*, 19(2), 232–253.
Schifirnet, C. (2012) 'Tendential Modernity', *Social Science Information*, 51(1), 22–51.
Schmidt, C. W. (2006). 'Unfair Trade e-Waste in Africa', *Environmental Health Perspectives*, 114(4), A232–A235 <http://www.ncbi.nlm.nih.gov/pmc/articles/PMC1440802/>, accessed 28 April 2011.
Schuerkens, U. (2003). 'Structural Change in Western Africa as a Legacy of European Colonialism: The Labour System in Ghana and the Ivory Coast', *Current Sociology*, 51(3–4), 287–304.
—— (2005). 'Transnational Migrations and Social Transformations: A Theoretical Perspective', *Current Sociology*, 53(4), 535–553.
Schulz, J. (2006). 'Vehicle of the Self: The Social and Cultural Work of the H2 Hummer', *Journal of Consumer Culture*, 6(1), 57–86.

Semmann, D., H. J. Krambeck and M. Milinski (2004). 'Strategic Investment in Reputation', *Behavioral Ecology and Sociobiology*, 56(3). 248–252.

Sheppard, E. (2002). 'The Spaces and Times of Globalization: Place, Scale, Networks, and Positionality', *Economic Geography* 78(3), 307–330.

Shepperson, G. (1985). 'The Centennial of the West African Conference of Berlin, 1884–1885', *Phylon* 46(1), 37–48.

Sherry, J. F. (1990). 'A Sociocultural Analysis of Midwestern America Flea Market', *The Journal of Consumer Research* 17(1), 13–30.

Sherwood, M. (2004). 'Britain, the Slave Trade and Slavery, 1808–1843', *Race & Class* 46(2), 54–77.

Shettima, K. (1993). 'Structural Adjustment and the Student Movement in Nigeria', *Review of African Political Economy*, 56, 83–91.

Shrum, W. (2005). 'Regency of the Internet, or, How I Became a Guest for Science', *Social Studies of Science*, 35(5), 723–754.

Silva, E. B. (2005). 'Gender, Home and Family in Cultural Capital Theory', *British Journal of Sociology*, 56(1), 83–103.

Smith, D. J. (2006). 'Cell Phones, Social Inequality, and Contemporary Culture in Nigeria', *Canadian Journal of African Studies*, 40(3), 496–523.

Smith, J. C. A. (2010). 'The Many Americas: Civilization and Modernity in the Atlantic World', *European Journal of Social History*, 13(1), 117–133.

Smith, K. E. (2009). 'The Constitution of Modernity: A Critique of Castoriadis', *European Journal of Social History*, 12(4), 505–521.

Smitherman, G. (1991). '"What is African to Me?": Language, Ideology, and *African American*', *American Speech*, 66(2), 115–132.

Soderman, B., and R. Carter (2008). 'The Auto Salvage: A Space of Second Chances', *Space and Culture*, 11(1), 20–38.

Sodhi, M. S., and S. Lee (2007). 'An Analysis of Sources of Risk in the Consumer Electronics Industry', *The Journal of the Operational Research Society*, 58(11), 1430–1439.

Srubar, I (1993). 'On the Limits of Rational Choice', *Rationality and Society*, 5(1), 32–46.

Standards Organisation of Nigeria (2009). *Substandard Goods – China Keen to Regain Nigeria's Confidence* <http://www.sononline.org/main/readNews.php?id=4>, accessed 2 November 2011.

Stolz, J. (2006). 'Salvation Goods and Religious Markets: Integrating Rational Choice and Weberian Perspectives', *Social Compass*, 53(1), 13–32.

Stone, J. C. (1988). 'Imperialism, Colonialism and Cartography', *Transactions of the Institute of British Geographers*, New Series, 13(1), 57–64.

Tade, O., and A. J. Adekoya (2012) 'Transactional Sex and the "*Aristo*" phenomenon in Nigerian Universities', *Human Affairs* 22(2), 239–255.

Thies, C. G. (2007). 'The Political Economy of State Building in Sub-Saharan Africa', *The Journal of Politics*, 69(3), 716–731.

Thomas, V. M. (2003). 'Demand and Dematerialization Impacts of Second-hand Markets: Reuse or More Use', *Journal of Industrial Technology*, 7(2), 65–78.

Thompson, R. F. (1970). 'The Sign of the Divine King: An Essay on Yoruba Bead-Embroidered Crowns with Veil and Bird Decorations', *African Arts*, 3(3), 8–17, 74–80.

Thorne, B. (2008). 'What's in an Age Name?' *Childhood*, 15(4), 435–439.

Thune, T., and A. Welle-Strand (2005). 'ICT for and in Internationalization Processes: A Business School Case Study', *Higher Education*, 50(4), 593–611.

Tofflemire, T. C., and P. C. Whitehead (1997). 'An Evaluation of The Impact of Day-time Running Lights on Traffic Safety In Canada', *Journal of Safety Research*, 28(4), 257–272.

Trentmann, F. (2009). 'Crossing Divides: Consumption and Globalization in History', *Journal of Consumer Culture*, 9(2), 187–220.

Uche, C. (2008). 'Oil, British Interests and the Nigerian Civil War', *The Journal of African History*, 49(1), 111–135.

Ukeje, C. (2006). 'Youth Movement and Youth Violence in Nigeria's Oil Delta Region'. In C. Daiute, Z. Beykont, C. Higson-Smith and L. Nucci (eds), *International Perspectives on Youth Conflict and Development*, 289–304. Oxford: Oxford University Press.

United Nations Development Programme (2008). *2008 Statistical Update (Nigeria): The Human Development Index – Going beyond Income*, <http://hdrstats.undp.org/2008/countries/country_fact_sheets/cty_fs_NGA.html>, accessed 28 August 2009.

United Nations Development Programme (2010) *Nigeria: Country profile of Human Development Indicators*, <http://hdrstats.undp.org/en/countries/profiles/NGA.html>, accessed 13 April 2011.

van Dalen, H. P., G. Groenewold and J. J.Schoorl (2005). 'Out of Africa: What Drives the Pressure to Emigrate?', *Journal of Population Economics*, 18(4), 741–778.

Van Der Bly, M. C. E. (2005). 'Globalization: A Triumph of Ambiguity', *Current Sociology*, 53(6), 875–893.

Vanberg, V. J. (2002). 'Rational Choice vs Program-Based Behaviour: Alternative Theoretical Approaches and their Relevance for the Study of Institutions', *Rationality and Society*, 14(1), 7–54.

Vandi, A. (1979). 'Symbolism in Developing Countries: A Perspective', *Journal of Black Studies*, 10(1), 69–77.

Vaughan, O. (2003). 'Chieftaincy Politics and Communal Identity in Western Nigeria, 1893–1951', *The Journal of African History*, 44(2), 283–302.

Veen, K. V., J. Bezemer and L. Karsten (2011). 'Diffusion, Translation and the Neglected Role of Managers In The Fashion Setting Process: The Case Of MANS', *Management Learning*, 42(2), 149–164.

Velia, M., I.Valodia and B. Amisi (2006). *Trade Dynamics In Used Clothing: The Case of Durban, South Africa*, Research Report 71, <http://sds.ukzn.ac.za/files/RR71%20Velia.pdf>, accessed 27 April 2011.

Velikonja, M. (2003). '*In Hoc Signo Vinces*: Religious Symbolism in the Balkan Wars 1991–1995', *International Journal of Politics, Culture and Society*, 17(1), 25–40.

Vogiatzoglou, K. (2009). *Determinants of Export Specialization in ICT Products: A Cross-Country Analysis* International Network for Economic Research INFER, Working Paper 3.

Wagner, P. (2011). 'From Interpretation To Civilization – And Back: Analysing The Trajectories Of Non-European Modernities', *European Journal of Social Theory*, 14(1), 89–106.

Waldman, M. (1996). 'Durable Goods Pricing when Quality Matters', *Journal of Business*, 69(4), 489–510.

——(2003). 'Durable Goods Theory for Real World Markets', *Journal of Economic Perspectives*, 17(1), 131–154.

——(2004). *Anti-Trust Perspectives for Durable-Goods Markets.* CESIFO Working Paper No. 1306.

Walker, E. A. (2000a). '"Happy Days Are Here Again": Cocoa Farmers, Middlemen Traders and the Structural Adjustment Program in Southwestern Nigeria, 1986–1990s', *Africa Today*, 47(2), 151–169.

——(2000b). 'Structural Change, the Oil Boom and the Cocoa Economy of Southwestern Nigeria, 1973–1980s', *The Journal of Modern African Studies*, 38(1), 71–87.

Wallerstein, I (1976). *The Capitalist World Economy.* Cambridge: Cambridge University Press.

——(1980). *The Modern World-System II: Mercantilism and the Consolidation of the European World-Economy, 1600–1750.* Bingley: Emerald Group Publishing.

——(1984). *The Politics of the World-Economy. The States, the Movements and the Civilizations.* Cambridge: Cambridge University Press.

——(1986). *Africa and the Modern World.* Trenton, NJ: Africa World Press.

——(1989). *The Modern World-System, vol. III: The Second Great Expansion of the Capitalist World-Economy, 1730–1840s.* San Diego: Academic Press.

Ward, J. (2003). 'Producing "Pride" in West Hollywood: a Queer Cultural Capital for Queers with Cultural Capital', *Sexualities*, 6(1), 65–94.

Wariboko, W. E. (2004). '"I Really Cannot Make Africa My Home": West Indian Missionaries as "Outsiders" in the Church Missionary Society Civilizing Mission to Southern Nigeria, 1898–1925', *The Journal of African History* 45(2): 221–236.

Watts, M. J. (2004). 'Antinomies of Community: Some Thoughts on Geography, Resources and Empire', *Transactions of the Institute of British Geographers*, New Series, 29(2), 195–216.

Williamson, K. (1962). 'Changes in the Marriage System of the Okrika Ijo', *Africa: Journal of the International African Institute*, 32(1), 53–60.

White, S. (2011). *American Cars Find Second Life in Nigeria.* <http://234next.com/csp/cms/sites/Next/Home/5734936-146/american_cars_find_second_life_in.csp>, accessed 26 November 2011.

Whiteman, K. (2008). 'Obituary: Babatunde Jose: Legendary doyen of Nigerian journalism', *The Guardian*, Monday 25 August 2008, <http://www.guardian.co.uk/media/2008/aug/25/pressandpublishing2>, accessed 7 October 2011.

Williams, A. F., and K. A. Lancaster (1995). 'The Prospects of Daytime Running Lights for Reducing Vehicle Crashes in The United States', *Public Health Reports*, 110(3), 233–239.

Williams, G. C., and C. Paddock (2003). 'Reconciling Economic and Cultural Explanations for Participation in Alternative Consumption Spaces', *Geografiska Annaler*, 85(3), 137–148.

World Bank (2010). *Nigeria: Merchandise Imports*, <http://search.worldbank.org/quickview?view_url=http%3A%2F%2Fdatabanksearch.worldbank.org%2FDataSearch%2FLoadReport.aspx%3Fdb%3D2%26cntrycode%3DNGA%26sercode%3DTM.VAL.MRCH.CD.WT%26yrcode%3D>, accessed 12 June 2011.

World Bank (2011). *Nigeria*, <http://siteresources.worldbank.org/INTPROSPECTS/Resources/334934-1199807908806/Nigeria.pdf>, accessed 2 May 2011.

Ya'u, Y. Z. (2004). 'The New Imperialism & Africa in the Global Electronic Village', *Review of African Political Economy* 31(99): 11–29.

Yokoo, H. (2010). 'An Economic Theory of Reuse', *Sustainability Science*, 5(1), 143–150.

Yoshida, A., and A. Terazono (2010). 'Reuse of Second-hand TVs Exported from Japan to the Philippines', *Waste Management* 30(6), 1063–1072.

Yurchisin, J., and K. K. P. Johnson (2004). 'Compulsive Buying Behaviour and its Relationship to Perceived Social Status Associated with Buying, Materialism, Self Esteem and Apparel-Product Involvement', *Family and Consumer Sciences Research Journal*, 32(3), 291–314.

Zafirovski, M. (1999). 'Unification of Sociological Theory by the Rational Choice Model: Conceiving the Relationship between Economics and Sociology', *Sociology*, 33(3), 495–514.

Archival Sources

CSO 26 File No. 10260 *Complaints Against Customs Department.* Ibadan: National Archives.
CSO 26 File No. 11772 Vol. IX *Customs Department Annual Reports.* Ibadan: National Archives.
CSO 26 File No. 11772/S.3 *Customs Department Annual Trade Report, 1942 1943.* Ibadan: National Archives.
CSO 26 File No. 39439/S. 295 *Bulking Textiles: USA Allocations 1946.* Ibadan: National Archives.
CSO 26 File No. 50753 *Nigerian Motor Traders Association.* Ibadan: National Archives.
Daily Times 13 February 1950 p. 9.
Daily Times 2 June 1951 p. 6.
Daily Times 21 April 1950 pp. 6–7.
Daily Times 26 January 1950 p. 1.
Daily Times 6 January 1950.
Daily Times Saturday 26 may 1951 p. 3.
Daily Times Saturday, April 14 1951 p. 4.
DCI 1/1 File No. 1043/S.2 *Cars and kit Cars, Western Zone.* Ibadan: National Archives.
DCI 1/1 File No. 195/S.6 *Kit Cars.* Ibadan: National Archives.
DCI 1/1 File No. 195C/7 *New Motor Cars: Requirements 1947/53.* Ibadan: National Archives.
DCI 1/1 File No. 195C/S.45 *New Cars: Application 1947/1952.* Ibadan: National Archives.
DCI 1/1 File No. 195C/S.65 *Requirements for Controlled Vehicles 1947/52.* Ibadan: National Archives.
DCI 1/1 File No. 195D/S.19 *Requirement for Controlled Vehicles* 1947/51. Ibadan: National Archives.
DCI 1/1 File No. 4032/C.7 *Import Control: Consumer Goods.* Ibadan: National Archives.
DCI 1043/S.5 *New Motor Vehicles.* Ibadan: National Archives.
Federation of Nigeria (1953). *Annual Report of the Department of Commerce and Industries for the Year 1950–1952.* Lagos: Federal Government Printer.
Federation of Nigeria (1955). *Annual Report of Her Majesty's Customs and Excise Department for the Year ended 31st March, 1954.* Lagos: Government.
Nigeria (1954). *Annual Report of Her Majesty's Customs and Excise Department for the Year Ended 31 March, 1953.* Lagos: Government Printer.

Webliography

Aljazeera (27 July 2010). *Witness: Mitumba: The Second-hand Road: The Saga of What Really Happens to Your Old Clothes When You Give Them Away.* <http://english.aljazeera.net/programmes/witness/2008/07/200871193825622661.html>, accessed 14 April 2010.

Youtube (2007). *BBC News – Electronic Waste*, <http://www.youtube.com/watch?v=dJ8nL2RBF4E&feature=related>, accessed 26 April 2011.

Youtube (2008). *Where does e-waste end up?* <http://www.youtube.com/watch?v=oJZey9GJQPo>, accessed 18 October 2010.

Youtube (2009a). *Toxic Electronic Waste Sent To Ghana*, <http://www.youtube.com/watch?v=fdP8fOlk74E>, accessed 15 October 2010.

Youtube (2009b). *Following the E-waste Trail*, <http://www.youtube.com/watch?v=LEmOsq7aWD8&feature=channel>, accessed 18 October 2010.

Youtube (2009c). *Toxic U.S. E-Waste: Third World Problem.* <http://www.youtube.com/watch?v=-j_Zohgg4S8&feature=related>, accessed 26 April 2011.

Youtube (2009d). *E waste China, India, Nigeria.* <http://www.youtube.com/watch?v=YeDw6yHQVbI&feature=related>, accessed 26 April 2011.

Youtube (2009e). *Global crisis favours Ivorian second-hand market*, <http://www.youtube.com/watch?v=rZSQnbkk2ok>, accessed 14 October 2010.

Youtube (2009f). *Experience an African Second-hand Clothing Market*, <http://www.youtube.com/watch?v=iYDIP9Yz-zs>, accessed 12 October 2010.

Youtube (2009g). *Prices Of Second-hand Clothes To Go Up*, <http://www.youtube.com/watch?v=8_dxC7zcOiA&feature=related>. accessed 26 April 2011.

Index

Africa in Development

Series Editor: Jeggan C. Senghor
Institute of Commonwealth Studies, University of London

While African development remains a preoccupation, policy craftsmen and a multiplicity of domestic and international actors have been engaged in the quest for solutions to the myriad problems associated with poverty and underdevelopment. Academic and scholarly responses have built on traditional and non-traditional analytical frameworks and promoted a multidimensional discourse on, for example, conflict management, peace and security systems, HIV/AIDS, democratic governance, and the implications of globalization.

This series is designed to encourage innovative thinking on a broad range of development issues. Thus its remit extends to all fields of intellectual inquiry with the aim of highlighting the advantages of a synergistic interdisciplinary perspective on the challenges of and opportunities for development in the continent. Of particular interest are studies with a heavy empirical content which also have a bearing on policy debates and those that question theoretical orthodoxies while being grounded on concrete developmental concerns.

The series welcomes proposals for collected papers as well as monographs from recent PhDs no less than from established scholars.

Book proposals should be sent to oxford@peterlang.com.

Volume 1 Jeggan C. Senghor: The Politics of Senegambian Integration, 1958–1994. 335 pages. 2008.

Volume 2 Finex Ndhlovu: The Politics of Language and Nation Building in Zimbabwe. 243 pages. 2009.

Volume 3 Sabelo J. Ndlovu-Gatsheni: Do 'Zimbabweans' Exist? Trajectories of Nationalism, National Identity Formation and Crisis in a Postcolonial State. 426 pages. 2009.

Volume 4 Suzanne Mulligan: Confronting the Challenge: Poverty, Gender and HIV in South Africa. 207 pages. 2010.

Volume 5 Johnson W. Makoba: Rethinking Development Strategies in Africa: The Triple Partnership as an Alternative Approach – The Case of Uganda. 287 pages. 2011.

Vols 6–8	Forthcoming
Volume 9	Edward Cavanagh: The Griqua Past and the Limits of South African History, 1902–1994. 152 pages. 2011.
Volume 10	Ayokunle Olumuyiwa Omobowale: The *Tokunbo* Phenomenon and the Second-Hand Economy in Nigeria. 216 pages. 2013.
Vols 11–12	Forthcoming
Volume 13	Emefiena Ezeani: Cooperative Collegial Democracy for Africa and Multi-ethnic Societies: Democracy without Tears. 215 pages. 2013.

FSC
www.fsc.org
MIX
Papier | Fördert
gute Waldnutzung
FSC® C083411

Kolibri 360 GmbH
Ferdinand-Jühlke-Straße 7
99095 Erfurt, Deutschland
produktsicherheit@kolibri360.de